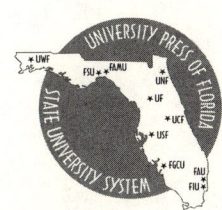

Florida A&M University, Tallahassee
Florida Atlantic University, Boca Raton
Florida Gulf Coast University, Ft. Myers
Florida International University, Miami
Florida State University, Tallahassee
University of Central Florida, Orlando
University of Florida, Gainesville
University of North Florida, Jacksonville
University of South Florida, Tampa
University of West Florida, Pensacola

Intellectual Trends in Twentieth-Century Iran: A Critical Survey

Edited by Negin Nabavi

University Press of Florida
Gainesville Tallahassee Tampa Boca Raton
Pensacola Orlando Miami Jacksonville Ft. Myers

Copyright 2003 by Negin Nabavi
Printed in the United States of America on acid-free, TCF (totally chlorine-free) paper
All rights reserved

08 07 06 05 04 03   6 5 4 3 2 1

Library of Congress Cataloging-in-Publication Data
Intellectual trends in twentieth-century Iran : a critical survey / edited by Negin Nabavi.
p. cm.
Includes bibliographical references and index.
ISBN 0-8130-2630-X (cloth: alk. paper)
1. Iran—Intellectual life—20th century. I. Nabavi, Negin, 1965–
DS316.4.I58 2003
955.05'086'31—dc21   2003040244

The University Press of Florida is the scholarly publishing agency for the State University System of Florida, comprising Florida A&M University, Florida Atlantic University, Florida Gulf Coast University, Florida International University, Florida State University, University of Central Florida, University of Florida, University of North Florida, University of South Florida, and University of West Florida.

University Press of Florida
15 Northwest 15th Street
Gainesville, FL 32611–2079
http://www.upf.com

Contents

Note on Transliteration vii
Acknowledgments ix

Introduction 1

Part I. Intellectual Discourse in Pahlavi Iran

1. The Ambivalent Modernity of Iranian Intellectuals 11
   Mehrzad Boroujerdi
2. Khalil Maleki: The Odd Intellectual Out 24
   Homa Katouzian
3. Ahmad Shamlu and the Contingency of Our Future 53
   Hamid Dabashi and Golriz Dahdel
4. The Discourse of "Authentic Culture" in Iran in the 1960s and 1970s 91
   Negin Nabavi

Part II. Intellectual Expressions and Dynamics in Postrevolutionary Iran

5. Crossing the Desert: Iranian Intellectuals after the Islamic Revolution 111
   Morad Saghafi
6. Religious Intellectuals and Political Action in the Reform Movement 136
   Hamidreza Jalaeipour
7. Improvising in Public: Transgressive Politics of the Reformist Press in Postrevolutionary Iran 147
   Farideh Farhi
8. Sacral Defense of Secularism: Dissident Political Theology in Iran 180
   Mahmoud Sadri
9. Women's Rights and Clerical Discourses: The Legacy of 'Allameh Tabataba'i 193
   Ziba Mir-Hosseini

Select Bibliography 219
Contributors 223
Index 225

Note on Transliteration

The system of transliteration used here is a simplified version adapted from the standard set by the International Journal of Middle East Studies. With the exception of ' for *hamzeh* and ' for *ayn*, all diacritical marks have been omitted. Besides the two diphthongs that are represented by *ey* and *aw*, the remaining vowels are transliterated as they are pronounced in Persian.

Acknowledgments

This book is a collection of essays, many of which originated as presentations at a conference held at Princeton University on 21 October 2000 on this same theme of "Intellectual Trends in Twentieth-Century Iran." I would like to thank all those who sponsored and made the conference possible: the Department and Program in Near Eastern Studies; Mamdouha S. Bobst Center for Peace and Justice, Politics Department; the History Department; and the Institute for the Transregional Study of the Contemporary Middle East, North Africa, and Central Asia at Princeton University. I am also grateful to my colleagues in the Near Eastern Studies Department who encouraged me in this venture, in particular Sükrü Hanioglu, Andras Hamori, Jerry Clinton, and Norman Itzkowitz.

Thanks are also due to acquiring editor Amy Gorelick, project editor Jacqueline Kinghorn Brown, and copy editor Carolyn Russ for their efficiency and hard work, the anonymous readers of the University Press of Florida for their helpful remarks, and to Ahmad and Azar Ashraf for their support, wisdom, and good advice.

A version of Morad Saghafi's chapter "Crossing the Desert: Iranian Intellectuals after the Islamic Revolution" has appeared in *Critique: Journal for Critical Studies of the Middle East*, no. 18, spring 2001; it can also be found on the journal's website at http://www.tandf.co.uk/journals. A version of Mahmoud Sadri's chapter, "Sacral Defense of Secularism: Dissident Political Theology in Iran," has been published in *International Journal of Politics, Culture, and Society* 15, no. 2 (winter 2001); and, finally, a Persian version of my own essay has appeared in *Iran Nameh: Majalleh-ye Tahqiqat-e Iranshenasi* 19, no. 3 (spring 2001), pp. 263–77. I am grateful to the editors of these journals for graciously allowing versions of the articles to be included here.

Introduction

In recent years, much has been written about the fate of the "public intellectual" in the West. The question that has particularly preoccupied observers is whether, at the end of the twentieth century, the era of the detached and independent intellectual critic engaged with universal issues is coming to an end. Writers and commentators such as Russell Jacoby, Régis Debray, and Edward Said have pointed out how, in an era of growing specialization and professionalization, there is a danger that intellectuals will withdraw from the public realm and no longer fulfill their role of "calling foul." In a different vein, Bernard-Henri Lévy, the French "New Philosopher," reflected playfully on the predicament of the intellectual in the post-modern age.[1] In his book *Éloge des intellectuels* (published in 1987) he imagined an entry for the word *intellectual* in a hypothetical French dictionary to appear in the year of the millennium. "Intellectual: noun, masculine; a social and cultural category born in Paris at the moment of the Dreyfus affair, dead in Paris at the end of the twentieth century; apparently was not able to survive the decline of belief in Universals."[2]

In Iran, however, the fate of the public intellectual has not been so sealed. Even if subject to abuse and intimidation by various pressure groups in the country, the figure of the intellectual is very much present. In recent years, intellectuals, both religious and secular, have engaged in discussing and interpreting important ideas; concepts such as civil society, pluralism, and the relationship between tradition and modernity have become the watchwords of many contributing to the debates, filling the pages of many Iranian journals and newspapers. This volume therefore examines the major intellectual trends in twentieth-century Iran from a number of perspectives and explores the role that the intellectual has played in shaping the debates and political culture in both prerevolutionary and postrevolutionary Iran. It considers the major themes and concerns of the intellectuals, both secular and religious, in the course of the century and points to some of the dynamics that have been at work in this period.

On the Concept of the Intellectual: From *Monavvar al-fekr* to *Rawshanfekr*

There are no unequivocal definitions of what an intellectual is.³ Scholars have varied greatly in their description of this term. Some have attributed it widely to all those who "create, distribute, and apply culture," whereas others, in an attempt to narrow the category, have qualified the word with distinct characteristics. Among this latter approach, Edward Said's description is one example: "An intellectual . . . [is] someone whose whole being is staked on a critical sense, a sense of being unwilling to accept easy formulas, or ready-made clichés, or the smooth, ever so accommodating confirmations of what the powerful or conventional have to say, and what they do."⁴ In a historical sense, however, the term has been used as one of self-description: that is, a loose term used by those who so describe themselves to define their role in society.⁵ And this usage is pertinent to our purposes, since as some of the essays show, the understanding of what constitutes an intellectual has changed over the years.

Contrary to the European context, in which the emergence of the notion of intellectuals as a self-conscious group with a sense of mission and collective identity is generally dated back to the Dreyfus affair in the late nineteenth century, there is no one incident in the Iranian context that can be considered as having heralded the advent of the "intellectual." A brief examination of the two terms used in Persian to denote the concept of the intellectual, together with the group that each refers to, is evidence of the gradual evolution of this idea. *Monavvar al-fekr,* adopted from the idea of the French Enlightenment and best translated as "enlightened of the mind," was the term used for earlier intellectuals, from the second half of the nineteenth century to about the Second World War. The term *rawshanfekr,* which gained currency following the abdication of Reza Shah Pahlavi in 1941, varies slightly in connotation, in spite of being a direct translation into Persian of the Arabic *monavvar al-fekr.*

Mirza Fath ʿAli Akhundzadeh (1812–1878), Mirza Aqa Khan Kermani (1853–1896), and Mirza ʿAbd al-Rahim Talebof (1834–1910) are often cited as examples of early *monavvar al-fekr.* They can be characterized as writer-reformers who had little sense of dilemma with regard to their role. That is, they admired the French *philosophes,* aspired to the achievements of a cultured Europe, and saw their task to be that of changing the attitude prevalent in Iranian society according to the Western model. In this sense, they have often been compared to the Russian intelligentsia, an educated elite who, in the words of Isaiah Berlin, were "united by something more than mere interest in ideas . . . [They were] devoted to the spreading of a specific attitude in life."[6] There were two aspects to this sense of purpose. They were early critics of the traditional society and believed that by introducing Western thought as well as Western institutions, they could find a place for their own, and in their eyes, "marginal" civilization in the wider world of which they had become aware. At the same time, disillusioned with the "despotic" state, which claimed to be the defender of Islam, and in order to guard against charges of "europhilia," they inverted their understanding of past history. While previously Islam had been regarded to have signaled the beginning of civilization and the pre-Islamic age to have exemplified that of ignorance *(jahiliyya)*, they now tended to depict the pre-Islamic past as an enlightened age *('asr-e monavvar)* that mirrored nineteenth-century Europe, and Islam as an age of ignorance, misery, and despotism. In this way, they attempted a process of historical dissociation from the Arab-Islamic culture and instead identified with the European, whose commendable manners they appropriated by claiming that they had been of Iranian origin.[7]

The later *monavvar al-fekr*s of the 1920s and 1930s continued to act as transmitters of European ideas and demand social change. Similarly, they persevered in glorifying the idea of the pre-Islamic past, in their quest to regain a sense of national pride and a footing among the world's nations. To this end, several among their ranks engaged in scholarly activity of one kind or other. Whether it was the publication of studies in the history and myths of ancient Persia by figures such as Hasan Pirniya (1873–1935), the research into Zoroastrianism and its sacred texts by Ebrahim Purdavud, or the compilation of the first volume of the monumental lexicon by 'Ali Akbar Dehkhoda (1876–1956), all aimed to further strengthen and draw attention to national Persian culture. Of course, the strict censorship prevalent during Reza Shah's rule must have certainly deterred intellectuals from any form of political expression, but it also meant that intellectuals at this time did not necessarily derive their sense of identity from political activity alone, as they were to do later.

The term *rawshanfekr*, by contrast, seems to have become prevalent following the emergence of the Communist Tudeh Party in 1941. The Tudeh was the first "modern" and "progressive" political party that came into being following twenty years of Reza Shah's rule, when change was being sought in the conditions of the country. This development, together with the fact that the Tudeh seemed unrivaled in providing a forum for the discussion of new ideas, may explain why it enjoyed the prestige that it did among the young and educated sectors of society, and why a majority of Iranian intellectuals became drawn to it, either as members or as sympathizers.

As the notion of the *rawshanfekr* came to have Marxist connotations, embodying the belief in the idea of a revolutionary struggle against the status quo and the state in power, intellectuals too, by and large, positioned themselves on the left of the political spectrum. Although by the 1960s many had become disillusioned with the Tudeh and were in search of an alternative, the fact remains that the new *rawshanfekri* had established its tradition within the ideological framework of opposition to and rejection of the state. In this sense, the concept of the *rawshanfekr* was politicized. To borrow a phrase from Jeremy Jennings, whose observation concerns French intellectuals but which could also be applied to the Iranian context after 1941, the "intellectual becomes an intellectual precisely at the point where he enters that area of public space known under the general title of the world of politics."[8] In short, while the *monavvar al-fekr* would have considered his task to be that of transmitting new ideas and reforming society, the *rawshanfekr* came to be primarily preoccupied with a demand for political change. Of course the notion of the *rawshanfekr* did not remain static and continued to change throughout the years,[9] but it would not be inaccurate to say that from 1941 until 1979, intellectual discourse was shaped to a large degree by the political atmosphere, both on the domestic and the international fronts.

Following the revolution, not only did the concept of the *rawshanfekr* undergo great changes but there also emerged the new phenomenon of the *rawshanfekr-e dini* or religious intellectual. Although those describing themselves as religious intellectuals appeared as rivals to the secularists in the early years, in recent times they seem to have developed into interlocutors of sorts, moving toward common liberal values, thus bringing about the possibility of a dialogue between secular and religious intellectuals, a theme that a number of the authors in this volume address.

The contributions that follow are organized in two parts. Part I, which covers the intellectual discourse in Pahlavi Iran, considers four major themes that colored much of the intellectuals' worldview between 1926 and 1979. Mehrzad Boroujerdi discusses the intelligentsia's preoccupation with and ambivalence toward the West and modernity throughout the twentieth century. That many Iranian intellectuals aspired to things Western, he points out, did not necessarily mean that they were particularly comfortable with the idea of the West or modernity. The way in which the early encounters with the West took place, together with the fact that the perception of the West was often closely linked to the political developments within the country, he suggests, may in part explain this paradoxical tendency and hesitation to embrace modernity fully. Homa Katouzian points to the exclusionist belief shared by left-leaning intellectuals, especially from the 1940s onward, concerning the role of the intellectual. For them, being an intellectual necessarily consisted of opposing the state and making no compromises with those in power. Therefore, if one such as Khalil Maleki attempted to present an alternative approach, he became an "odd intellectual out" at best, or a "collaborationist" who was moreover isolated and ostracized. By contrast, Ahmad Shamlu, the subject of the essay by Hamid Dabashi and Golriz Dahdel, in the words of the authors, represented the "very summation of the age that celebrated him." If he came to embody this quality for many of his contemporaries, it was because he succeeded in integrating the idea of "literary commitment" into his poetry. That is, he shared the belief adopted from Jean-Paul Sartre and held by many in Shamlu's generation that literature, like political action, had to be inspired by the needs of the here and now, take a stance, and resist power. Thus Shamlu, by "fusing the lyrical and the political," to use the words of the authors of this essay, became the "romantic revolutionary" that suited the times. Finally, in my essay on "the discourse of authentic culture," I discuss another concern that gained increasing importance in the late 1960s and 1970s, namely, that of defining an authentic culture, or of defining the characteristics of an Eastern as opposed to a Western culture. I speculate that this discourse, even though vague, may have been partly responsible for the unquestioning backing that secular intellectuals gave the religious opposition to the Pahlavi regime, resulting in the revolution in 1978–79.

Part II, concerning intellectual expressions and dynamics in postrevolutionary Iran, examines the significant developments that have taken place on the intellectual scene since 1979. Morad Saghafi discusses the predicament of these same secular intellectuals, who, in spite of their alliance with the religious forces at the time of the revolution, became marginalized and subject to accusations of different kinds soon after. Ironically, as argued by Saghafi, it may be precisely because they were marginalized and ignored for much of the first decade after the revolution that they managed to keep their autonomy, which enabled them to make a comeback to the public domain, once disillusionment set in with the state. Hence, in his words, "[T]he more the public turned against the state, the more it looked toward intellectuals, who in the absence of political organizations, seemed to be the only group capable of having a sociopolitical discourse."

The next three essays consider the relatively new phenomenon of the religious intellectual from different perspectives. Hamidreza Jalaeipour, a religious intellectual himself, examines the question of what it means to be a religious intellectual and the role that religious intellectuals have played in the reform movement. Arguing that religious intellectuals do not constitute one homogeneous group and that a distinction needs to be made among the different leanings, he directs his attention to the "secondary intellectuals," namely the journalists and essayists of the reformist movement. Similar to Saghafi, Jalaeipour suggests that if religious intellectuals gained a political role and moved beyond the cultural domain, it was because they were unintentionally pushed into it by the conservative forces. That is, in the absence of political associations, they were left with no choice but to emerge in the public domain and take on the mantle of public intellectuals. The impact of religious intellectuals is taken up once again in the next essay by Farideh Farhi, but this time it is examined from the angle of the dynamics of the public sphere in which they operate. By focusing on one aspect, namely the reformist press during its short life span of two years, Farhi points out its improvisational and open-ended nature and argues that regardless of the end result, this episode began a process that can only contribute to a changing political culture. The following essay by Mahmoud Sadri centers on the domain of ideas and discusses three major religious thinkers whose writings have come to represent, in different ways, a secularizing trend and a challenge to the hegemony of the clerical order from within. Though not as accessible as the reformist press, their arguments have had resonance beyond the ivory tower, perhaps because they embody a move away from ideology and absolutism and toward a pluralism of interpretation. Finally, in the last essay, Ziba Mir-Hosseini examines another recent development within the religious discourse, namely, the debate about women and women's rights in clerical circles as reflected in an article published in *Payam-e Zan,* a woman's journal published by the Propagation Office of the Qom Seminaries. By translating and contextualizing an article that appeared in this journal in the mid-1990s, she points to the challenges and paradoxes inherent in such an undertaking. That this subject is discussed is itself a sign of the recognition, at least among some elements in the clerical circles, that such issues can no longer be avoided. However, that this question is addressed in the form of a favorable commentary on the writings of a prerevolutionary religious scholar who did not believe in gender equality points to the obstacles and difficulties that those in search of change have to grapple with in the years to come.

Thus, in spite of their varied and disparate approaches, the essays collected here point to the changing panorama of what has constituted the intellectual scene over the past hundred years. Whereas the prerevolutionary era seems to have been dominated by outside models and exclusionist ideas of what it meant to be an intellectual, the postrevolutionary intellectual scene, two decades after the revolution, is not so clear. However, one fact is apparent. That is, in spite of having had their activities curtailed and their newspapers shut down, intellectuals, whether secular or religious, have not lost their relevance. Perhaps part of their appeal lies in their recognition that these uncertain times require a shift in consciousness and that answers no longer necessarily lie in age-old ideologies but in dialogue, new arguments, and approaches.

Notes

1. Bernard-Henri Lévy, *Éloge des intellectuels* (Paris: Bernard Grasset, 1987). See also Russell Jacoby, *The Last Intellectuals: American Culture in the Age of Academe* (New York: Basic Books, 1987); Régis Debray, *Le scribe* (Paris: Éditions Grasset et Fasquelle, 1980); Edward Said, *Representations of the Intellectual: The 1993 Reith Lectures* (London: Vintage, 1994).

2. The translation is by David Schalk in "Are Intellectuals a Dying Species? War and the Ivory Tower in the Post-modern Age," in J. Jennings and A. Kemp-Welch, eds., *Intellectuals in Politics: From the Dreyfus Affair to Salman Rushdie* (New York: Routledge, 1997), p. 271.

3. An earlier version of this section has been published in *Iranian Studies* 32, no. 3 (summer 1999).

4. Edward Said, *Representations of the Intellectual: The 1993 Reith Lectures* (London: Vintage, 1994), p. 17.

5. See, for example, Sunil Khilnani, *Arguing Revolution: The Intellectual Left in Postwar France* (New Haven: Yale University Press, 1993).

6. Isaiah Berlin, "The Birth of the Russian Intelligentsia," in *Russian Thinkers*, eds. Henry Hardy and Aileen Kelly (London: Hogarth Press, 1978), p. 117.

7. For a study of the reshaping of language and history by the nineteenth-century thinkers, see Mohammad Tavakoli-Targhi, "Refashioning Iran: Language and Culture during the Constitutional Revolution," *Iranian Studies* 23, nos. 1–4 (1990), pp. 77–101.

8. Jeremy Jennings, "Mandarins and Samurais: The Intellectual in Modern France," in *Intellectuals in Twentieth Century France*, ed. J. Jennings (New York: St. Martin's Press, 1993), p. 13.

9. See Negin Nabavi, "The Changing Concept of the 'Intellectual' in Iran of the 1960s," *Iranian Studies* 32, no. 3 (summer 1999), pp. 333–50.

Part I

Intellectual Discourse in Pahlavi Iran

The Ambivalent Modernity of Iranian Intellectuals

Mehrzad Boroujerdi

In 1922, at the unripe age of twenty-seven, a brilliant Iranian writer named Hasan Moqaddam (1895–1925) published a play titled *Ja'far Khan az farang amadeh* (Ja'far Khan is back from Europe). The play, mocking a *dépaysé* Westernized Iranian named Ja'far Khan, remains popular in Iran to this day. Having returned to his homeland after seeing what gadgetry and material amenities Europe has to offer, Ja'far Khan has become rather contemptuous of his indigenous traditional culture with its stultifying rituals and primordial values. Meanwhile, he considers Europe as the embodiment of prestige, progress, possibility, and privilege. Ja'far Khan both resembles and radically differs from the character Bazarov depicted by Ivan Turgenev in *Fathers and Sons* some sixty years before. Both are members of an up-and-coming generation that is severely judgmental and horridly arrogant. They have poor opinions of their compatriots, oppose adulation of native values, admire the West for its scientific and technological precocity, and disapprove of the ignorance or obdurate hostility of their predecessors toward the West.

However, Ja'far Khan is nothing like the autodidact, iconoclastic, and self-assured Bazarov. Instead, he comes across as a superficial idiot savant skilled in the slavish imitation of Westerners but defective in his knowledge of the West. While the reader can easily identify with the nihilist yet genuine Bazarov, one is hard-pressed to develop any sympathy for the musings of Ja'far Khan. So what accounts for the unfailing popularity of *Ja'far Khan az farang amadeh,* even among intellectuals, some eighty years after it was first published?

Perhaps the attraction of this play can be attributed to the author's mystifying personality, a Swiss-educated literator who died at the tender age of thirty. Another explanation may be that Iranians take delight in mocking their own deficiencies and deceitfulness. One can even say that by humorously reprobating Ja'far Khan's lack of empathy for the local culture, Moqaddam echoed the acerbic and cynical view of a contemporaneous Ottoman statesman who, speaking of students dispatched to Europe, once remarked that they came back "syphilized, not civilized."[1] However, I contend that this play still resonates with educated Iranians for two main reasons: first, because it addresses through art the questions of "identity" and "uprootedness," themes that have consistently preoccupied and engaged Iranian intellectuals; and second, it deftly portrays the dominant feeling of ambivalence that Iranians have exhibited toward "modernity"[2] and "modernism."[3]

The latter point constitutes the principal contention of this essay. By briefly chronicling the history of Westernization in Iran, I will argue that for over a century the Iranian intelligentsia have embraced modernity while at the same time keeping a critical distance from it.[4] This is largely because the view of modernity subscribed to by most Iranian intellectuals has closely conformed to the country's political standing at the time. Considering the tumultuous nature of Iran's domestic and foreign policy over the last century, the intellectuals have mainly opted for a guarded, qualified, and utilitarian embrace of Western modernity. Hence, they have shared a widespread proclivity to advocate selective assessment, modified adaptation, and discreet assimilation of Western philosophical and techno-scientific culture. By and large, the Iranian intelligentsia viewed their procurement of Western modernity as an adulterous affair or a Faustian bargain, which they could neither openly brag about nor necessarily be proud of. How can we make sense of this disposition?

Chronicle of an Ambivalent Modernity

Iran's ties with modern Europe can be traced back to the time of Shah 'Abbas in the sixteenth century, when Persia entered the community of nations. Yet Europe's intellectual revolution between 1600 and 1800—as exemplified in the works of Bacon, Descartes, Galileo, Hobbes, Hume, Kant, Montesquieu, Newton, Pascal, Rousseau, and Voltaire—hardly affected Iran's lettered strata. The seventeenth- and eighteenth-century educated Persians viewed the West less as a philosophical threat and more as an exotic cultural edifice worthy of a voyeuristic gaze. Hence, unlike their Turkish counterparts, Iranian intellectuals shied away from openly embracing Anglo-Saxon scientific pragmatism or positivism.

Beginning in the early nineteenth century, various military defeats at the hands of rival states (especially Russia) coupled with formidable Western exploits, interference, and permeations managed to change the West's image in the minds of many Iranians. The century of humiliation that was to follow transformed Iran's image of the West from a nebulous entity into a real and concrete political adversary, a cultural opponent, and an ideological threat.[5] Magnanimity toward foreigners soon gave way to a wounded sense of national pride that showed traces of haughtiness, megalomania, and xenophobia.[6] Exhibitions of Anglophobia and Russophobia became a national pastime as well as a favorite way to ignore the social ills besetting the country.

A glance at the historical lineage of Westernization during this period quickly reveals that even as Iranian intellectuals tried to embrace modernity and adopt its extensive vocabulary, they did not cease paying tribute to tradition. The curbing of the pioneering fetters of modern thought was part of the defensive arsenal of a traditional society uneasy with modernity. This point has not escaped the attention of the perceptive historian Mangol Bayat, who reminds us that, while convinced that the "secret" of European power and prosperity was rooted in constitutional government and scientific knowledge, nineteenth-century, reform-minded intellectuals and statesmen such as Mirza Fath 'Ali Akhundzadeh (1812–1878), Mirza Taqi Khan Amir Kabir (1807–1852), Mirza Malkam Khan (1833–1908), Mirza Hoseyn Khan Sepahsalar (1826–1881), and even Mirza 'Abd al-Rahim Talebof (1834–1910) were not willing to give up the full panoply of traditional thinking and culture. Bayat writes,

> The so-called modernist thought of the turn of the century, despite its loud call for Westernization, was in spirit and form, if not in content, deeply rooted in tradition, bearing as much the mark of the Irano-Islamic heritage outwardly rejected by some of its spokesmen, as of the European systems it strongly wished to emulate.

She continues:

> In their attempt to define the new society, despite their conscious or unconscious desire to emulate some of the sociopolitical practices of Western Europe, nineteenth-century reformers projected the neo-Platonic view of the heavenly city on earth, the classical "Virtuous City" of the medieval philosophers, where the Perfect Man, the philosopher-king, rules over the masses, rather than the concept of a pluralist society where the sovereignty of the people is recognized and where a representative government implements the will of the majority.[7]

In other words, while a good number of the late-nineteenth- and early-twentieth-century intellectuals believed in fighting superstitious beliefs by promoting modern values, they also attached various amendments and conditions as to how the original European code of modernity—humanism, man's dynamic role in the universe, conquest of nature, history as progress, and reason as a critical tribunal—could be adopted. The existing rancor between science and religion did not necessarily convince intellectuals to forgo the religious inheritance of their society or to engage in a vigorous critique of Islamic jurisprudence or mysticism.[8] The "sacral" intellectual strata held on to the desideratum that Islam was a once-great-but-now-fallen religion that could be restored to its pristine vigor and virtue only if we were to understand it correctly and cleanse it of its false and fatigued accretions.[9] The insights of the sociologist Edward Shils help us understand why these intellectuals were willing to sacrifice "actual history" in order to protect a "revelation betrayed." Shils maintains that in underdeveloped countries that "possessed conspicuous evidence of great indigenous achievements in the past" and now felt enfeebled and degraded, the development of political life is often accompanied by an "impassioned effort of religious and moral self-renewal."[10]

Nonetheless, one can still brand this early generation as modernist, not so much because of its answers but on account of its questions. More importantly, this generation's significance as architects of political life cannot be easily dismissed. As Shils points out, "[T]he gestation, birth, and continuing life of the new states of Asia and Africa, through all their vicissitudes, are in large measure the work of intellectuals."[11] In other words, it is impossible to analyze the trajectory of modernization, nation building, and secularization in lesser-developed countries such as Iran without discussing the social significance of the intelligentsia. As the carriers of such concepts as culture, historical consciousness, modernism, and nationalism, the intelligentsia tried to bridge the rift created by the process of Westernization and mitigate the alienation that naturally accompanied it.[12] As instigators of ideas and executants of power, these "liaison officers" were expected to negotiate with a potent modernity while simultaneously keeping the West politically at bay.[13]

Finally, as secular ministers, they were expected to celebrate, concoct, and revive national myths while emblematizing national identity.[14] This tendency was fully on display in Iran from the 1920s to the 1950s, a period that Eric Hobsbawm has accurately called "the heyday of nationalism" around the world. Again, Edward Shils helps us understand this inclination:

The first generation of constitutional politicians in most underdeveloped countries were relatively highly "Westernized." The usual antagonism toward the older generation made the next, younger generation more antagonistic toward Western culture, and encouraged their rudimentary attachment to the indigenous traditional culture to come forward a little more in their minds. This provided a matrix for the idea of a deeper national culture and, therewith, of the nation which had only to be aroused to self-awareness.[15]

As the twentieth century got further under way, the cumulative impact of a host of events made many of Iran's intellectuals skeptical about the fervent Enlightenment discourse of internationalism and encouraged them to develop greater affinity for nationalism and traditional culture. Those of the interwar generation, in particular, experienced the full brunt of Western civilization as they witnessed such tragic events as World War I, the Great Depression, the Gulag, Fascism, the Holocaust, World War II, the explosion of the atomic bomb, the 1941 Allied invasion of Iran, and the sacking of Reza Shah.[16] The 1953 coup toppling Premier Mohammad Mosaddeq delivered yet another psychological blow by startling the post–World War II generation.[17] The American-orchestrated coup and the subservient behavior of the Tudeh Party toward the Soviet Union disillusioned many intellectuals as to the altruism of the great powers and further solidified nationalistic sentiments.

The 1960s and 1970s further prolonged the ambivalence of Iranian intellectuals toward the West. The prefabricated and montage-style modernization pursued by the shah, the cleft between new education and old religion as well as between technology and tradition, the rise of anticolonial movements in the third world, and the philosophical self-doubts expressed by Western thinkers cast a shadow of doubt over Western modernity's aura of prestige.[18] The cumulative impact of the aforementioned factors is no doubt partly to blame for the unwillingness of Iranian intellectuals to face their own ineptitude, myopia, and obscurantism.[19]

Two Types of Alienation

In *The Crisis of the Arab Intellectual,* the Moroccan scholar Abdallah Laroui argues that the West created not only an intellectual crisis but a crisis of the intellectuals as well. Laroui emphasizes that what is essential in understanding how Arab intellectuals have responded to the West is the issue of "historical or cultural retardation."

The intellectual is molded by a culture; the latter is born of a consciousness and a politics. Now there are two types of alienation: the one is visible and openly criticized, the other all the more insidious as it is denied on principle. Westernization indeed signifies an alienation, a way of becoming other, an avenue to self-division (though one's estimation of this transformation may be positive or negative, according to one's ideology). But there exists another form of alienation in modern Arab society, one that is prevalent but veiled: this is the exaggerated medievalization obtained through quasi-magical identification with the great period of classical Arabian culture.[20]

The two types of alienation singled out by Laroui are also discernable in the encounter of Iranian intellectuals with the West. If the uprooted Ja'far Khan represented the literary alienation of Westernized intellectuals, the conservative intellectual-statesman Mehdi Qoli Hedayat (Mokhber al-Saltaneh), whose life span covered half of the nineteenth century and half of the twentieth century (1863–1955), represented the second type of alienation. A resolute critic of Western modernity and civilization, Mokhber al-Saltaneh lamented such developments as the abolition of private property, the formation of big cities, the modern spatial organization of the household, the rise of the urban proletariat, revolutionary movements, and women's suffrage. The conservative views of this German-educated man of letters and politics, who served for a while as Iran's prime minister under the "modernizing" monarch Reza Shah, bore striking resemblance to the "antimodernist" camp in Germany.[21] Comparing the present invidiously with the past, he decried modernity's complexities, ethical decay, fragmentation, impersonality, irreverence, materialism, and self-interested individualism. He prescribed moral remedies such as generosity, inner policing, and restraint for solving abstruse social problems.[22] One should bear in mind that Mokhber al-Saltaneh advocated a nostalgic return to a serene, yet noble and resplendent past, while Max Horkheimer and Theodor Adorno were formulating a critique of instrumental reason—reason defined by the adequacy of means for the realization of predetermined ends—in the pages of *Dialectic of Enlightenment*.[23]

The vast majority of the Iranian intelligentsia were not willing to object to the moralistic and pedantic intellectualism of the likes of Mokhber al-Saltaneh, who was engaged in the audacious denunciation of Western modernity.[24] Fewer still were convinced of the utter futility of such a pursuit. The well-worn dichotomies between a spiritual Orient and a materialistic Occident, Anglo-Saxon scientific pragmatism and Asiatic romantic aestheticism, or the genuinely local and the appropriating global never lost their sway. Having an inadequate knowledge of Western history and a tenuous grasp of Western philosophy meant that Mokhber al-Saltaneh and most members of his generation could hardly comprehend the organic complexities, the multilateral character, or the runaway quality of Western modernity.[25] Hence, alas, they vacillated between admiring and disparaging, craving and abhorring, and finally emulating and rebuffing the West.

Everlasting Incertitude?

So far I have maintained that when we examine the actual versus the fictional history of Westernization in Iran, we are struck by how very few real Ja'far Khans indeed existed. In the annals of Iranian history, one can find very few intellectuals who were so enamored of Western culture as to advocate a forgoing of Iran's cultural heritage in order to surmount the country's economic, social, and scientific retardation.[26] This proclivity was widespread despite the fact that the modern intelligentsia had a keen awareness of the gradual diminution of Iran's civilizational grandeur. It is therefore appropriate to ask what has been gained from adopting an ambivalent attitude toward the regime of modernity.

In my view, the most important lesson has been the realization that the whimsical imitation of the West is a charade, and submissive pandering to the past is futile. Today, the absence of unanimity and monological discourse regarding a host of issues indicates that the Iranian intellectual world is more heterogeneous and reflexive than it has ever been in the past. Gone are the days when the preponderance of one ideological viewpoint bestowed a uniform yet feeble quality on Iran's intellectual life. As far as acceptance of Western modernity is concerned, there are promising signs of change. Copious and vindictive diatribes and eulogies for a cul-de-sac modernity are becoming trite or are falling by the wayside. Iranian intellectuals are coming to terms with the fact that the omnipotence of modernity's worldview and the omnipresence of its regalia can now be felt the world over.[27] The utopian strivings of more and more of Iran's intellectuals are now impregnated with modernist sensibilities and theoretical givens, such as the legitimacy of the separation of religion and state, the individual nature of faith, and the essentiality of political pluralism. While condemnation of Western governments for their historical and neocolonial arrogance, belittlements, denigrations, domination, plunders, and slights continues unabated, the discourse of "anti-Westernization" is undergoing a serious interrogation. This may be partly attributed to the fact that an increasing number of Iran's educated classes now recognize that "the West" is an inextricable constituent of their inchoate identity and an internalized part of their swelling self-consciousness.

This group can more and more identify with the following sentiment expressed by the Palestinian historian Hisham Sharabi:

> Today, I am inclined to see the West mostly as a collective singular, a figure of speech, an entity in constant flux, a different thing at different times—Christianity, Modern Europe, Industrial Society, Imperialism, Technology, Violence—without center or inner unity. The West is centered unity only from the outside, from the standpoint of the non-West, that of the societies/cultures (India, China, Islam) that have been the target of Western violence and domination.[28]

Abandoning this "unity-centered" view of the West is not going to be an easy task for Iran's lettered classes. They recognize that modernity, both as a phenomenon and as a spirit, has brought along monumental revolutions as witnessed by the transition from "man" to "individual" and from "status" to "contract." Yet, in societies such as Iran where modernity was acquired mostly as a technique, the indispensable cultural and social rudiments for the above typed transitions have either been missing or meager. Hence, unsurprisingly, the acquisition of material and imagined modernity could not be devoid of debilitating fear, keen skepticism, or mordant cynicism. In a cultural setting saturated with metaphysical beliefs and deference to ancient traditions, many remain fearful that modernity will diminish the sense of inwardness and the distinctiveness of the individual and erect a world where contempt for religion and an impersonal, routinized, and uniformed logic will rule supreme. Even for some of those thinkers who are persuaded that articulating an alternative account of modernity is unattainable, the idea of domesticating modernity or staging symbolic resistance to it remains enduringly appealing. This disposition may be partly attributed to the fact that most Iranians could not easily pardon past and present Western violence and will to dominate.

Nonetheless, cataloguing the theoretical shortcomings of Iran's intellectuals should not prevent us from recognizing the ills and harms of modernity. After all, modernity was not merely about self-assertion and individual liberty. It was also about bureaucratization, commercialization, violence, and social engineering. Modernity enabled the modern state to spread its tentacles as never before and create newer types of violence. Large-scale inspection, systematic surveillance, technologies of torture and total war, use of gratuitous violence, and well-organized exterminations testify to modernity's penchant for discipline and punishment while ecological disasters and overpopulation testify to some of its other evils.[29] In other words, one has to acknowledge that modernity has camouflaged, redeployed, and sanitized violence without necessarily diminishing it.

We also need to concede that modernity's claim to provide complete, final, and universal answers and solutions to problems besetting humankind was, in retrospect, naive, arrogant, and pernicious. As Aziz al-Azmeh has reminded us, such nineteenth-century utopias as historical inevitability and unilinear progress have been dealt a coup de grace.[30] Furthermore, modernity may have been disseminated worldwide, but it was still developed locally. Marx was correct in considering the railroad as India's passport to modernity, but he did not live to see that in India—as well as in most other parts of the developing world—modernity did not manage to render impotent local repertoires nor did it bring the same remunerations as in the West.[31] Moreover, modernity surely had Europe as its cradle, but its present caretakers are dispersed all throughout the globe. Hence, modernity has come to denote different things to different people.

Certainly, Iranian intellectuals can benefit from as well as contribute to the ongoing debate concerning a reassessment of the status and values of modernity. As the contours of the Iranian intellectual life further mutate in the direction of celebrating an eclectic consciousness, the intelligentsia will be further reassured that this plural identity is the best cultural safeguard for democratic practice because pluralism can inhibit the cruelty of a single belief, the vanity of one standard of value, and the banality of one code of conduct, be it traditional or modern.

Notes

1. Quoted in Roderic H. Davison, "Westernized Education in Ottoman Turkey," *Middle East Journal,* vol. 15 (summer 1961), p. 299.

2. Anthony Giddens defines modernity as a historical condition of difference and associates it with "(1) a certain set of attitudes toward the world, the idea of the world as open to transformation by human intervention; (2) a complex of economic institutions, especially industrial production and a market economy; (3) a certain range of political institutions, including the nation-state and mass democracy." See Anthony Giddens and Christopher Pierson, *Conversations with Anthony Giddens: Making Sense of Modernity* (Stanford, Calif.: Stanford University Press, 1998), p. 94.

3. I have relied on the definition of modernism proposed by Marshall Berman

in *All That Is Solid Melts into Air* (New York: Penguin Books, 1988). Berman maintains that "modernism" is "any attempt by modern men and women to become subjects as well as objects of modernization, to get a grip on the modern world and make themselves at home in it" (p. 5). He continues: "To be modern is to find ourselves in an environment that promises us adventure, power, joy, growth, transformation of ourselves and the world—and, at the same time, that threatens to destroy everything we have, everything we know, everything we are" (p. 15). "Modernization" consists of the "social processes that brings this maelstrom into being" (p. 16).

4. By "Westernization" I mean a mode of thinking and praxis that corresponds to Western (i.e., mainly European) rather than native ways.

5. This type of reaction was not peculiar to Iran. As Adnan Adivar explained, next door in the Ottoman Empire, the "official pressure against the penetration of Western thought was such that toward the end of Abdul Hamid II's reign, just before the revolution of 1908, the very word *hikmet* (philosophy) was taken out of the dictionaries by order of the government." Abdulhak Adnan Adivar, "Islamic and Western Thought in Turkey," *Middle East Journal,* vol. 1 (July 1947), p. 275.

6. This attitude may partly be seen in the following quotation attributed to Naser al-Din Shah, the Qajar king who ruled Iran for almost the entire second half of the nineteenth century (1848–1896): "I wish that never a European had set foot on my country's soil; for then we would have been spared all these tribulations. But since the foreigners have unfortunately penetrated into our country, we shall at least make the best possible use of them." Quoted in William S. Haas, *Iran* (New York: AMS Press, 1966), p. 35.

7. Mangol Bayat, *Mysticism and Dissent: Socioreligious Thought in Qajar Iran* (Syracuse, N.Y.: Syracuse University Press, 1982), pp. 173–4.

8. While such literary figures as Mehdi Akhavan-Sales (1928–1990), Zabih Behruz (1890–1971), and Sadeq Hedayat (1903–1951) criticized Arabs and Islam through humor or poetry, one should perhaps single out Ahmad Kasravi (1890–1946) and ʿAli Dashti (1895–1982) as the two notable figures who undertook somewhat scholarly critiques of Islam.

9. On "sacral" intellectuals see Edward Shils, "The Intellectuals and the Powers: Some Perspectives for Comparative Analysis," *Comparative Studies in Society and History,* vol. 1 (1958–59), pp. 5–22.

10. Edward Shils, "The Intellectuals in the Political Development of the New States," in *Political Change in Underdeveloped Countries: Nationalism and Communism,* ed. John Kautsky (New York: John Wiley and Sons, 1963), p. 223.

11. Ibid., p. 195.

12. It is fair to say that in addition to helping the formation of new classes (i.e., the urban proletariat, the middle class), Westernization also changed the overall structure of the educational, political, economic, literary, and family structure in Iran as well as elsewhere.

13. Arnold J. Toynbee describes the intelligentsia as "a class of liaison officers

who have learnt the tricks of the intrusive civilization's trade so far as may be necessary to enable their community, through their agency, just to hold its own in a social environment in which life is ceasing to be lived in accordance with the local tradition and is coming more and more to be lived in the style imposed by the intrusive civilization upon the aliens who fall under its dominion." Arnold J. Toynbee, *A Study of History*, vol. 1 (abridged ed., New York: Dell Publishing Co., 1971), p. 451.

14. It is interesting to note that in Iran and many other lesser-developed countries, the "Westernized" intellectuals have also been the most ardent advocates of "nationalist" causes.

15. Shils, "Intellectuals in Political Development," p. 209.

16. Nonetheless, the ideas of Western thinkers heavily influenced the deliberations of Iranian intellectuals during this period, among them, Auguste Comte (1798–1857), Denis Diderot (1713–1784), Alexandre Dumas (1802–1870), Anatole France (1844–1924), Victor Hugo (1802–1885), Jean de La Fontaine (1621–1695), Immanuel Kant (1724–1804), Alphonse de Lamartine (1790–1869), Gustave Le Bon (1841–1931), Vladimir Lenin (1870–1924), John Locke (1632–1704), Karl Marx (1818–1883), Molière (1622–1673), Charles-Louis de Secondat Montesquieu (1689–1755), Blaise Pascal (1623–1662), Jean-Jacques Rousseau (1712–1778), Leo Tolstoy (1828–1910), and Émile Zola (1840–1892).

17. The coup may have shocked the intelligentsia, but it did not necessarily diminish their social significance. Writing around that time, T. Cuyler Young Jr., a professor of Persian language and history at Princeton University, who had acquired an intimate knowledge of Iran by working there, first as a missionary and later as cultural and political attaché at the American Embassy, spoke of the importance of Iranian intellectuals in the following fashion:

> Probably the most important group furnishing present support and future promise is that of the intellectuals. The spread of modern education has greatly increased their numbers to proportions of relative importance. For all the predominance of the emotional and aesthetic in Iranian personality, Iranian culture has been characterized by an unusually distinguished and persistent intellectual tradition. The cultivation of the mind has always been encouraged and honored in Iran, where the mind has ever been remarked for its native intelligence and curiosity, flexibility, and speculative bent. Professional intellectuals have been rooted in and supported by large sections of the masses who, illiterate but not untutored, have enjoyed the literary and artistic accomplishments of their leaders. T. Cuyler Young Jr., "The Social Support of Current Iranian Policy," *Middle East Journal* 6, no. 2 (spring 1952), p. 129.

18. During this period, Iranian intellectuals were most captivated by the ideas of such thinkers as Che Guevara (1928–1967), Henry Corbin (1903–1978), Frantz Fanon (1925–1961), Erich Fromm (1900–1980), Réné Guénon (1886–1951), Martin Heidegger (1889–1976), Vladimir Lenin, Herbert Marcuse (1898–

1979), Tibor Mende (1915–1984), Bertrand Russell (1872–1970), Jean-Paul Sartre (1905–1980), and Oswald Spengler (1880–1936).

19. Some of these issues have been addressed in Mehrzad Boroujerdi, *Iranian Intellectuals and the West: The Tormented Triumph of Nativism* (Syracuse, N.Y.: Syracuse University Press, 1996).

20. Abdallah Laroui, *Crisis of the Arab Intellectual: Traditionalism or Historicism?* (Berkeley: University of California Press, 1976), pp. 155–6.

21. For views of the antimodernists in Germany, see Kevin Repp, *Reformers, Critics, and the Paths of German Modernity: Anti-politics and the Search for Alternatives, 1890–1914* (Cambridge, Mass.: Harvard University Press, 2000).

22. See Mehdi Qoli Hedayat (Mokhber al-Saltaneh), *Tohfeh-e mokhberi ya kar-e bikari* (The gift of reporting or a leisurely profession) (Tehran: Chapkhaneh-e Majles, 1954).

23. Max Horkheimer and Theodor W. Adorno, *Dialectic of Enlightenment*, translated by John Cumming (New York: Continuum, 1986). It is important to remember that Mokhber al-Saltaneh's view of modernity differed from that of Rousseau, who was equally convinced of the corrupt nature of urban society and believed that humans should rescue themselves from the plight of modernity. Mokhber al-Saltaneh did not share the latter's negative view of private property as a cause of avarice and inequality, nor did he embrace the French philosopher's advocacy of a general will or a social contract. To this day, while in the West the attack on Enlightenment thought is increasingly coming out of leftist circles, in Iran it is still the Right that objects to the rational universalism and secular humanism of Enlightenment.

24. After all, Mokhber al-Saltaneh was by no means the only one in his generation who was critical of Iran's Westernization. Other men of letters such as Mohammad ʿAli Foroughi (1876–1942), Qasem Ghani (1893–1952), Seyyed Vali Allah Nasr (1876–1946), ʿAllameh Mohammad Qazvini (1877–1949), Gholamreza Rashid Yasami (1896–1951), Seyyed Fakhr al-Din Shadman (1907–1967), and ʿAli Shayegan (1902–1981), while supportive of state modernization, used to castigate the Westernization and Europeanization of Iran.

25. See Anthony Giddens, *Modernity and Self-Identity: Self and Society in the Late Modern Age* (Stanford, Calif.: Stanford University Press, 1991), p. 16.

26. Mirza Fath ʿAli Akhundzadeh (1812–1878), Mirza Malkam Khan (1833–1908), and Seyyed Hasan Taqizadeh (1878–1970) are often offered as such examples. However, we should bear in mind that even though Taqizadeh advocated a wholesale imitation of the West in the early 1920s, he retracted this argument by the early 1960s. See Seyyed Hasan Taqizadeh, *Khatabeh-ye Aqa-ye Seyyed Hasan Taqizadeh dar akhz-e tamaddon-e khareji* (Seyyed Hasan Taqizadeh's address on the adoption of Western civilization) (Tehran: Entesharat-e Bashgah-e Mehregan, 1960–61), p. 7.

27. In this regard, it helps to remember the argument of Anthony Giddens regarding the separation of space and place under modernity. Giddens writes:

"The advent of modernity increasingly tears space away from place [the physical settings of social activity] by fostering relations between "absent" others, locationally distant from any given situation of face-to-face interaction. In conditions of modernity, place becomes increasingly *phantasmagoric:* that is to say, locales are thoroughly penetrated by and shaped in terms of social influences quite distant from them. What structures the locale is not simply that which is present on the scene; the 'visible form' of the locale conceals the distanciated relations which determine its nature." Anthony Giddens, *The Consequences of Modernity* (Stanford, Calif.: Stanford University Press, 1990), pp. 18–9.

28. Hisham Sharabi, "Modernity and Islamic Revival: The Critical Task of Arab Intellectuals," *Contention: Debates in Society, Culture, and Science* 2, no. 1 (fall 1992), p. 129.

29. For two works on violence, see Anthony Giddens, *The Nation-State and Violence* (Berkeley: University of California Press, 1985); and John Keane, *Reflections on Violence* (London: Verso, 1996).

30. Aziz al-Azmeh, *Islams and Modernities* (London: Verso, 1993), p. 20.

31. As the Indian thinker Nirad Chaudhuri put it, "The West conferred subjecthood on us but withheld citizenship."

2

Khalil Maleki

The Odd Intellectual Out

Homa Katouzian

A Note on Iranian Intellectuals

The modern intellectual elite—that is, the growing body of people known as *monavvar al-fekran* and, since the 1940s, as the *rawshanfekran*—emerged during the constitutionalist movement of the late nineteenth century. There were two principal outside models for this new elite. One was the contemporary Russian intelligentsia, whose ideas and attitudes had a great impact on the thinking and aspirations of *monavvar al-fekran*. The other, a less obvious but in certain respects more important and more enduring model, was the French intellectual movement.

In effect the French are the inventors of modern intellectualism and the intellectual elite, in the narrower and more specialized sense of the term employed in this essay. The first discernible body of modern intellectuals in history, although they were not then so-called, were the eighteenth-century *philosophes,* such men and women as Voltaire, Diderot, d'Alembert, Helvétius, d'Holbach, Émilie (Marquise) du Châtelet, and Madame de Staël, most of whom were otherwise known as the Encyclopedists.[1] The term "intellectual"—as a noun (rather than an adjective) and in the sense meant here—was first used toward the end of the nineteenth century, especially in the wake of the campaign led by Émile Zola and his supporters in the Dreyfus affair. It was applied by Georges Clemenceau—later to become the French war leader—to the men of letters and knowledge such as Anatole France who had signed the manifesto in support of Zola's campaign against the French military leaders' great injustice to Captain Dreyfus.[2]

From then on *les Intellectuels* referred to a fairly well defined and generally controversial elite. Julien Benda's *La trahison des clercs* (1927) and Raymond Aron's *L'Opium des intellectuels* (1955) are two of the most celebrated critical essays on French intellectuals. In its usage in France, the appellation "intellectual" usually excluded academics and other intellectuals who were either establishmentarian or quietist. When Raymond Aron, the distinguished French sociologist and erstwhile fellow-student of Jean-Paul Sartre at l'École Normale, described Marxism as "the opium of intellectuals," he clearly did not regard himself as an intellectual in the special sense that the term was normally applied in that country. In Iran, likewise, the Iranian intellectual elite was and remained an essentially dissident group. The term was used in that sense and usually excluded non-dissident academics and intellectuals. (Jalal Al-e Ahmad may well have been aware of Benda's essay when he first wrote the article "Dar khiyanat-e rawshanfekran" [On the betrayal of intellectuals], since he accuses French intellectuals of the same offense although for different reasons. Of course, Al-e Ahmad's critique, in that article and his later book, refers entirely to the Iranian experience.) At the risk of overemphasizing the point, it should be stressed that the distinction made here between dissident and nondissident is not intended as anything except compliance with the normal usage of the term at the time and in the countries concerned; it is not based on a definition or a value judgment by the author.

Even though the French and the Russians provided the paradigms for modern Iranian intellectuals, both *monavvar al-fekran* and *rawshanfekran*, the phenomenon was not unfamiliar in Iranian history and had a counterpart in various forms throughout the ages. It had existed in the shape of thinkers and intellectual critics like Farabi and Ibn Sina, radical poets and campaigners such as Naser Khosraw, and countless mystic thinkers, leaders, and poets such as Bayazid, Abu Saʿid, ʿAttar, Sohravardi, Rumi, ʿAyn al-Qozat, and others. Such men were the traditional vehicles for social and political (including religious) protest and dissent since they considered shunning the state and state-related power to be among their highest duties. It is well known that Shiʿi theory did not regard government as legitimate except by the anointed Imams, despite the fact that, in practice, the ʿulama coexisted with the government and many drew privileges from it. However, the ongoing conflict between state and society in Iran was a familiar phenomenon from much earlier—in fact, ancient—times: it arose from the arbitrary nature of government and (corresponding) chaotic tendencies of society.[3] Thus, society saw the state as an alien force; and, perforce, dissident thinkers, mystics, and poets represented, and sometimes articulated, the society's views and sentiments.

In 1941, intellectuals, mainly Marxist, some of whom had just been released from jail, founded the Tudeh Party. It was not yet a Communist party, whether in name, politics, outlook, or methods. It resembled more closely a popular or democratic front run by Marxist intellectuals and activists, similar to those groups that were active in occupied Europe to resist Nazi rule. From about 1949 it became a solidly Communist party in language, ideas, and international allegiance, having put behind it three crucial events: the Azerbaijan revolt of 1945–46, the ensuing party split of January 1948 (led by Khalil Maleki), and the official banning of the party in February 1949.[4]

The story of Iranian intellectuals in the 1940s and 1950s is largely the story of the Tudeh Party, including those who remained faithful to it, those who led its splinter group and founded other left-wing movements, and those who left it quietly and gave up political activism. Ahmad Kasravi was perhaps the only leading (dissident) intellectual of the 1940s and 1950s who was not a Tudeh member or "fellow traveller" in the early 1940s, although many others later became disillusioned with Communism and some even actively opposed it.[5] Thus, in the 1940s and 1950s, the general outlook of the main body of Iranian intellectuals—whether Tudeh or non-Tudeh—was leftist, though not necessarily Communist. There were sometimes major differences among them concerning, for example, their attitude toward Mohammad Mosaddeq's government or toward the Soviet Union and the Eastern bloc, but to varying degrees they were anti-imperialist, secular, and modernist. They were poets, writers, critics, essayists, journalists, and translators, though hardly any of them made a living from these activities. They either taught at schools and similar institutions or had lower- or middle-ranking jobs in a public office.

The Odd Intellectual

The hallmark of Iranian intellectuals, at least until the 1960s, was to be modernist, forward looking, and in conflict, overtly or covertly, with the state. On the face of it, Maleki's position did not seem to be very different from this general intellectual outlook. What singled him out and made him into an "odd intellectual" was his approach, together with his attitude and method. That is, it was not so much *what* he believed in, which clearly did not remain absolutely the same over time, as it was a matter of how he arrived at his beliefs, how he held and applied them, and how and on what basis he revised them. In other words his views were fundamentally different from those of other intellectuals largely because of the approach, attitude, and methods that had given rise to them.

There were three interrelated aspects to this. First was his lack of uncritical adherence to any particular social or intellectual framework, which was the main reason for his unusual originality, or the fact that he was, as they sometimes say even in the academic community, "too original." Second was his general lack of dogmatism and his readiness to suggest or consider principled compromises, that is, his belief in the "politics of imperfection" as opposed to the "politics of elimination."[6] And last, he had an unshakeable commitment to his fundamental principles and invariably refused to give them up either for power or popularity. Indeed, the immediate cause of his personal tragedy was that he was prepared to become almost totally isolated, not least from the intellectuals or the opposition, if he thought that the latter's views or methods did not best serve the general good, including their own.

His lack of complete adherence to any given intellectual or analytical framework did not just constitute a rejection of ideology in the sense that that term is often used in recent times, namely a system of thought uniquely held and believed to provide the best answers to all questions. It went further than that. It involved an open outlook of the kind that is advocated most persistently by Karl Popper both in science and society. Such openness, or readiness to ignore or contradict sacred ideals and symbols, or established paradigms (as Thomas Kuhn might have put it), is not easily tolerated even among natural scientists of modern times. Darwin was not denounced just by a few religious bigots. Einstein found himself isolated in the field of physics before the eclipse of 1919 because his theory of relativity cast doubt on the validity of established traditions. Both of them were "too original" even for the scientific community.

Yet Darwin and Einstein do not supply the best examples, because they eventually succeeded in their own lifetime. Galileo's example is more apt; so is the example of Jan Hus as compared with that of Martin Luther. Committing scientific or social (let alone religious) sacrilege, even if in the name of truth or the ideal, against attitudes and methods nominally upheld by established science and society, carries a serious risk of isolation and personal failure. This is a universal truth that may be demonstrated in politics, science, art, or, indeed, any other sphere of social life, notably religion. "Heresy," after all, is originally a religious concept, although it may also be applied in science and other spheres of human activity where a body of knowledge is held to be more or less sacred by powerful individuals and institutions.⁷ Abbé Siéyès, one of the very few leading figures of the French Revolution of 1789 to survive all the turbulent seasons until his peaceful death under Louis Philippe in the 1830s, once said that "people want to be pleased and let you flatter them; but will not put up with education." "Let us hold our tongues" was his refrain.⁸ Putting aside rare exceptions, experience everywhere seems to be consistent with this common expression of the problem, an observation that is more unfortunate than unreal.

This does not mean that the intellectual, the scientist, the artist, the political leader, or the activist has no choice at all but to conform or be condemned. Usually there are both soft and hard choices. The adherents of hard choices are called nonconformists, whether Puritans, Baptists, or Quakers before and after the English Revolution [English Civil War], cubists and surrealists of the early twentieth century, Marxists in undemocratic countries, or democrats in totalitarian states. Yet, however hard it might be to belong to such groups in a bigoted society, members receive warmth and comfort from their own people, their own sect, their own framework. The real test and trial is not so much to drink the hemlock of martyrdom, but to be martyred for a cause that no sect, group, or party of power and importance claims to be its own.

Except for the periods 1943–48, when Maleki was in the Tudeh Party, and 1949–53, during the oil nationalization and Mosaddeq's government, Maleki was generally isolated from all the main seats of power and politics, whether in government or opposition. Even in those two exceptional intervals (characterized by an unusual political openness) he did not entirely conform to the movements that he generally supported; that is, even then, he was no more than a nonconformist in the sense described above.

He did not wantonly seek this as "freaks" may do. It was just that he viewed things more or less from the outside. And, given his high intellectual potential and the amount of time he was prepared to devote to political activity and analysis, he tended to be far ahead of the existing political fashions in his diagnoses and prescriptions. Yet, this might not have led to the kind of isolation that he normally experienced had he not insisted on publicly advocating views that were too complex even for his intellectual public to understand and, in the few exceptional cases, too costly to support.

The second series of *'Elm va Zendegi,* the occasional journal of Maleki's group in the late 1950s, regularly boasted the following motto at the top of its front page: "The test applied by this journal is truth and nothing but the truth; not populism or fear of being rejected by the populace." And this "populace" ranged from leading intellectual figures on the far Left to many leaders of the Popular Movement (Nehzat-e Melli) and one or the other groups that were listened to. One is reminded of Byron telling his publisher in 1819, "I have written from the fullness of my mind ... but not for [the public's] 'sweet voices'—I know the precise worth of public applause."[9] But Byron was a radical romantic poet, not a political intellectual and activist who spent almost all of his time trying to convince those in power (whether in government or opposition) of the correctness of his policy prescriptions. This position was at once the chief cause of Maleki's success in analyzing situations with clarity and his failure in persuading any powerful body of people. There were only two exceptions to this, both occurring when his predictions proved to be right. The first occasion was in 1947, in the wake of the collapse of the Azerbaijan revolt, which he had insisted the Tudeh Party should not support uncritically. The second occasion was in 1965, when he participated in the formation of the Third National Front with Mosaddeq's backing only because major policy errors that Maleki had consistently warned against had led to the collapse of the Second National Front. But even these were empty victories precisely because success came only with the demoralization or collapse of a movement. In the former case, his "success" ended with the party split of January 1948; and in the latter, it was followed by his arrest and military trial in August 1965.

Alluding to a regular radio program during which "successful men" *(mardan-e movaffaq)* were introduced, he once said in 1960 that if the producers wished to do the same for "unsuccessful men" *(mardan-e na-movaffaq),* they should first go to him.[10] He was therefore aware that he was often courting failure and seemed to be proud of it. Whatever the psychology behind his attitude and behavior, he thought it unethical to support positions that he believed were wrong or that would end up in the failure of movements to which he more or less belonged. This ethical posture was already implicit in the slogan quoted on the front page of his journal. His posture was more explicitly expressed in the motto that regularly appeared on its back page: "For man will be immortal so long as he does not give up."

In short, Maleki was an unusual phenomenon in modern Iranian politics and society. His ideas made him many enemies across the political spectrum. Ironically, he is now being acclaimed by the democratic parties and groups of both Right and Left as a sincere and astute political thinker and activist, too far ahead of his time to have been understood and appreciated before the recent lessons of Iranian history. Indeed, a growing number of former Marxist-Leninist groups and individuals who have now turned to parliamentary socialism regard him as their "great precursor."

A Short Biography

Khalil Maleki was born in Tabriz in 1901 and died in Tehran in 1969. His father, Hajj Mirza Fath 'Ali, was a well-to-do merchant and a supporter of the Constitutional Movement. As a little boy Maleki witnessed the siege of Tabriz following Mohammad 'Ali Shah's coup d'état, during which their home was looted more than once by government forces. The death of his father and subsequent remarriage of his mother found the young Maleki in Soltan-Abad (later Arak), where he went to the traditional schools, *maktab* and *madreseh*. In the early 1920s he attended the German Technical College in Tehran and, following that, succeeded in the difficult competition for a state scholarship in Europe. He had already been attracted to politics and socialism in Tehran and cites, in a series of unfinished autobiographical essays, his somewhat disillusioning meeting with Soleyman Mirza, the then parliamentary Socialist leader. This interest was to be widened as well as deepened because of the rising political conflict in Europe (which at the time was probably at its height in Berlin, where he studied chemistry), the reemergence of arbitrary rule in Iran, and his contact with other radical students, notably, Taqi Arani.

The much-valued state scholarship was withdrawn after a student committed suicide and Maleki insisted on a full investigation, which the Iranian embassy staff was trying to avoid.[11] They branded him a Communist (which he was not) and sent him back to Tehran where he studied philosophy and education *(falsafeh va 'olum-e tarbiyati)* to become a secondary school teacher in chemistry.[12]

Early in 1937 he was arrested on the false charge of belonging to a "collectivist" [*eshteraki*] organization, tried, and convicted as one of the "Group of Fifty-three." Like most of the others in the group, he was not yet a Marxist but became one in prison. By all accounts, notably that of Bozorg 'Alavi's *Panjah va seh nafar* (The fifty-three), he behaved with exceptional courage and dignity while in jail.[13] But, as he later explained in numerous places, he became disillusioned and disappointed with many of his comrades, hence his reluctance to become a founding member of the Tudeh Party in 1941, when Reza Shah abdicated in the wake of the Allied occupation of the country. But within a year or so, some of the party's leading young intellectuals persuaded him to join the party with the express purpose of helping them to reform its leadership and program. The party opposition thus became known as the Reformist wing (Jenah-e Eslah-Talab). Their complaints were growing, including the leadership's bureaucratic attitude within the party and its conservative policy outside the party, and its submissive tendencies toward the Soviet embassy in Tehran. The party somehow managed to survive its ongoing internal conflicts, notably those over the First Party Congress and the unsuccessful Soviet demand for an oil concession.[14]

But the Azerbaijan crisis brought matters to a head. As the head of the provincial Tudeh Party in Azerbaijan, Maleki had been critical of the attitude and behavior of both the Soviet occupying forces and Ja'far Pishevari's Democrats. He opposed with equal force the Tudeh Party's formal affiliation with the Democrats in Azerbaijan and its very short-lived participation in Ahmad Qavam's coalition government. (Maleki's objection in the latter case arose simply because he thought Qavam would dispose of them at the first opportunity, as he in fact did.)

The catastrophic failure of these policies, and the internal party struggles that followed, heightened the conflict within less than a year of the collapse of the Azerbaijan Democrats. The young Reformist intellectuals—led by Al-e Ahmad—were in contact with both the young and fiery theorist Eprime Eshag and with Maleki, who was considered the elder statesman of the party opposition. It was they who persuaded Maleki to lead the famous split of January 1948.[15]

The Soviet Union immediately denounced the split and branded its leaders agents of British imperialism. The group therefore abandoned the idea of launching another party and decided to lie low for a time. The time for reflection led Maleki to conclude that the problem lay in Soviet Stalinism, on the one hand, and Marxist-Leninist ideology, on the other. He openly denounced the former and moved beyond the latter by making it clear that he was no longer a Leninist and did not subscribe to the Marxist ideology, although he still used Marxian concepts wherever suitable.

The campaign at the close of the Fifteenth Majles against the Supplemental Oil Agreement (better known as the Gass-Golsha'iyan agreement) quickly widened into a movement for free elections and democratic government, shortly to be known as the Popular Movement (Nehzat-e Melli). This happened almost at the same time as the banning of the Tudeh Party that followed an attempt on the shah's life in February 1949. The popular democratic forces closed ranks and began to form a broad-based coalition. Mosaddeq, who was not a Fifteenth Majles deputy, was brought out of his self-imposed political retirement to lead the movement. The National Front was formed during the struggles for free elections in Tehran. Mozaffar Baqa'i was leading his very effective Action Group for Free Elections (Sazman-e Nezarat bar Azadi-ye Entekhabat) when, in September 1949, he launched his weekly newspaper *Shahed*.[16]

Shortly afterward, Al-e Ahmad joined *Shahed*'s voluntary staff and persuaded Maleki to write for the newspaper.[17] The immediate result was the series of articles later published in a volume titled *The Conflict of Ideas and Opinions,* the Persian title of which (Barkhord-e 'aqayed va ara) was one of the many social and political terms and phrases coined by Maleki, later to become standard in the Persian language. The cooperation with *Shahed* continued until May 1951, when, in the wake of Mosaddeq's assumption of office, Maleki and the remnants of the Tudeh splinter group, together with Baqa'i and his Action Group formed Hezb-e Zahmatkeshan-e Mellat-e Iran, or the Toilers Party. This was to become a serious rival to the Tudeh Party in attracting students, youths, and working people, especially following Baqa'i's split and the creation of the Third Force Party—although inevitably it was a considerably smaller organization.

The relationship between Baqa'i and Mosaddeq began to run into difficulty within the first year of Mosaddeq's premiership. Their public cooperation was to endure only until the successful revolt of July 1952 against Ahmad Qavam's short-lived premiership. Baqa'i's view at that time—that the Toilers Party should go into public opposition against Mosaddeq's government—was rejected by Maleki's wing of the party, whereupon Baqa'i arranged the party split of October 1952, and the Maleki wing continued its activities under the title of the Third Force.[18]

Henceforth, the Third Force grew at a rapid rate, while the government's position tended to weaken, not least because of the split within the movement's leadership, with Baqa'i, Ayatollah Seyyed Abolqasem Kashani, and a few others first criticizing, then attacking it. The conflict came to a head on 28 February 1953, when the movement's splinter group supported the riots against Mosaddeq because of the announcement that the shah intended to visit Europe. In the event, the Third Force played a visible role in saving the situation, and Mosaddeq formally thanked them by inviting Maleki and thirty of the party activists to his home.[19]

When in July of that year Mosaddeq decided to hold a referendum to close the Seventeenth Majles and have fresh elections, Maleki and his party tried to dissuade him on the grounds that the recess would offer a golden opportunity for the openly anticipated coup attempt. Many other Popular Movement leaders likewise thought it an unwise move. Mosaddeq disagreed. There followed a private meeting—witnessed by Karim Sanjabi—that ended with Maleki speaking the now famous prophetic words: "The path you are treading will lead straight to Hell; but we shall accompany you to it, nonetheless."[20]

The coup of August 1953 saw Maleki in jail. He had been the leader of a lawful party with no responsibility in the government, thus no charges could possibly be brought against him. He was therefore jailed for a year without trial and held (deliberately, he believed) along with a group of Tudeh leaders, workers, and intellectuals in Falak al-Aflak, a medieval citadel in Khorramabad. He never ceased to complain of the mental torture that that experience inflicted on him.[21]

In 1960, when the government's economic problems and difficulties in foreign relations made political activity somewhat less restricted, Maleki led the formation of the Socialist League of the Popular Movement of Iran shortly after the establishment of the Second National Front. In the next four years, the Socialist League's criticisms of the Front's policies as the biggest organization within the Popular Movement were increasingly echoed by others such as Mehdi Bazargan's Freedom Movement, Daryush Foruhar's People of Iran Party, and the highly effective and influential student movement based at the University of Tehran. Eventually, Mosaddeq himself intervened in the matter via secret correspondence from his internal banishment and attacked the Front's leadership. They thus resigned their positions, while Mosaddeq and their other critics organized the Third National Front.[22]

It was too late. A few months after the formation of the new Front, of which the Socialist League was a member, Maleki and three other leaders of the league who were still free were arrested in August 1965, tried in a military court on the familiar charge of "planning to overthrow the regime of constitutional monarchy," and sentenced to three years' imprisonment. He was released after serving half of his sentence, because of continuing pressure on the regime by human rights groups, the Socialist International, and European socialist parties and governments (including the Austrian president's personal intervention with the shah). Two years later he died in isolation and depression.[23]

Maleki's Politics

Maleki is renowned due to a number of factors: the Tudeh split of 1948, his founding of a parliamentary socialist movement, his campaign against Stalinism both in Iran and within the world context, his general theory of the Third Force, his organized and systematic, though not uncritical, support of Mosaddeq's government, and his systematic persecution by virtually all the country's political power centers, including many of those in opposition.[24] Yet there are deeper and less obvious, although historically more important, sides to his political approach and views, which also happen to be most relevant to contemporary Iranian politics. Therefore, attention here will be focused on these aspects of his political thought and activities, which may be analytically discussed under two general headings: rejection of the conspiracy theory of politics; and dialogue, democracy, and reform.

Rejection of the Conspiracy Theory of Politics

The conspiracy theory of politics in Iran is not merely a product of modern colonial relations. On the contrary, it has deep roots in the country, running into the long history of arbitrary government. Arbitrary rule meant that there were no independent rules and procedures for the protection of life and property, even of the most privileged people in the land. It followed that there was no long-term aristocracy or any system through which the social classes and their membership could persist in the long run; hence, this author's designation of Iran as the "short-term society" as compared with Europe's "long-term society."[25]

Arbitrary rule meant that life and property were extremely tenuous and unpredictable, depending on the will and whims of rulers and local governors, pure chance or kismet, as well as the manipulative and conspiratorial skills of the persons concerned. From this followed the social psychology that every event was the product of a conspiracy, and from approximately the middle of the nineteenth century, these events were increasingly attributed to superhuman decisions and actions by the great powers. The great powers obviously were there to promote their own interests, but the magical powers attributed to them were more in line with the country's rich legendary and mythological culture than with reality. In time, this theory became a self-fulfilling prophecy: the foreign powers became far more influential in the country's politics than they might otherwise have been, by virtue of the fact that they were believed to be absolutely invincible. Modern theories of imperialism tended to enhance this tradition later in the twentieth century, but beneath the intellectual veneer of such theories the old conspiracy theory and xenophobia could be recognized at the point of application.

As early as 1949, and in the midst of the oil nationalization movement and public indignation against the Anglo-Iranian Oil Company, the raging

Cold War, and international anti-imperialist movements, Maleki launched a campaign against conspiracy theory as a most destructive barrier to the country's social and political development. He noted that he did not at all wish to underrate the power, influence, interference, and unequal position of the great powers, past or present, in Iran or in other colonial and semicolonial countries. But he opposed commonly held views regarding the great powers, namely, that (a) all the country's ills were due to colonialism and imperialism; (b) all (including even minor) events in the country's affairs were due to the underhanded machinations of these powers; (c) all the main actors in the Iranian government, politics, and opposition were agents of one or another of the great powers; (d) it was not possible for the country to develop and progress except by joining one or the other of the Cold War blocs; and (e) all seemingly independent efforts and achievements were bound to be smokescreens motivated by a great power so as to throw dust into the people's eyes and get in through the back door.

The contemporary reader without close knowledge or experience of this Iranian conspiracy theory and its length, breadth, depth, and coverage at the time might find Maleki's views and arguments commonplace if not altogether bland. Such a reader must refer to the country's political literature to be able to appreciate the extraordinary nature of Maleki's systematic argument against conspiracy theory, which in part helped reinforce his detractors' heavy charges against him and his ideas.[26] If there was one thing on which almost the whole of the country's intellectuals, and representatives of virtually all the political trends and tendencies—ranging from the shah through to the conservatives, the Tudeh Party, and the Popular Movement—were united, it was this theory, first as it pertained to the role of Russia and Britain, then Britain and the Soviet Union, and last but not least, the United States, although Britain was never quite lost sight of, even up to the revolution of 1979.

There was no other political thinker, intellectual leader, or activist leading a campaign (albeit a largely futile one at the time) against this conspiracy theory from the late 1940s through the late 1960s. In his 1949 article "Kabus-e badbini" (The nightmare of pessimism), Maleki described conspiracy theory as the main cause of pessimism among the intelligentsia concerning the country's prospects:

> [They] have turned the British Empire—which is in a process of decline, and is losing her bases one after the other—into an omnipotent, supernatural, and invincible power. In our country's capital one

can find intellectual politics-mongers who think it impossible to have a political movement independent from foreigners. If you mentioned India's freedom to them, they would immediately smile and express surprise at your naïveté not to realize that Nehru, Gandhi, and the whole of the Indian freedom movement . . . are nothing but a farce. As we all know, some people also regard Hitler (certainly) and Stalin (probably) as stooges of the British.[27]

In a subsequent article, "Maraz-e este'mar-zadegi" (The disease of being struck by imperialism), for the first time in the language of politics, Maleki used the Persian suffix *zadegi* to indicate a pathological affliction. He argued that British imperialism had been made into a terrifying specter, resulting in the Iranian people's complete loss of self-confidence. The society was "struck," he wrote, by the illusion of British omnipotence, and this had led to the belief that the Iranians were no more than puppets in the hands of foreign powers, utterly incapable of improving their own lot. The phobia had gone so far, he argued, that if one were to suggest some positive steps for social progress, most would react by saying, "But they won't allow it," clearly referring to the agents of British imperialism. "There can be no doubt about the strength of imperialism," he wrote, "but we must find out where this strength lies and what is at the source of this force, which has so effectively penetrated the roots of our society and has become the turn of phrase of these gentlemen, who are struck by imperialism."[28] He went on to say that, in fact, much of this strength lay precisely in the illusion of its invincibility. It was a complex phenomenon consisting of two different parts, "objective" and "subjective." The objective part corresponded to imperialism's real power, presence, and ability to interfere in the country's affairs, whereas the subjective aspect was a figment of the imagination and had "no counterpart in reality." If those who had given up all hope out of fear of the "*illusion* of imperialism" would only try to overcome that illusion and assess its strength as being no more or less than it actually was, without underrating the strength of the Iranian people, then it would be possible for Iranians to overcome the "real" and "objective" strengths of imperialism. "Some . . . individuals who suffer from the disease of being struck by imperialism," he argued, "do not even think in terms of reform, let alone take any steps toward it. This group of politics-mongers and intellectuals, who suffer from the paranoia of the omnipotence of imperialism and the impotence of Iranians (and similar peoples), must justly be called 'struck by imperialism.' It is very difficult to argue with those who suffer from this sickness."[29] "The exaggeration of the strength of imperialism," he wrote in the subtitle to another article, "serves the interests of Britain today and those of the Soviet Union tomorrow, but it will never serve the interests of Iran."

As noted above, Maleki published these articles in 1949. He was to continue in the same spirit for the rest of his life, in theory as well as in practice, saying that unreasonable fear of the great powers would work against the country's interests and its ability to improve its domestic and international situation. Hence, although he was critical of Soviet domestic and international politics, he nevertheless believed that the best line of action toward the Soviet and American blocs was to establish friendly but independent relations with both of them.

For example, at the end of January 1953, when Mosaddeq's government nationalized Caspian shipping, turning down the Soviet request for an extension of their expired concession, the Tudeh press vehemently condemned the decision while the daily *Niru-ye Sevvom* published several articles supporting it. Yet, on the day the former Caspian Fishing Company passed into Iranian hands, *Niru-ye Sevvom*'s leading article, written by Maleki, ran the following headline:

> The Iranian government's refusal to renew the Soviet fishing concession must not be put down to an unfriendly attitude [toward the Soviet Union]. The Iranian people *(mellat)* wish to have friendly relations with the Soviet people, and to maintain their political, economic and cultural links with them . . . The Soviet government can be absolutely sure that the Iranian people have no wish to break up their friendship with the Soviet Union. But this friendship must not be based on the old lines. If the Soviet government does not respect the freedom and independence of the Iranian people, it should not expect a friendly attitude from them.[30]

Maleki's antixenophobia, and his distrust of conspiracy explanations and analyses and the use of libel and defamation in politics, went further than may be conveyed by the above. After his last term in jail in the mid-1960s, and a couple of months before his death, a three-volume book on Iranian Freemason societies and their membership caused a frenzy in Tehran. SAVAK documents published later, in the 1980s, revealed that SAVAK had secretly aided and financed that project, in all probability to discredit those named (and, often, pictured), most of whom belonged to the social and political establishment. Freemasonry at the time was universally regarded as a den of the most hardened and corrupt "British spies." Maleki's view of the subject was more realistic as well as more fair to

Iranian Freemasons. In a letter he wrote at the time, he incidentally mentioned the publication of that book, saying, "In the last two months, the publication of *Faramushkhaneh ya Feramasonry dar Iran* (Faramushkhaneh or Freemasonry in Iran) has been the topic of conversation in the social and political circles of Tehran. In Iran they attach more importance to this organization than in fact is fitting, and show its members in a worse light than they deserve."[31]

Both during Maleki's lifetime and after—certainly as late as the early 1990s—almost all Iranian political leaders who were somehow associated with the shah's regime were branded agents or spies of Britain or the United States. But Freemasonry was perhaps the worst charge that could have been levelled against anyone, and in some cases it did not even have a basis in fact.

The xenophobia was such that, while the dissidents often thought that the shah's regime was little more than a puppet of the United States, the shah and his entourage—and, later, many who themselves had supported the revolution—believed that the revolution of February 1979 had been engineered by the Americans. There was even suspicion by some poets committed to the classical style of Persian poetry that modernism was a product of foreign conspiracies.[32] The few public figures (such as Seyyed Hasan Taqizadeh) who did not believe in conspiracy theories were often reluctant and unhappy members of the establishment, and, in some cases, were themselves unjustly believed to be foreign agents. Putting those very few aside, it would be difficult to think of anyone—certainly anyone in opposition—apart from Maleki who did not see foreign agents everywhere in Iranian politics.[33]

Dialogue, Democracy, and Reform

Maleki's political paradigm was complex and largely of his own making. He was a socialist but no longer a Marxist, although he did make use of some Marxian concepts and categories in his approach to social and economic development. But he firmly believed in personal freedoms, the people's free vote in parliamentary elections, and parliamentary democracy itself. Early in 1951, in the wake of the nationalization of Iranian oil, he wrote that oil nationalization had been a great achievement but that it was just the beginning for fundamental political development:

> The popular forces must be organized in order to establish real parliamentary democracy based on political parties, so that the people would really and genuinely be able to govern the country through

their parliamentary deputies.... This is an important function of the National Front Coalition, and to succeed in this historical duty, its leaders and progressive members must not simply follow the existing regional and international trends, but must rely on their own initiatives.... The people must be taught and educated so as to be able to earn and protect both bread and freedom.... In other words, measures must be taken to enable every cook to learn the art of governance and of participation in government.

And he went on to add that a system had to be created whereby it would be possible to have both bread and freedom, and to serve the society's interest without sacrificing the rights of individuals: "In my view, the National Front's most important historical duty is to create . . . a civilization in which neither the society shall be sacrificed to the individual nor shall it be forgotten that the society is not an abstract entity but is the sum of its individual members."[34]

In September 1952, in an article whose central point was the need for public order and political discipline (very rare commodities in the 1940s) as well as social and economic legislation for development, he wrote, "[D]emocratic discipline must replace chaos and indiscipline." "Yet," he went on to emphasize, "the great difference between disciplined work based on social planning and priorities suggested by us, as compared to totalitarian systems, is its democratic nature. We must not sacrifice individual freedoms to public institutions, nor must we allow absolute dominion of such institutions over personal liberties."[35] Years later he was to write on the front page of an issue of *'Elm va Zendegi:* "Communists sacrifice freedom for bread, while reactionaries sacrifice bread for freedom; we hold that bread, freedom, and social welfare are not mutually exclusive."[36]

This was in 1960, when the postcoup regime was at its weakest point and radical idealism was exceedingly rife among its opponents. But Maleki still believed that the country's best chance was in the establishment of the rule of law and peaceful political and economic reform. Here is a short selection of Policy Point IV of the Socialist League's manifesto published in September 1960:

> It seems that the substance of a social system is more important than its form.... The League shall respect the present constitution and try to establish the rule of law. With land reform and the abolition of remnants of the *moluk al-tavayefi* (feudal) system, it may be possible to create social stability and equilibrium and give real meaning

to the right to vote. If we succeed in securing the essence of parliamentary constitutionalism by obtaining the [true] right to vote for all the people of both town and country, we shall be able to hit major targets by making good use of it.

But democracy and freedom, the manifesto emphasized, were far from chaos. "Some people confuse libertarianism with lawlessness and chaos. *The Socialist League regards this kind of freedom as a necessary prelude to dictatorship.*" On the other hand, there must be serious respect for individual freedoms and decentralization of administration across the country:

> While the League regards as necessary government intervention in the economy and elsewhere, it also puts a premium on personal freedoms and private initiative. Government intervention or control should never be at the expense of individual freedoms. For the same reasons, the League . . . believes that, gradually and as far as possible, central government functions must be relegated to the local authorities.[37]

In the 1951–53 period, when Mosaddeq was prime minister, Maleki led a systematic campaign for major social reforms. The political atmosphere was such that almost no other political force or leader, either pro- or anti-Mosaddeq, offered concrete proposals (as distinct from millenarian slogans) for long-term reform. The Tudeh Party looked forward to radical and comprehensive change achieved by an imminent revolution led by them. National Front parties other than Third Force were preoccupied with the Anglo-Iranian oil dispute and were not as concerned about long-term social development.

Maleki was conscious of the fact that as long as the Anglo-Iranian oil dispute continued—indeed, went on escalating—there would simply not be sufficient domestic peace and strength to make major reform possible. Therefore, both in the interest of domestic peace and stability and for the sake of long-term political and economic progress, he advocated the best possible settlement for the oil dispute, even if it was not a completely just one from Iran's viewpoint. But before reaching a settlement of the oil dispute, he thought it necessary to remind both the state and the society of the urgency of major social reforms. They included a number of fundamental measures, but the two most important from his own point of view were land reform and equal rights for women.

He advocated a comprehensive reform of Iran's land tenure system—

"the liberation of 80 percent of the population from bondage and deprivation"—both for reasons of justice and morality, and in the interest of social and economic development. On the question of women, he did not miss an occasion to advocate the full franchise and integration into the civil society of "the one-half of the society that brings up the other half on its lap" and the need to mobilize the country's full capacity by bringing women into the sphere of public life and social activity.[38] Indeed, in his long and important open letter to Ayatollah Seyyed Abolqasem Kashani, written in October 1952 just after some of Kashani's activists helped Baqa'i's men to evict the Toilers Party cadre forcefully from the party premises, he wrote, "I seek honor in what I have written about women's rights, and state with utmost courage that—in our time, and in the prevailing conditions of the world—it will not be possible to keep more than half of the society in a state of paralysis. All nations of the world, today, make use of the most of their human resources, in the interest of peace or war [as the case may be]. If we do not manage, or do not want to involve women in social life, in all matters that affect the management of society, we shall not be able to defend our independence."[39]

When, in January 1953, Mosaddeq was considering the enfranchisement of women through a comprehensive electoral reform, and some very influential 'ulama let it be known that they would not tolerate it, Maleki and the Third Force launched a relentless and vociferous campaign in favor of the vote for women. Nonetheless, the government had to shelve the proposed bill because it lacked the strength to face a populist opposition to it on religious grounds.[40]

As noted, the arguments and programs for women's rights, land reform, parliamentary democracy, personal liberties (as opposed to license and chaos), and social welfare continued after the 1953 coup and into the early 1960s, despite the fact that the public attitude toward the regime had become very uncompromising, and this, as we shall soon see, was a strong factor in supplying more cannon fodder to Maleki's detractors. In 1956, Maleki suggested a comprehensive political program to party leaders (who later organized the Second National Front in 1960). At the time, they thought that there would be no hope of political activity for years, perhaps even decades, to come.[41] Maleki believed that the opportunity would arrive sooner or later and they needed to be ready for it. He put forward a comprehensive set of proposals regarding domestic politics, foreign relations, and social and economic reform.

In domestic politics, he wrote, they should enter a "life-and-death struggle" against corruption, strive for the establishment of the rule of law, and promote "constitutional and parliamentary democracy based on a welfare state." However, they should accept the existing system of constitutional monarchy. This did not mean "unprincipled politicking"; rather, it was a quest for "revolutionary aims by the use of peaceful means."

The proposed social reform program contained a fairly detailed land reform policy and an industrialization policy based on planning and state participation that explicitly rejected *étatisme*. With regard to foreign policy, it called for the establishment of friendly relations with both East and West without compromising the country's independence.[42]

To many members of the Iranian intelligentsia, intellectuals, political parties and groups, and leading reformers today, this should look like a very reasonable and progressive package of reforms and a responsible attitude toward politics and society. Yet, at the time, to most of them it smacked of "collaborationism" and opportunism at best, but more often as betrayal. Indeed, within the couple of years that separated the publication of the two above-mentioned documents, Maleki and his colleagues were showered with a barrage of political abuse.

Yet, and in spite of all that, in 1960 Maleki was to supply the seemingly most convincing evidence for his detractors' charges against him. In October of that year, Asadollah 'Alam met him a couple of times and repeated an invitation by the shah for the two men to meet. Maleki had once met the shah (also at the latter's bidding) early in 1953, after obtaining the full consent of his party's central committee and the support of Mosaddeq. But this time, things were different, and his meeting with the shah could be used—and in fact it was—as evidence of the "collaborationism" of which a growing circle had already begun to accuse him.

This time, too, Maleki obtained the unanimous agreement of his colleagues and the support of Gholam Hoseyn Sadiqi and Karim Sanjabi, two of the most prominent and respected leaders of the Second National Front. Two years later, in his long letter to Mosaddeq, he briefly described how he had met the shah again and what they had talked about: "[In October 1960] Mr. 'Alam visited me three times, each time for two hours, and tried to convince me to have a meeting with the shah . . . In those days the ruling regime was weak and was prepared to give many concessions to the [Second] National Front. The very insistence that I should go and see the shah was evidence of that weakness." To the question of why "a few other Popular Movement leaders had not been likewise invited," 'Alam answered that Maleki had "made clear [his] respect for the Constitution" and that his attitude "toward the Tudeh Party was well known."

'Alam explained that the others would also be invited once they clarified their positions with regard to those two questions, and that the meeting with Maleki was intended to clear the way for a wider meeting. "In the end," wrote Maleki in his letter to Mosaddeq, "I visited the shah, with the agreement of our [Socialist League's] executive committee, and after direct consultation with Messrs. Sadiqi and Sanjabi." "In this meeting," he continued, "just like the previous meeting that had taken place after informing and consulting with your excellency, I obtained permission to speak—with respect to the substance of my talk—as one human being [would] to another, and not according to courtly protocols. At least insofar as it concerned me, the [one-on-one] discussions [that took three hours] were plain, clear, and direct." In the end the shah said it did not make any difference to him who ran the government, even if it was the likes of the "Salehs" or the "Sanjabis." He had to be assured, however, on two points. "They must, first, make their position clear with regard to [their] respect for the Constitution (by which he meant respect for the monarchy) and, secondly, vis-à-vis the Tudeh Party." Maleki then went on to complain bitterly to Mosaddeq that, as a result of the lack of response of the Front's leaders, the whole movement had suffered a great setback by the time of writing his letter to Mosaddeq:

> At the time when the establishment was considerably weak, and all sorts of concessions could have been extracted from them in the interests of the Popular Movement, the announcement of a couple of words about the Constitution and the Tudeh Party could have clarified the movement's position both on the domestic and on the foreign standpoints. But the [Second National Front] leaders maintained silence over these two subjects until they themselves became defenders of the Constitution and constitutional monarchy. That is, in response to the charges that SAVAK leveled against them, they found it necessary, many times, to issue public statements against the Tudeh Party and the Persian radio broadcasts from Eastern Europe. Had they clarified their position in the first place, they would not have been forced to respond to such charges [to the extent that they were later obliged to do].

Maleki concluded this part of his long letter by referring to further developments when he argued once again that the movement's leaders had made a fatal mistake by adopting a sentimentalist, uncompromising attitude, this time toward 'Ali Amini's government: "During Dr. Amini's premiership [April 1960–July 1961] there was another kind of opportunity.

There was a split within the ruling establishment, and it was quite possible [for the Popular Movement] to succeed Amini. Yet, with their amazing mistakes, the Front's leaders also threw that opportunity away."[43]

The argument over Amini's government is yet another important episode in Maleki's "strange politics." 'Ali Amini was a loyal establishment politician with a major land reform policy, who also believed that the shah's extraconstitutional powers should be curtailed. The shah neither liked nor trusted Amini. Yet the latter took advantage of the shah's domestic and foreign troubles and became prime minister.

Briefly, Maleki's analysis of the situation was that Amini represented the regime's reformist wing, that he was serious in his land reform policy, and that he was prepared to grant more freedoms to the Popular Movement vis-à-vis the shah and the landlords. The Second National Front, he argued, should therefore take advantage of the new situation and organize itself into a shadow government by putting forward a more progressive social and political program and acting as constructive opposition to Amini's government. However, the Front led a purely negative campaign against Amini until his fall in July 1962, and this led to their own failure and defeat shortly after.[44]

It was no wonder, therefore, that—given the country's political underdevelopment—Maleki was isolated, attacked, and vilified by government and opposition alike. Thus, when he was arrested for the last time before his death, the official report of his arrest looked like reports of the arrest of men like Bukharin in Stalin's time. The long report's conclusion is fully representative of its entire text:

> The above-mentioned person showed in the end that he was a born adventurer and anarchist who would abuse the vulnerabilities of the country's youth in order to achieve his filthy ends and would not shy away from resorting to any ugly means. It is unfortunate that the country's security forces sometimes adopt a forgiving attitude toward such treacherous and subversive elements and only begin to prosecute them when a number of innocent young people have already been struck by their poisonous spell. It is to be hoped that henceforth . . . the security forces and responsible organizations will not give such elements so much opportunity to enable them, by means of their evil ideas, to propagate their deviant, destructive, and antireligious thoughts among the impressionable youth and individuals.[45]

Conclusion

Khalil Maleki was thus an "odd intellectual" in two senses of the term. In the first place, he was "odd" in the sense of formulating and publicly campaigning for theories and policies that were not acceptable to the large majority of his contemporary intellectuals and the political power centers (whether in government or in opposition). In other words he was "too original" and, as such, would have been isolated anywhere, not just in Iran, although he would not have paid such very high costs for it in a politically advanced society. Second, and by corollary, he was an "odd intellectual out" in the sense that he contradicted the main political tenets of his time in Iran. This led him to campaign against the seemingly immutable conspiracy theory of politics, advocate parliamentary socialist democracy and respect for individual freedoms, and reject *étatisme* in planning for development. Furthermore, he endorsed and practiced political dialogue and campaigned for major social and political reform rather than revolution, mainly in the areas of democracy, land reform, and women's rights. No wonder that he was rejected, denounced, and persecuted by various political power centers—whether in government or in opposition—until 1990, when he began to come back into vogue. In short, Maleki's intellectual legacy is thus not just in the policies that he advocated at the time in Iran, but, even more, in his critical, open, and nondogmatic attitude, from which lessons may be learned by traditionalists and rationalists alike.

Appendix: Report of the Arrest of Khalil Maleki

The following report is an excerpt from the newspaper *Keyhan*:

It has been announced that in the last few days, Khalil Maleki and some of his colleagues have been arrested by the security forces on charges of spreading Marxist and collectivist [*eshteraki*] ideas, poisoning [people's] minds and taking action against the security of the country. . . .[46]

According to past records, Khalil Maleki has been one of the prime promoters of the *eshteraki* ideology in Iran, and together with fifty-two other leaders of the Tudeh Party [sic], founded that party [sic]. . . . Afterward, when, as a result of his own personal ambitions, he ran into conflict with the party's leaders over gaining high position within the party, he managed to win the support of a group [of party members] and seceded from it.

The above-mentioned person, while keeping to his [original] ideology, had been looking for an opportunity to implement his malicious ideas. Mosaddeq's government, especially in its later period, when various destructive factions were acting against Iran's territorial integrity, [was in power at just such a time]. . . . [Maleki's] clique was the first group to demand the declaration of a republic during the dark days of 16 to 19 August [1953], and he was imprisoned and banished for this very reason following the national uprising of 19 August.

After a time, according to the [Arabic] expression "Public amnesia is my shield" *[nisyan al-nas hisni],* he exploited the forgetfulness of some people, especially the young. In the name of sympathy for the working classes, securing public welfare, extending social justice, and other such-like deceptive notions, he inculcated dreams and mirage-like ideas in the minds of a small number of people who were prepared to work with him, hoping that in this way he would acquire some power and finally, manage to satisfy his passion for high position.

At this juncture, as a result of the 6th Bahman [January 1963] White Revolution and [other] progressive projects, Iranian society was led toward a prosperous standard of living, and consequently Khalil Maleki's group lost its deceitful propagandist weapon. When Maleki (who had one day promised the reform of the workers' and peasants' living standards as if it were a dream, believing that [such a thing] could only be attained through a series of revolutionary actions involving devastation and massacre) realized that better reforms had been carried out without any bloodshed . . . and that the Iranian nation looked forward to a hopeful and brilliant future and would pay no attention to the balderdash put out by him and his friends, he looked for a new weapon. He declared the subversive riots of 5 June [1963], which had caused much financial and spiritual damage to the motherland, to be a national [or popular] revolt, hoping that in this way, he would achieve his perverse and power-seeking aspirations.[47]

Following that, he collaborated with other subversive cliques—whose nature is known to all the compatriots—inside and outside the country. At the same time, taking advantage of the radical sentiments of some young people, he decided to use certain Marxist theories in order to sow the seeds of anarchism, terrorism, chaos, and turmoil in [people's] minds and, so to speak, lead them toward a red revolution. The above-mentioned person showed in the end that he was a born adventurer and anarchist who would abuse the vulnerabilities of the country's youth in order to achieve his filthy ends and would not shy away from resorting to any ugly means.

It is unfortunate that the country's security forces sometimes adopt a forgiving attitude toward such treacherous and subversive elements and only begin to prosecute them after a number of innocent young people have already been struck by their poisonous spell. It is to be hoped that henceforth, in accordance with public expectations, the security forces and responsible organizations will not give such elements so much opportunity to enable them, by means of their evil ideas, to propagate their deviant, destructive, and antireligious thoughts among the impressionable youth and individuals whose existence will certainly be of value for the reconstruction of Iran.

Notes

1. References on the *philosophes* and the Enlightenment are virtually innumerable. See, for example, Isaiah Berlin, *The Age of Enlightenment: The 18th Century Philosophers* (New York: New American Library, 1956); Otis E. Fellows and Norman L. Torrey, eds., *The Age of Enlightenment: An Anthology of Eighteenth-Century French Literature* (New York: F. S. Crofts, 1942); Kingsley Martin, *French Liberal Thought in the Eighteenth Century: A Study of Political Thought from Bayle to Condorcet* (London: E. Benn, 1929); Isaiah Berlin, *Against the Current: Essays in the History of Ideas,* ed. Henry Hardy (London: Pimlico, 1997).

2. A good knowledge of the Dreyfus affair and the campaigns of the Dreyfusards and anti-Dreyfusards is indispensable for an appreciation of the emergence and implications of the concept of the intellectuals in France. As H. A. L. Fisher wrote in his voluminous *A History of Europe,* "It is difficult for those who did not live through the feverish years 1894–1903 to form a conception of the passions which were aroused by the fate of this young Jewish officer . . . Half France vehemently held that Dreyfus was guilty, the other half with equal vehemence that he had been cruelly wronged. Lifelong friendships were ruptured, the peace of families was ruined, the conscience of individuals was racked and tortured." See *A History of Europe* (London: Edward Arnold, 1936), pp. 1005–6. The affair itself is described and discussed in countless sources, including biographies of Zola, Clemenceau, Anatole France, Georges Sorel, Maurice Barrès (a leading anti-Dreyfusard), and others.

3. The causes, patterns, and implications of persistent state-society conflict have been discussed elsewhere, both extensively and intensively. See, for example, Homa Katouzian, *State and Society in Iran: The Eclipse of the Qajars and the Emergence of the Pahlavis* (London and New York: I. B. Tauris, 2000); Katouzian, "European Liberalisms and Modern Concepts of Liberty in Iran," *Journal of Iranian Research and Analysis* 16, no. 2 (November 2000), pp. 9–29; Katouzian, "Towards a General Theory of Iranian Revolutions," *Journal of Iranian Research and Analysis* 15, no. 2 (November 1999), pp. 145–62; Katouzian, "Arbitrary

Rule: A Comparative Theory of State, Politics and Society in Iran," *British Journal of Middle Eastern Studies* 24, no. 1 (1997), pp. 49–73; Katouzian, "The Aridisolatic Society: A Model of Long-term Social and Economic Development in Iran," *International Journal of Middle East Studies* 15, no. 2 (May 1983), pp. 259–81. See also other essays reprinted in Katouzian, *Iranian History and Politics: The Dialectic of State and Society* (London: Routledge Curzon, 2003).

4. See, for example, Homa Katouzian, *The Political Economy of Modern Iran: Despotism and Pseudo-Modernism, 1926–1979* (London and New York: Macmillan and New York University Press, 1981); Katouzian, *Musaddiq and the Struggle for Power in Iran,* 2d ed. (London and New York: I. B. Tauris, 1999); Katouzian, *Sadeq Hedayat: The Life and Legend of an Iranian Writer* (London and New York: I. B. Tauris, 2002); Ervand Abrahamian, *Iran between Two Revolutions* (Princeton, N.J.: Princeton University Press, 1982); Babak Amir Khosravi, *Nazar az darun beh naqsh-e hezb-e Tudeh-ye Iran* (An inside look at the role of the Tudeh Party of Iran) (Tehran: Entesharat-e Ettela'at, 1996).

5. For a detailed discussion of individual intellectuals and their ideas, see Ali Gheissari, *Iranian Intellectuals in the Twentieth Century* (Austin: University of Texas Press, 1998); Mehrzad Boroujerdi, *Iranian Intellectuals and the West: The Tormented Triumph of Nativism* (Syracuse, N.Y.: Syracuse University Press, 1996); Negin Nabavi, *Intellectuals and the State in Iran: Politics, Discourse, and the Dilemma of Authenticity* (forthcoming).

6. "The politics of elimination" is this author's term and concept for politics in an arbitrary state and society. See Katouzian, "Problems of Democracy and the Public Sphere in Modern Iran," *Comparative Studies of South Asia, Africa, and the Middle East* 18, no. 2 (1998), pp. 31–7; Katouzian, "European Liberalisms"; Katouzian, "Towards a General Theory."

7. The issues alluded to in the above paragraph are too wide and complicated to enable an extended treatment in this essay, although they are vital to understanding Maleki's predicament. See, for example, Karl Popper, *Conjectures and Refutations: The Growth of Scientific Knowledge* (London: Routledge & Kegan Paul, 1963); Popper, *Objective Knowledge: An Evolutionary Approach* (Oxford: Clarendon Press, 1972); Popper, "The Myth of the Framework," reprinted in *The Myth of the Framework: In Defence of Science and Rationality,* M. A. Notturno, ed. (London and New York: Routledge, 1994); T. S. Kuhn, *The Structure of Scientific Revolutions,* 2d ed. (Chicago: University of Chicago Press, 1970); Homa Katouzian, "The Hallmarks of Science and Scholasticism: A Historical Analysis," in *The Yearbook of the Sociology of the Sciences* (Dodrecht, Boston, and London: Reidel, 1984); Katouzian, *Ideology and Method in Economics* (London and New York: Macmillan and New York University Press, 1980), chaps. 4 and 5; Katouzian "T. S. Kuhn, Functionalism and Sociology of Knowledge," *British Journal for the Philosophy of Science* 35, no. 2 (June 1984), pp. 166–73. For an unspecialized discussion of the problem, see "Khalil Maleki va mas'aleh-ye adam-e ghayr-e 'adi" (Khalil Maleki and the problem of the unusual person), in *Yadnameh-ye Khalil*

Maleki (Essays in memory of Khalil Maleki), ed. H. Katouzian and A. Pichdad (Tehran: Sherkat-e sahami-ye Enteshar, 1991).

8. See "Siéyès," in J. M. Thompson, *Leaders of the French Revolution* (Oxford and New York: Blackwell, 1988), p. 11.

9. Quoted in Andrew Sanders, *The Short Oxford History of English Literature* (Oxford: Clarendon Press, 1994), p. 380.

10. See *'Elm va Zendegi,* nos. 1–11 (1960–61).

11. There was another protester, Ahmad Hami, who was likewise forced to return home because his scholarship was withdrawn. But he had powerful connections who helped restore his grant, enabling him to return to Berlin.

12. There are no known written sources on Maleki's childhood and youth, and the basic information that is available is a result of oral accounts by himself and/or his half brother Hoseyn Malek. Fortunately, however, he did write a series of articles about his public life experiences in the 1920s in a column titled "Trazhedi-ye qarn-e ma" (The tragedy of our century), published in the weekly *'Elm va Zendegi,* nos. 1–11, throughout the year 1960–61. After this date, the publication was banned for good.

13. See Bozorg 'Alavi, *Panjah va seh nafar* (The fifty-three) (Tehran: Amir Kabir, 1978); Hamid Ahmadi, ed., *Khaterat-e Bozorg 'Alavi* (The memoirs of Bozorg 'Alavi) (Sweden: Nashr-e Baran, 1997); Anvar Khameh'i, *Panjah nafar va seh nafar* (The fifty and the three) (Tehran: Entesharat-e Hafteh, 1982); Homa Katouzian, ed., *Khaterat-e siyasi-ye Khalil Maleki* (The political memoirs of Khalil Maleki) (Tehran: Sherkat-e sahami-ye Enteshar, 1989).

14. See, for example, Maleki's text as well as Katouzian's introduction to *Khaterat-e siyasi,* and the text of Maleki's letter to Abdolhoseyn Nushin reprinted in the appendices of the same book. Homa Katouzian and Amir Pichdad, eds., *Khalil Maleki: barkhord-e 'aqayed va ara* (The conflict of ideas and opinions), 2d ed. (Tehran: Nashr-e Markaz, 1997); Anvar Khameh'i, *Forsat-e bozorg-e az dast rafteh* (The big opportunity that was lost) (Tehran: Entesharat-e Hafteh, 1983); Turaj Atabaki, *Azerbaijan, Ethnicity, and the Struggle for Power in Iran* (London and New York, I. B. Tauris, 2000); Abrahamian, *Iran between Two Revolutions.*

15. For full information on the arguments and events, see Khalil Maleki, *Daw ravesh baray-e yek hadaf* (Two approaches to the same objective) (Tehran: Jam'iyat-e Sosialist-e Tudeh-ye Iran, 1948); Katouzian, *Khaterat-e siyasi* (text and introduction); Katouzian and Pichdad, *Barkhord-e 'aqayed;* Jalal Al-e Ahmad, *Dar khedmat va khiyanat-e rawshanfekran* (On the service and betrayal of intellectuals) (Tehran: Ravaq, 1978), chap. 6; Anvar Khameh'i, *Az enshe'ab ta kudeta* (From the secession to the coup d'état) (Tehran: Entesharat-e Hafteh, 1984); Eprime Eshag, *Cheh bayad kard* (What is to be done?) (Tehran: 1946); Alatur [Eprime Eshag], *Hezb-e Tudeh dar sar-e daw rah* (The Tudeh Party at a juncture) (Tehran: n.p., 1947); conversations with Eprime Eshag in Oxford over many years; Katouzian, *Musaddiq and the Struggle for Power;* Katouzian, *Sadeq Hedayat: The Life and Legend,* chap. 9; Katouzian, *Political Economy;* Abrahamian,

Iran between Two Revolutions; Maziar Behrooz, *Rebels with a Cause: The Failure of the Left in Iran* (London and New York: I. B. Tauris, 1999); Babak Amir Khosravi, *Nazar az darun,* chap. 8.

16. See Katouzian, *Musaddiq and the Struggle for Power;* Katouzian, *Political Economy;* Katouzian, introduction to Maleki's *Khaterat-e siyasi;* Khameh'i, *Az ensheh'ab;* Abrahamian, *Iran between Two Revolutions;* Fakhreddin Azimi, *Iran: The Crisis of Democracy 1941–1953* (London and New York: I. B. Tauris, 1989); Nikki Keddie, *Roots of Revolution: An Interpretive History of Modern Iran* (New Haven, Conn.: Yale University Press, 1981).

17. See Al-e Ahmad, *Dar khedmat,* chap. 6; Katouzian and Pichdad, *Yadnameh.*

18. See Katouzian's introduction to Maleki's *Khaterat-e siyasi* and Maleki's open letter to Ayatollah Kashani in the appendices of the same book. Katouzian, *Musaddiq and the Struggle for Power; Niru-ye Sevvom* (The Third Force) (daily), 14 and 18 October 1952; *Shahed* (Witness), 15 October 1952; Amir Khosravi, *Nazar az darun.*

19. In various issues of the daily *Niru-ye sevvom,* for the period of two weeks after 28 February 1953, reports were included of the meeting between Maleki and Mosaddeq, together with a large photo of the two leaders among Third Force activists at Mosaddeq's home. See Muhammad Musaddiq, *Musaddiq's Memoirs,* ed. Homa Katouzian (London: Jebheh, 1988), pp. 261–305, 482–6; Katouzian's introduction to Maleki's *Khaterat-e siyasi;* Azimi, *Crisis of Democracy;* Amir Khosravi, *Nazar az darun.*

20. Sanjabi related this to the author in Tehran in October 1960, and this statement was included for the first time in the author's introduction to Maleki's *Khaterat-e siyasi,* p. 103.

21. See his unfinished articles on the Falak al-Aflak experience in several issues of the weekly *Ferdawsi* in 1956, as well as his long letter of March 1953 to Mosaddeq, published in *Khaterat-e siyasi,* pp. 412–29. Also, see his "Letter to the Establishment" (Nameh-ye Khalil Maleki beh awliya'-ye omur), pp. 433–8.

22. See Katouzian, introduction to Maleki's *Khaterat-e siyasi; Musaddiq and the Struggle for Power,* chaps. 16 and 17.

23. See Katouzian, introduction to Maleki's *Khaterat-e siyasi.*

24. All or some of these issues have been discussed in Katouzian's introduction to Maleki's *Khaterat-e siyasi;* Katouzian, *Musaddiq and the Struggle for Power;* Katouzian and Pichdad, *Yadnameh;* Abrahamian, *Iran Between Two Revolutions;* Amir Khosravi, *Negah az darun.*

25. For a detailed account of the theory of arbitrary rule, see the references in note 3 mentioned above. The concepts of "short-term society" and "long-term society" have been discussed in a number of my articles. See, for example, "Liberty and Licence"; "Problems of Democracy"; "Iran's Fiscal History and the Nature of State and Society in Iran," *Journal of the Royal Asiatic Society* 11, no. 2 (2001).

26. Examples abound. For three well-known historical sources, all of them

showing visible symptoms of the conspiracy theory, domestic and—especially—foreign, see Hoseyn Makki, *Tarikh-e bist-saleh-ye Iran* (A history of Iran, 1921–41) (Tehran: Amir Kabir, 1979); Mahmud Mahmud, *Tarikh-e ravabet-e siyasi-ye Iran va Inglis* (The history of the political relations of Iran and Britain), vols. 1–8 (Tehran: Eqbal va Shoraka', 1949–54; Khan-Malek-e Sasani, *Siyasatgaran-e dawreh-ye Qajar* (The politicians of the Qajar era) (Tehran: Ketabkhaneh-ye Tuhuri, 1959).

27. See Maleki, "Kabus-e badbini: ancheh mored darad va ancheh bimored ast" (The nightmare of pessimism: That which is relevant and that which is irrelevant), in *Barkhord-e 'aqayed va ara*, ed. Katouzian and Pichdad, p. 41.

28. Maleki, "Maraz-e Este'mar-zadegi" (The disease of being struck by imperialism), in *Barkhord-e 'aqayed va ara*, p. 43.

29. Ibid., p. 44.

30. *Niru-ye Sevvom* (31 January 1953). For the reaction of the Tudeh press see, for example, *Mardom* (People), the official party organ (11 February 1953), and several issues of *Beh su-ye ayandeh* (Toward the future) published in February 1953. For further discussion of the subject, see Katouzian, *Musaddiq and the Struggle for Power*.

31. See Maleki's letter (from Tehran) to Amir Pichdad (in Paris), 26 June 1969, in *Namehha-ye Khalil Maleki*, ed. Homa Katouzian and Amir Pichdad (The letters of Khalil Maleki) (Tehran: Nashr-e Markaz, 2003).

32. At least three poets, two of them prominent, made such a claim; two of them attributed it to imperialism, the third to international Communism.

33. For Taqizadeh's private comments on conspiracy theory, see his posthumously published memoirs, *Zendegi-ye tufani* (A tempestuous life), ed. Iraj Afshar (Tehran: 'Elmi, 1993); *Namehha-ye Landan* (Letters from London), ed. Iraj Afshar (Tehran: Farzan, 1996).

34. Maleki, "Vazifeh-ye tarikhi-ye Jebheh-ye Melli" (The historic duty of the National Front), in *Barkhord-e 'aqayed*, p. 230.

35. See "Sarnevesht-e tarikhi-ye liberalism dar daw qarn-e akhir" (The historic fate of liberalism in the last two centuries), *'Elm va Zendegi*, no. 7 (September 1952), reprinted in Khalil Maleki, *Nehzat-e Melli-ye Iran va 'edalat-e ejtema'i* (The Popular Movement of Iran and social justice), ed. 'Abdollah Borhan (Tehran: Nashr-e Markaz, 1999), p. 37.

36. See *'Elm va Zendegi* (9 August 1960).

37. See the Socialist League's manifesto, *Bayaniyeh-ye Jame'eh-ye Sosialistha-ye Nehzat-e Melli-ye Iran* (September 1960), pp. 42–3, reprinted in Borhan, *Nehzat-e Melli*, pp. 195–246.

38. See, for example, "Sarnevesht-e tarikhi-ye liberalism" (The historical fate of liberalism) and "Sharayet-e edameh-ye piruzmandaneh-ye Nehzat-e Melli" (The conditions for the successful continuation of the National Movement), *'Elm va Zendegi* (October 1952), reprinted in Borhan, *Nehzat-e Melli*; "'Alami az naw bebayad sakht" (A world must be built afresh), *'Elm va Zendegi*, reprinted in

Borhan, *Nehzat-e Melli*, pp. 53–69; "Daw rah-e hal bara-ye moshkel-e keshavarzi" (Two solutions for the problem of agriculture) in *Barkhord-e 'aqayed*, pp. 226–8. Note that these examples refer to the years 1950–53 and not the following period, which contains more extensive as well as intensive material on the subject of land reform and the vote for women. See the issues of *Nabard-e Zendegi* pertaining to the years 1955–57, as well as *'Elm va Zendegi* in the years 1958–61; *Ferdawsi*, in the period 1961–62; and *Bayaniyeh-ye Jame'eh*.

39. *Khaterat-e siyasi*, p. 442.

40. See, for the evidence, Katouzian, *Musaddiq and the Struggle for Power*, and the sources cited therein.

41. See Maleki's long "Letter to Mosaddeq" (March 1963) reprinted in *Khaterat-e siyasi*, p. 419; Katouzian, *Musaddiq and the Struggle for Power*, p. 217.

42. See "Tashkil-i Jame'eh-ye Sosialistha ra mitavan mored-e motale'eh qarar dad" (The formation of the Socialist League can be studied), *Nabard-e Zendegi* (May 1956), reprinted in Borhan, *Nehzat-e Melli*; see, further, Katouzian, *Musaddiq and the Struggle for Power*, pp. 217–8.

43. See Maleki, "Letter to Mosaddeq," *Khaterat-e siyasi*, pp. 412–29.

44. For more on Amini's government and the attitudes of Maleki and the Second National Front toward it, see Katouzian, *Musaddiq and the Struggle for Power*, chap. 16; Katouzian, *Political Economy*, chap. 11; Katouzian, introduction to Maleki's *Khaterat-e siyasi*; the long analysis of the Socialist League in *Sosialism*, no. 5 (November 1962); Abrahamian, *Iran between Two Revolutions*; Keddie, *Roots of Revolution*.

45. The report, almost certainly written by some intelligence authority, was published in the daily *Keyhan* 12, no. 2157 (5 Sept. 1965), two weeks after his arrest. See the appendix in this chapter for the full text.

46. Ibid.; also published in *Khaterat-e siyasi*, pp. 462–4.

47. As a matter of fact, Maleki had been undergoing a heart operation in Austria before the June revolt and returned to Iran a few months after it. See the introduction to Maleki's *Khaterat-e siyasi*.

3

Ahmad Shamlu and the Contingency of Our Future

Hamid Dabashi and Golriz Dahdel

> You are the most familiar with my work and my disposition, a familiarity combined with the necessary courage and power of imagination. Your poetry is passionate and alive because you harbor this very familiarity, having discovered the specific conditions in which I compose each one of my poems.
> —Nima Yushij (1951)[1]

> As a matter of principle, art itself is not committed. It is the person of the artist who must feel committed. But this commitment must be human and social, away from ideological sectarianism and party lines, one that moves from politics toward the culture of the society at large. Much of what is called committed poetry will soon disappear because it is not poetry, just slogan. My point is that before anything else a poem ought to be a poem. In other words, it will have to be first poetry and then committed.
> —Ahmad Shamlu (1986)[2]

The way we ordinarily think of the pioneering generation of modern Iranian poets is that Nima Yushij was principally responsible for constituting the Iranian subject in modernity, and Mehdi Akhavan-Sales provided it with a genealogy for its morals, a past for its future. Ahmad Shamlu gave that subject and the agency of its morality the powerful contingency of a future and thus the possibility of hope. As Nima imagined and delivered the Iranian subject as a historical agent, Ahmad Shamlu gave it a future to imagine. Shamlu's reading of Hafez in particular was quintessential to the lyrical cast of his own poetic character, and his detailed attention to colloquial language gave texture and dexterity to his politics. Both in his lyricism and his politics, Shamlu was the very summation of the age that celebrated him.[3]

Born on 11 December 1925 in Tehran, Shamlu received his early education in Zahedan, Birjand, Mashhad, Gorgan, Reza'iyyeh, and Torkaman Sahra. His father was a military officer and constantly on the move. He dropped out of school in the tenth grade, never again pursuing formal education. By 1945, during the Allied occupation of Iran, Shamlu became politically active and was briefly incarcerated. Yet before the end of the war, he began his career as a literary journalist. His first poems appeared in 1951. During the next two decades, Shamlu established himself as one of the major voices in modernist poetry and became a leading public intellectual. In his long and illustrious career, Shamlu became a prominent literary journalist, translated prose and poetry, made documentary films, organized public poetry readings, collected and published folklore, and edited a critical edition of Hafez's *ghazal*s. But above and beyond everything else, he published, one volume after another, poems that became the moral alpha and the political omega of his generation and provided the very language with which they fought and fell in love. Before his death on 24 July 2000, Shamlu was universally recognized as one of the most prominent poets of the twentieth century. Despite years of forced silence and seclusion after the Islamic revolution, tens of thousands of Iranians young and old poured into the streets to pay their last respects to Shamlu, collectively canonizing him as "our national poet."[4]

The honorific title was not given in vain. It is impossible to exaggerate the significance of Shamlu as the leading public intellectual of his time. In the half century between the early 1950s when his first poems began to appear and his death in July 2000, Shamlu was by far the most celebrated public intellectual of his generation. Although he engaged in a wide range of literary and scholarly activities in a variety of genres, it was ultimately as a poet that he became the most eloquent spokesman of his nation. There is in fact something far more significant about Shamlu than simply being a spokesman; in his poetry, he did not just represent but in effect constituted the collective aspirations of an entire culture of defiance. Our purpose in this essay is to map out the specific contours of Shamlu's poetic imagination, the most enduring legacy of his half century of gracing a nation with its highest hopes, its most noble aspirations.

In mapping out the particular features of Shamlu's topography of sentiments, one senses the uncanny fusion of the lyrical and the political, the most enduring aspect of his poetry. No one had yet so successfully collapsed the presumed separation of the poetic reality and political predicament together. In the emotive cast of what was to come, Shamlu brought the *lyrical reality* and the *political act* together in a language and diction never before or again realized. From this creative cohesion arose an erotics of the real, sustained through a politics of the possible. Yet this fusion of the lyrical and the political in Shamlu's poetry is not an end onto itself—we read that seamless fusion as a preliminary stage toward the commencement of an aesthetics of uncertainty that poetically rises in order to politically replace an ossified metaphysics that long suffocated the creative energy of the culture. But even that aesthetics of uncertainty should not be considered an end onto itself: We propose that the poetic constitution of the aesthetics of living doubt, especially in its creative replacement of a metaphysics of dead certainties, was in response to the deterritorialization of the very idea of a homeland occasioned by the colonial encounter. The aterritorial nature of the colonial conquest—when a landless, amorphous enemy comes from nowhere to conquer and plunder—had estranged the very conception of (home)land. Thus the inhabitants of that land each came to live within their own amorphous body. This mental mutation of the body was by far the most radically destabilizing consequence of colonial conquest, when a people no longer live in the land they occupy, nor occupy the very body they inhabit.

Shamlu intuitively grasped and poetically celebrated that deterritorialized land and that amorphous body. While the rest of society was busy producing a terrigenous metaphysics, increasingly losing its grip on a deterritorialized land, Shamlu shifted the cornerstone of that misplaced metaphysics and built an aesthetics of uncertainty that thrived on the aggressively deterritorialized land and celebrated the jubilant ephemerality of an amorphous body. Suddenly an entire nation of ideas began to ebb and flow, sing and dance to the rising fluency of that emancipatory language. It was, we believe, the poetic discovery of this celebratory language that ultimately led Shamlu to the spectacular articulation of a semiotics of defiance with which his legacy will always be identified. The Persian classical semiology crumbled under the epistemically corrosive presence of the European Enlightenment and its economic logic of capitalist modernity. Following the thrust of Nima, Shamlu crafted a semiotics of defiance that replaced the presumed but discredited classical signature of the culture. The result was the birth of a new nation of ideas, with Shamlu poetically navigating the course of its contingent future.

The Fusion of the Lyrical and the Political

Today we view Shamlu as chiefly responsible for taking the rugged mountaineer that was Nima to the glorious city of his own poetry and urbanizing him. Without Nima, Shamlu would have been impossible. Without Shamlu, Nima would have remained the Olympian oracle of incomprehensible genius. Born and raised on the summit of the Nimaic heights, Shamlu descended into the city to proclaim the oracle in a lyrically seductive language: urbane, expansive, melodious, political, emotive, and mobilizing. There is something very specific about Shamlu's poetry when we think of him in the context of his contemporary poets. By far the most ingenious and uncanny achievement of his poetic imagination was a forging of the *lyrical reality* and the *political act*. The lyrical poetry of Rumi, Sa'di, or Hafez was on the light side of the Persian poetic mind, and the political poetry of Dehkhoda, Eshqi, or Farrokhi Yazdi on the dark side. How could these two relate? Impossible. Yet Shamlu dreamed and delivered it. On his glorious pages the two turned and twisted: the lyrical assumed political power, the political became lyrically seductive.[5]

As early as the summer of 1951, when a demonstration against an American envoy to Tehran was brutally suppressed, Shamlu's first celebrated poem, "Twenty-three" (for the 23rd of the month of *Tir* 1330 of the Persian calendar, corresponding to 13 July 1951), marked the occasion with this uncanny melding of the erotic and the political:

> The bare body of the street
>   Fell into the embrace
> Of the city and droplets
>   Of pubescence trickled up
> The thighs of the avenues
> A warm summer of breathing—
> Drunken by the dream of wet forests—
>   Dripped in the palpitations of love's heart.
> The naked street
> With its pearl cobble-stone teeth
>   Parted its mouth—
> So the painful pleasures of
> Love could suck away the poisons of its palate.
> And the city wrapped himself around her
> Held her tightly
> In the tantalizing arms of his embrace.
> The virgin history of a love
> That had given her
> Hot girlish body
>   To take in a youth
> Bloodied the bed of that fate-less city.[6]

The erotic energy of this vivid description soon begins to fall flat when we realize that we are not reading the description of a lovemaking but in fact witnessing the description of a massacre in the streets. "The arrogant death" has just announced itself; it is then that anger begins to take momentum:

> Hey!
> Careless
> Witless hands of the
> What-am-I-to-do's
> Of fate!
> Behind the bars and filigrees of nobility
> Behind the silence and behind the gallows
> Behind the turbans and cloaks of duplicity
> Behind accusations, behind the walls
> Behind today and behind the birth day—
> With its broken black frame—
> Behind the pain, behind the No, behind the dark
> Behind persistence, behind thickness
> Behind the stubborn disappointment of your masters
> And even, even behind the thin chamber of my heart-in-love:
> The beauty of a history
> Submits the red paradise of its body's flesh
> To those men whose bones are the bricks of a building
> Their kisses furnaces and their voices drums
> And the steel pillow of their bed
>   A sledge.

In this modular interfusion, Shamlu molded an art that made love earthly, and the political, human. Soon in his poetry, the features of "our future," as he saw and suggested them, became poetically evident. A whole new conception of art emerged from this poetic union that was no longer in the domain of an over-aestheticized assumption of poetry. Art, in and through his poetry, emerged distinctly as the "will to resist power."[7] The "will to resist power" as knowledge—which in the colonial endgame seemed more pertinent than the "will to power as knowledge" and thus truth—was resisted with the "will to power" as art as aesthetics. But a double reversal became evident in Shamlu's poetic defiance that negated the "will to power as colonial knowledge" by art as the "will to resist power." Shamlu's poetry emerged as the very definition of that art as the "will to resist power": Shattering the colonial will to power as knowledge—in the very constitution of our subject—we were attracted to Shamlu's poetry as a "will to resist power."

What we soon realized in the presence of Shamlu was that poetry as the will to resist power placed the poet at the center of a rebellious act, in fact, the very occasion of our resistance. The figure of Shamlu himself, poet par excellence, emerged in the height of Iranian modernity as the romantic revolutionary beyond the reach of prosaic politics. In effect, no revolutionary figure of Shamlu's generation could even have a claim to such a status without simultaneously submitting his credentials as a poet. Khosrow Golesorkhi and Sa'id Soltanpur were two prominent political revolutionaries of this generation who had to publish their poetic claims to legitimacy before they were executed, one by the shah's regime and the other by Khomeini's. The legacy goes back all the way to the early twentieth century and to such figures as Farrokhi Yazdi, a prominent socialist revolutionary who was murdered in Reza Shah's dungeons after he had established his reputation as a great poet. The entire spectrum of the constitutional revolution features a panorama of revolutionary poets who personified the defiant figure of the "will to resist power" as art. Mirza Aqa Khan Kermani among men and Tahereh Qorrat al-'Ayn among women are the primary models of romantic revolutionaries in the nineteenth century.

Shamlu soon emerged as both the voice and the vision of these romantic rebels, the center of the insurrectionary act, the occasion of the fusion that brought the lyrical and the political together. It was as if Shamlu had to sing the panegyric praise of the revolutionary martyrs before they were recognized as such. He in effect had to narrate them poetically into history so as to ensure that they would not have died in vain. Shamlu thus emerged as the conscience of his generation of revolutionary insurrection. "My unknown friends," he declared in "On the Stone Pavement" (1960),

>Like burnt-out stars
>Fell so thickly on the dark earth
>Cold
>>As if forever
>>>The earth remained
>>>>A starless night.
>Then
>>I,
>>>who was

The silent owl of my own dark nest of pain,
Put aside the broken-stringed harp,
Lifted the lantern and took to the street
And moved among the crowd, crying out loud,
Fire on my lips:
>"Ahai!
From behind the windows look at the street!
See the blood on the pavement!
Is this the blood of dawn
That so palpitates in its every drop
The very heart of the sun..."
A hasty wind blew
Upon the dead of the earth
And threw down the ruinous nest of the crow
From the naked branch of the old fig tree in the garden...
"The sun is alive
In this black night
[The dim-faced darkness
               From head to toe
All its soul turned into a mouth
                   To chew on hatred]
I have heard the majestic melody
Of the beating heart of the sun
Clearer
Angrier
Stronger
Than ever...
From behind the windows look at the street!
From behind the windows
Look at the street!
From behind the windows look
At the street!
From behind the windows...
The fresh leaves of the sun
Grow on the ivy by the side of the old garden.
The joyous lamps of the stars
Hang from the ceiling
On the sun's path...
I returned from the path,
All my soul in anticipation,

All my heart in palpitation.
                   I tightened and tuned
The broken-stringed harp
                   And sat by the window
                   And broke the cup of the cold lips
Of the martyrs of the street
By a song I sang
            Full of passion:
"Ahai!
Is this the blood of the dawn
On the pavement
That so palpitates in its every drop
The heart of the sun . . .
From behind the windows look at the street!
See the blood on the pavement!
See the blood
On the pavement!
See
The blood on the pavement . . ."[8]

A panegyric for revolutionary martyrs killed in street battles, this poem is Shamlu at his best, the voice and the vision of a social conscience otherwise mute and blind. Significant about "On the Stone Pavement" is how in the course of the poem, Shamlu's poetic voice sublates from a hesitant beginning, putting away his "broken-stringed harp" in the "dark nest of pain" in which he was living like a "silent owl," and walks out into the street to watch the dead bodies of his comrades laid out in full view. It is critical to note in this movement the ocular interval between the time when the poet is sitting like a "silent owl," with his "broken-stringed harp" out of tune, by his side, and the point at which he tightens up the strings and tunes his harp. The move from a broken vocal to a muted visual is bridged by the poet's *observation* of the dead bodies of his fallen comrades. It is this visual experience that restores his own vocal chords, for the first time after we have known him as the silent but observant owl of his own "nest of pain." It is a cry that first comes out of his mouth: "Ahai! / From behind the windows look at the street! / Watch the blood on the pavement!" The repetition of the phrase "From behind the windows look at the street!" in different shapes, forms, lengths, and tonality in effect vocally imitates the visual restoration of the tuned strings to the broken harp. Shamlu, or more accurately his poetic persona in this critical poem, is tuning his vocal chords after years of owl-like observation in silence so that he can now sing with the same perspicacity with which he has watched.

An Aesthetics of Uncertainty

The compelling contingency that captivated Shamlu's conception of "our future" was thus predicated on the figure of the romantic revolutionary who personified the creative fusion of the lyrical and the political. As "art as the will to resist power" thus took momentum, Shamlu himself became the very embodiment of the collective psyche he personified and represented, the martyrs whom he celebrated, aspects of his own revolutionary character. "For Blood and Lipstick" (1953) is one of the earliest poems of Shamlu in which we read this central figure of the poet as the "will to resist power." Mehdi Hamidi, a prominent opponent of the modernist movement in Persian poetry, had said in a poem addressing his beloved, "If you are the queen of all women, I am the God of all poets." Shamlu targeted this line and issued one of his earliest manifestos. "For Blood and Lipstick" is a defiance of the continual fixation of the poetry that Hamidi best represented with a lethargic kind of love that was perpetually unfulfilled. Then Shamlu turns the poem around to re/signify the color "red."

> Let it be thus
> That in our time
> The man knows
> Melody and color,
> Beauty, glory, and allure.
> That he knows life.
> While he ought to have looked for color
> In your yellow cheeks, Brother!
>   In your yellow cheeks
> And in this naked bruised shoulder,
> Whipped rhythmically
> By one even weaker than you—
> One carrying the heavy burden
> Of his docile soul
> Upon the shoulders of
> His body's wounds![9]
> Then he warns:

Hey!
> Poet!
>> Hey!

Red is red:
Lips and wounds!
But every time the lips of your beloved
In smiling reveal her teeth,
Long before your ailing eyes
Sees them like
"A string of wet pearls upon a pomegranate blossom"
In my eyes
A bloody wound appears
In its center the bone exposed
Since long before Hitler—
The butcher of Auschwitz—
Burnt my friends in death ovens
His accomplice
Had already filled many
Bottles of red frankincense
With the blood of black man
In Harlem and the Bronx
> Storing them perhaps
To make lipstick
For your beloved
The lips of your beloved!
Let your love
Cry in your poem . . .
Let my pain laugh
In mine . . .
And then the ultimatum:
Yet I
(This sin, this born of tyranny,
This life to darkness lost,
This from darkness and sorrow taken his name)
Without any boasting
Will put a chain
On you
The lie!
I will order the ripping of this lineage!
I will dig a grave

From my poetry
And will throw this ridiculous God—Head first—
Into it
And pour over its head
The black ashes of oblivion . . .

Here, it would be impossible to distinguish between Shamlu the public intellectual and Shamlu the poet. Poetic defiance translates into "art as will to resist power," while the poet emerges as the defiant revolutionary, with the same logic and tenacity with which the poetic act becomes a re/creative event, mocking and modulating divinity. This is a threat, a *liaison dangereuse,* far more serious than simply endangering the historical occurrence of any sacred claim on reality. All religion and all philosophy, all morality and all claims to truth, are ipso facto negated, whether Abrahamic or Platonic. Shamlu's poetry, in particular, was the retrieval and the restitution of the sensuous, the semblance, the transient, the materiality of the evidence of life, its generation, growth, corruption, and renewal. Retrieving the scattered and buried memories of a Khayyamesque quatrain here or a *ghazal* of Hafez there, Shamlu's generation of poetic uprising mapped out the contours of that material evidence, celebrating all its forgotten claims to re/creativity, mocking and modulating divinity, on an entirely new constellation that embraced the present world while casting it into a contingent future.

The collapse of the metaphysical dead certainties coincided with Shamlu's generation of a poetic movement that ipso facto replaced these convictions with an aesthetic of uncertainty, full-bodied and insurrectionary. The collapse of the Qajar dynasty in the aftermath of the constitutional revolution of 1906–11 ushered in the end of all metaphysical certainties that could not be put to effective political use. The metaphysics of Islamic certainties was successfully exorcised and deposited in the museums of outdated pieties, or alternately studied by orientalists, while its politics were launched into the making of the "Islamic ideology." The result was a complete metaphysical vacuum that the Nimaic poetic revolution could not but occupy and Shamlu's generation succeeded to animate. Shamlu's poetic imagination and drive was predicated on that Nimaic occupation of the metaphysical space by a poetics of possibility and gave immediacy to the defiant purposefulness of that poetics. In one critical stanza in "Until the Red Blossom of a Shirt" (1950), Shamlu summarized this commitment:

This is how I am:
Maybe I am an idiot!

> Who knows that I have to
> Carry the stones of my own prison
> On my shoulders
> Just like the Son of Mary
> His Cross, and
> Not like you who
> Cut the handle of your headsman's whip
>   From your brother's bone
> And weave strands of your executioner's lash
>   From the hair of your sister
> And place the broken teeth of your father
> As a gem on the whip of tyrants.[10]

The only way that this commitment could keep its sharp critical edge was to be equally self-critical, thus placing the fallibility of the individual at the center of the "will to resist power" as art. In "The Song of the Man Who has Killed Himself" (1951), Shamlu gives an account of destroying his own apolitical, and what he dismisses as "romantic," self:

> I gave him no water
> Nor did I recite a prayer.
> I put the dagger to his throat
> And in a long death
> I killed him.
> I told him:
>   "You speak the enemy's tongue!"
> And I killed him.
> He had my name
> And no one was as close to me as he
> And he made me a stranger
>   To you
> To you whose need for bread
> Beats impatiently in every vein.[11]

By thus locating a fallible historical agent, Shamlu manages to materialize life through his poetry, restoring the palpitation of uncertainty to it, without depoliticizing it. Materializing life meant to place the "will to art" above and beyond the "will to truth." Holding the aesthetic at that critical threshold meant that the "will to art" sustained a simulacrum of the "will to truth." Islam and, with it, the entire metaphysical underpinnings of the culture, had been eroded persistently and systematically since the onslaught of colonially mitigated modernity early in the nineteenth century. Islamic ideology borrowed heavily from that metaphysical underpinning and turned the ancestral faith into a site of political resistance, a configuration of ideological contestation. Meanwhile, the ancestral faith increasingly lost its moral and intellectual grip on the texture and reality of life. Truth was thus released from the exclusive sanctity of its metaphysical domain and let loose into a stream of conflicting claims, with Islamic ideology being one of the competing contenders among others. The rise of Persian poetry in general, that of Nimaic poetics in particular, and Shamlu's poetry even more specifically, coincided with this constitutional collapse of Islamic metaphysics. Nowhere is this tension-ridden substitution of Persian aesthetics for Islamic metaphysics more evident than when Shamlu and Morteza Motahhari battled over the legacy of Hafez and what he was supposed to mean and signify. Shamlu's critically edited version of Hafez utterly frustrated not only the academic professoriate for his having dared to transgress into the hallowed ground of such giants as Mohammad Qazvini but equally angered the Muslim ideologues who thought him to be appropriating a Muslim icon into the ranks of rebel poets.

The collapse of Islamic metaphysics in the Iranian context meant the final destruction of all metaphysics of dead certainties. In the Nimaic revolution that Shamlu's generation of poets brought to success, an aesthetics of living doubts came into being. Central to that aesthetics was a historical agent whose agency was precisely in his fallibility. This ultimately intimates an aesthetics of resistance, defiance, and insurrection. The reason that the fate of the Persian poetic imagination in modernity ought to be understood precisely contrapuntally to the will to power is that our predicament in the colonially conditioned encounter with modernity has inevitably been a will to resist power, whether domestic and tyrannical, or foreign and colonial. It has been constitutional to our agencial presence, and the very formation of our subject, in our modern history. This will to resist power, as opposed to power itself, and as the defining moment of our agencial presence in the time of our history, gives an entirely different disposition to our art, when our art is understood to be an expression of that same will as the will to resist power. The constitution of our subjectivity, as resisting power with art, is the ipso facto oppositional, dialogical reaction to the coloniality of our state. We were denied, by the colonial condition, our will to resist power, and to emerge into a positive aesthetic. Our aesthetic, instead, was negational and defiant at the very core of its insurrectionary disposition.

Precisely because of that negative dialectic at the root of this aesthetics of uncertainty, the Nimaic revolution has remained persistently undertheorized. As the true, the good, and the beautiful collapse and coalesce together in Shamlu's poetry, the poetic disposition assumes a reality sui generis, with the will to resist power as its defining moment. The principal aesthetics that generated and sustained that poetics remained entirely undertheorized not because it denied itself self-reflection but because that poetry was in and of itself a theoretical reflection on our state of being. The theorists of our predicament, the visionaries of the highest we should achieve from the depth of our embattled condition, were our poets, their defiant disposition our will.

The aesthetics of living doubts that became central to Shamlu's poetry defined not just the substance but its very formal disposition. The destruction of the Persian prosody, in which venture Shamlu was even more radical than Nima, is something far more significant than a mere iconoclastic antiformalism. What broke down with the formal tyranny of Persian prosody was the whole Aristotelian *hylî-morphî* distinction that had determined the course of the Persian poetics, at least since Shams Qays Razi's *al-Muʿjam fi maʿaʾir ashʿar al-ʿAjam* (circa thirteenth century).[12] Even before Shams Qays, as early as in Nezami Aruzi's *Chahar Maqaleh* (mid-twelfth century), we have known the poetic act as a creative art, or *senaʿat (technê)*. According to Nezami:

> Poetry is a craft with which the poet arouses the imaginative faculties and then fulfils the resulting expectations in such a way that the insignificant appears as prominent, the prominent as insignificant, the beautiful, ugly, and the ugly, beautiful. By means of metaphoric suggestions, he also excites the forces of anger and lust so that through such suggestions the natural dispositions are expanded and contracted and thus great deeds are implemented in the world.[13]

That conception of the poetic act as *senaʿat* has entitled the poets to a creative license that interjects them into the sacred realm of divinity. The Qurʾanic opposition to poets had already made of poetry a subversive act precisely on the grounds of its creative impulses. The critical point about *senaʿat* is that it designates craftsmanship and constitutionally resists overaestheticization. It is from this angle that Shamlu launches the conception of a poetry that is constitutionally life affirming. Thus in his poetry the Aristotelian *hylî-morphî* distinction collapses and a mode of poetic craftsmanship emerges that makes poetry contingent on reality. The canonical formalism of the *hylî-morphî* distinction no longer holds and the poet carries the poetic act into the contingent world of the real. "Poetry is an accident," Shamlu once said in an interview, and, continued:

> an accident that time and space have made possible but its formation takes place in language. . . . Words in a poem are not representations of things. They are the things themselves appearing in the poem through words, with all their color and taste, sound and volume, coarseness and softness, with all the effusions of which they are capable, all the suggestions in their command, all the weight they carry, all the culture they embody, the spectrum they create, all their history. All these things ought to have been known and experienced by the poet. The poet has to have experienced the entire world through the language. He cannot speak of the bitterness of poison without having tasted it, as he cannot compose a eulogy for death, except if he has indeed exposed himself to death. But he will not be able to benefit from these experiences in the creation of his poetry except if he has crafted an intimacy with the very soul of these experiences.[14]

Shamlu thus takes the poetic act through an aesthetics of contingency and subjects it to the brutal incidentality of the world. The result is a frontal assault against the conventional, legislated, scholastic, even, disposition of classical Persian poetry. With the formal destruction of the Aristotelian distinction between *hylî-morphî*, the canonical formalism of the poetic act yields to the contingent world and becomes integral to it. What this meant in Shamlu's poetry was that the fusing of the lyrical and the political made love worldly, and the political, human and diametrically interpolated.[15] This revolutionized the very texture of the Persian poetic imagination, and with it the very text of what was now emerging in Shamlu's poetry as the Iranian emotive universe. In demystifying the Persian poetic conception of love, Shamlu gave it material evidence and a palpable immediacy. Shamlu had inherited, and standing on Nima's shoulders, was destined to end and transfigure, the millennium-old mollification of earthly love and the embodied flesh yearning to unite. Glorious David against a monstrous Goliath, Shamlu threw his poem like a shooting star against the decadent temple of the giant and killed him without mercy. What emerged was the ebullience of the transient flesh, the impermanence of holding a hand, kissing passionately, holding two mortal arms extended to embrace the Copernican universe, and then, making love, as in:

> I am the spring, you the earth,
> I am the earth, you a tree,
> I am a tree,
> You are the spring—
> The caress of your raining fingers
> Turns me into a garden,
> Unmatched in all the forests.[16]

The impermanence of the world, its critical contingency, became the very defining moment of Shamlu's poetic disposition. "If living is so base," he declared in "Being" (1957):

> Then how shameless I be
> If I don't hang the lantern
> Of my life in all ignominy
> On the tall, barren pine
> Of my dead-end alley.
> If life is so pure
> Then how dirty I be
> If I were not
> To plant my faith
> Like a mountain
> A memorial permanent
> Upon the surface of the impermanent soil.[17]

The fusion of the lyrical into the political in Shamlu's poetry was tantamount to an active reconstitution of the violent into the moral. We became moral agents in the poetry of Shamlu precisely by his active restitution of the violent disposition of our political presence. The ephemerality of that presence became the reality in which Shamlu's poetry thrived. The result was the restoration of a vast emotive universe for his created moral agency to migrate. In thus crafting an emotive constellation, and thereby a future, for the moral agency that Nima had invented, Shamlu wove together the tapestry of a whole new texture of reality and its substantiating traces. The questions that emerged in his poetic space were geared toward this resolution. For example, he writes in "Nocturnal" (1957):

> Nocturnal a poem
> How could be written
> To speak of both
> My heart and my arm?
> Nocturnal

A poem thus
How could one write?
I am the cold ash that in me
Rises the flame of all rebellion.
I am the calm sea that in me
Cries the thunder of all storms.
I am the dark cavern that in me
Lights the fire of all convictions.[18]

As the lyrical corroded into the ethereal and restored the real, it began to mutate the very constitution of the political. The political lost its medieval roots in a vicious cycle of senseless violence and began to sublate into a morally anchored outrage. The moral was at once the right and the beautiful. At the lyrical end of Shamlu's poetry, the beautiful held the rope, just as at the political end the right held the other. Upon the tightly extended trapeze then walked the moral agency of a new historical person: "Iranian" in the very emotive fabric of her constitution, in the moral cast of his character.

A small tavern
Is the world
        In between a sin and hell.
The sun like a curse
                Rises and the day
An irreparable shame.
Oh
Before I drown in my tears
Say something.[19]

This is in the space of one stanza: The first part destroys the whole metaphysics of an afterlife and then links it to the shameless life of a nation at loss, and the second gasps for air in the bosom of one whom the poet loves. Love emerged from the battle scene of that mortal combat as the earthly moment of an insurrectionary culture, confident, competent, glorious, potent in its defiance. No more those ghastly candles and roses, no more those damned moths. No more Indian moles, Mongoloid eyes, no more cursed deadly eyebrow bows, no more poisoned arrows of long eyelashes, no more ropes to hang you by your throat from your fictive lover's locks. No. Entering into Shamlu's poetry was like walking into a universe of material imagination in which we were showered and washed, baptized like the Christians we were not, and ushered into a new birth. Shamlu interrupted our inherited world like no other revolutionary poet could ever dare. He recast us, made us anew, and changed forever the very alphabet of our moral demands upon the world, the very cosmogony of our emotive universe. In his poetry we were transubstantiated into forces we did not know, imploding our ancestral irrelevance, exploding onto the vision of our future. He sat us upon his shoulders and made us see what we could not on our own. "One day we will," he promised in "The Open Horizon" (1957):

> Find again our pigeons
> And kindness will hold
> The hand of beauty.
> A day when
> The shortest song we
> Sing is a kiss
> And when every human being
> Is a brother
> To another.
> A day when
> No one closes
> The doors to their houses
> When lock is a myth
> And a heart sufficient for living.
> A day when
> The meaning of every word
> Is to love.
> So that you won't have to look
> For your last word.
> A day when
> The melody of every word is life
> So that I won't have to suffer
> In search of a rhyme for my final poem.
> A day when
> Every lip is a song
> So that the briefest melody
> Be a kiss.
> A day when
> You come.
> Come forever
> And kindness and beauty bond.

A day when
We again throw seeds for our pigeons.
And I will wait for that day
Even on the day
That I no longer am.[20]

The emotive universe Shamlu thus crafted drove the lyrical and the political to a new destination, there to save and rescue the nation of ideas that Nima had made possible for posterity, for the future. In that conclusion, we commenced: born out of the ashes of our ancestral certainties, braving the elements of a whole new realm, with Shamlu's poetry being the very cast of our character, the very matter of our agency. Material and present to the core of its creative imagination, the world Shamlu molded was at once revolutionary and immediate, idealist and realist, hopeful and instantaneous. "Neither for the sun nor for the epic," he declared in "Of Your Uncles" (1957):

Just for the sake of the short shadow of his roof,
For the sake of a song
                Smaller than your hands.
Neither for the jungles nor for the sea,
Just for the sake of a leaf,
For the sake of a drop of water
                Brighter than your eyes.
Not for walls,
Just for a tent.
Nor for all humanity,
Just for the infant child of his enemy perhaps.
Not for the whole world, just for your home.
For your little certitude that
Man is a universe.
For the moment of my wish to be with you,
For your small hands in my big hands,
And for the sake of my large lips
On your innocent cheeks.
For a sparrow in the wind
When you are jumping in joy,
For the morning dew on a leaf
When you are asleep.
Just for the sake of your smile
When you see me by your side.

For the sake of a song,
For a story on the coldest nights,
On the darkest nights.
For the sake of your dolls
Not for the sake of important people.
For the sake of the stony path that brings me to you,
Not for distant highways.
For the sake of the spout
When it rains.
For the sake of beehives and little bees,
For the sake of the white candelabrum of clouds
In the vast peaceful sky.
For your sake,
For every small thing,
Every thing pure,
They fell to the dirt.
Remember!
Of your uncles I talk
Of Morteza I speak.[21]

The Deterritorialized Land, the Amorphous Body

What gradually becomes evident in Shamlu's aesthetics of uncertainty is the primacy of the body in evidencing the culture. By way of demystifying physical love through a poetic restitution of the Eros, Shamlu re/inscribed the body as the site of physical encounter with the real. A critical consequence of materializing the evidence of physical love was contemporizing the political act. As the metaphysical soul yielded to the physical body as the volatile site of the sensual, so did the pre-eternity of the political culture submit to the immediacy of the political present. This was indeed a strange but nevertheless evident inevitability. Shamlu approximated the erotic and the political so persistently that the more he materialized physical love, the more revolutionary politics became contemporized. He in effect gave immediacy to the political by giving primacy to the material nature of Eros. It is only after that association that we realized that the jaundiced nature of our political culture had a bizarre, though direct, connection to the sickly denial of the Eros in our poetic imagination, by virtue of its overmystification, the denial and burial of its physical evidence.

Through Shamlu's poetry, the body politic became as perishable as physical love was preciously precarious. The conclusion was quite simple:

Love passionately and fight immediately. That gave urgency to revolutionary politics, as it gave a transient exigency to the budding sensuality of a people, the physical evidence of their Eros, in the creative imagination of their most celebrated poet. Now, if we keep in mind that the materializing of our physical love, coterminous with contemporizing our politics, were both geared toward a future that Shamlu's poetry sought to assay, then we see how the physical body, magnificently perishable, gave a corporeal immediacy to the material evidence of the nation. Shamlu could not go too far from Nima, whose cosmic presence could be shot through a future only as far as it remained firmly grounded. Nima's cosmic present was thus extended to Shamlu's future only to the degree that it could validate the immediacy of the poetic act via the evidence of the erotic body.

The obvious question is how and why this primacy of the contingent body emerged in the creative imagination of an artist who was increasingly celebrated as the national poet of a people. The answer will have to be in the political context of our poetic imagination: Our colonial constitution as the subjugated had far-reaching implications beyond the historical exigencies of coloniality. The world at large appeared as having left us behind and it seemed that we could not reach it, no matter how fast we moved or how hard we tried. In this context, poetry became a kind of narrative defiance of our colonially constituted character. In this poetry we could defy our own selves as they were mapped out and interpreted as colonial, oriental, third-world, as the lower layers of a presumed social Darwinism. In this poetry, we could stand up and claim ourselves. More than anything else, colonialism was faceless, deterritorialized aggression. Its violence was entirely alien to the territorial warfare of the premodern times when the enemy was known and lived just across porous borders. The colonial officer (British, French, might as well be Martian) came out of nowhere, alien enemies from outer space, neither their faces nor their territory within navigational parameters. Under the pressure of the anonymity and aterritoriality of the colonial officer, the ground under the feet of the natives gradually gives in. We exited our own bodies, became volatile, amorphous, alien to our own land, strangers to our own worldly locale. The power of the anonymous, aterritorial enemy made the homeland amorphous, the very idea of it precarious, its disposition transient, deterritorialized. Once the navigational properties of the land were lost, so was the fictive permanence of the body.

The problem with the Persian poetic (indeed, with Iranian culture at large) that Shamlu's generation inherited was that it continued to correspond to a territorialized solidity about the land and a metaphysical permanence about the body which no longer existed. With the Nimaic revolutionary destruction of the Persian prosody, we began to float more easily about our amorphous land and in our deterritorialized body. But it was not until Shamlu's poetry that both were in fact poetically theorized. Consider the calendar of emotive events that he constructs in "Look!" (1957):

> Year of evil
> Year of wind
> Year of tears
> Year of doubt
> Year of longer days and of shorter endurance
> The year that pride went begging.
> Year of sordidness
>   Year of pain
>   Year of mourning
> Year of Pouri's tears
> Year of Morteza's blood
> The leap year . . .[22]

This is the constitution of an entirely different temporality for the land we inhabited and the body we owned. Shamlu poetically theorized us in our new habitat, both in our deterritorialized homeland and in our amorphous body, by generating an erotics of the real and fusing it with a politics of the evident. Shamlu's erotics of the real did not deny or gloss over our deterritorialized land and body. It celebrated them. What Shamlu carried forward from his earliest poetic experiments, what he would later falsely dismiss as "neoromanticism," was precisely a revolutionary erotics that foregrounded the body as the site of cultural contestation.

The road to the active celebration of the deterritorialized land and the amorphous body was paved from the political site of our predicament and worked toward our emancipatory poetics. It was not until Shamlu's erotics of the real that one of our greatest living poets began to celebrate our deterritorialization. In his poetry, Shamlu generated and sustained this erotics by salvaging an earlier poetic experiment he later dismissed as "romantic," sublating it into a poetic celebration of impermanence. In his erotics of the real Shamlu subconsciously found the sole way to remain true to an amorphous land and a deterritorialized body and link them to the politics of the predicament. The sustained correspondence between the erotics of the real and the politics of the possible was Shamlu's way of extending our deterritorialized land and body to the compelling contingency of a future.

The colonial conditioning of an amorphous land meant a simultaneous globalization of the very idea of homeland. Shamlu consistently identified with the anticolonial and revolutionary movements throughout the world. "The Magnificent Hymn" (1951) is dedicated to a Korean comrade, Shen-Cho, on the occasion of the American invasion of Korea.

> Shen-Cho!
>   Where's the war?
> In your home
>   In Korea
>   In the Far East?
> But you
>   Shen
>   My dear yellow-skinned brother!
> Never think separate
> That straw-walled, clay-roof cottage
> From my shelter and abode.
> It is clear
>   Shen
>   That your enemy is my enemy
> And that stranger who is drunk with your blood
> From the dark blood of my sons
> Neither
>   Can wish to
>   Wash his hands.[23]

Whether Korean, French, Greek, Spanish, Latin American, Indonesian, or Jewish, Shamlu's global attention to his comrades-in-arms has the simultaneous effect of acknowledging and celebrating the deterritorialized homeland and of the amorphous body throughout the world. In 1950 Shamlu wrote "The Panegyric for the Person of the Month of Bahman" on the occasion of the murder of Taqi Arani, a prominent Marxist, in Reza Shah's prison. The poem also celebrates the impermanence of the body in an entirely unexpected way.

> You don't know how the cry of majesty
> When it does not moan
> Under the torture of defeat
>   Rises like a mountain!
> You don't know how the unfaltering gaze
> Of one condemned for his certitude

> Staring into the fearful eyes of a tyrant
>   Looks an ocean!
> You don't know how dying
> When man has defeated death
>   Is life!
> You don't know what life is
> What victory is
> You don't know who Arani is
> And you don't know when
> With the skin of dust
> And the bone of brick
> You have covered his grave
> And as your lips blossom
> Into a smile of content and
> As your throat explodes
> Into laughter
> And as you think
> You have severed
> The meat of his life
> From the bone of his body
> How he beats the red drum
> Of his life
> In the pulse of Zirab
> In the heart of Abadan.[24]

Both the deterritorialized land and the amorphous body are the *condito sine qua non* of the erotics of the real constitutional to Shamlu's poetry. Shamlu's lyricism dwells on and celebrates the impermanence of the emotive moment, taking pleasure in the certainty of an arrival, while waiting, as in "Golku" (1957):

> Night is not about to sleep.
> Runs in the veins of the garden
> The wind like a fierce fire howling.
> Trails its fingers on the window glass
> The branch of a dried-out ivy
> Fearful the storm
> Might steal it away.
> I am not about
> To find disappointment
> In the hope

That gave me patience.
Let the wind turn
With the night and let
The willow dance
With the wind.
Golku will come
Smiling Golku will come.
Golku will come
I know,
Stubbornly as the wind
        Grabs at her skirt
On the crumbling narrow path.
Golku will come
With all the enmity of this cold night
Hiding the trace
Of this path
Under its cloak.
The night is not about to sleep.
The blighted branch
Of dried-out ivy
Caresses the window glass.
I am not about
To lose hope
Under the impatience of night
From the distance approaches
The steady pulse of footsteps.[25]

From the erotics of the real there is only a short distance to the politics of the possible. In his "Last Word" (1957), Shamlu issues this manifesto:

Neither Fereydun am I
        Nor Vladimir[26]
                Who put a bullet
Like a dot
At the end of a sentence
Which was the severed edge
Of his history.
Neither I return
        Nor do I die.
Because I—
[Who am Alef of Morning[27]

And it has not been long since
I threw to the dirt my own foreign self
Just like a huge oak tree
Upon the crossroads of a desert
And it has not been long since
I threw to the dirt my own foreign self
Just like his entire self that Vladimir
Killed].
In the center of the gambling table
Of you journalistic pimps
Of highfalutin verses
I slam the ace of my heart.
Since you
      The stupid morons who ridicule Nima,
And you the murderers of the likes of Vladimir,
This time around
Have come to battle with an unbroken mule of a poet
Who leaps and horses through
All the dusty old collections of poetry.
And a forgotten kind of death
      A sweet desire that like sugar melts in his heart.
I ask of you
The honorable pimps of prostitute poems!
If instead of all your historical references
I rear-end your snout
What would you do?
But if you prefer that
      Poets vomit in front of you
What you have eaten for many long years,
What can Morning do whose poetry
Is the noble sentiments of a tomorrow
That now
Are but embryos of suggestiveness.
What can the Morning do if tomorrow
Is the shadow-by-shadow twin
Of Victory?
What can Morning do if yesterday
Is a grave from which grows
Nothing from its every bush but regret
With the bitter seed of experience

In its black fruit?
What could Morning do
If the future
Were to lose to the past
Then Doctor Hamidi the Poet[28]
Would have had still to be
        A single amebic creature incurably
Stranded in the distant waters of time?
And I who am Alef of the Morning,
Just to rhyme,
With uncertain respect
Do warn you
[The dead of a thousand
Graveyards!]
That your efforts are futile,
Because between me and the people
We who like rebels grasp each other
        In tight embrace
                Stands not even the thin wall of a shirt.
Above all the sullen wipe-cloths
Of your collections of poetry
That I have thrown at the diseased women
Of my dirty copulations,
And above all the tall ladders of fake poetry
That I have muddied with the heavy tread
Of my passing feet,
Above all the bickering of bespectacled professors
The members of the fossil dwelling of panegyrics and quatrains,
Members of the Association of *mafaʿelun*s and *faʿalatun*s,
Guards at the gate of the bordello-houses of journals
I have spat on,
The cry of this bastard infant
Of poetry will hang you!
"You the pimps of old prostitute poems!
You are dealing with me:
I—not any old fun-loving whoremonger!
And I neither return nor do I die!
Part with your nameless names
As I am neither Fereydun nor
Am I Vladimir!"[29]

This fusion of the lyrical into the political, of the erotics of the real into the politics of the possible, finds one of its most glorious expressions in "From the Wounds of Aba'i" (1957):

> Young women of the valleys!
> Young women of waiting!
> Young women of tight hope
>   In boundless vales
> And of boundless hopes
>   In tight-hearted times!
> Young women of the dream
> Of a new canopy
>   Under canvas one hundred years old!
> Were you to blossom
> Out from the armor of your dress
> The mad wind
> Would dishevel
> The long mane
> Of the horse of desire . . .
> Young women of the muddy brook!
> Young women of a thousand columns
> Of flame high
> To the tall dome of smoke!
> Young women of distant lovers
>   Days of silence and toil
>   Nights of exhaustion!
> Young women of days
>   Running tirelessly nights
>   disappointed!
> In the hidden garden
> And manly privacy
> Of what love,
> In the pious dance
> In gratitude
>   Of what desire fulfilled
> Will you raise
>   Your fountainous arms?
> Alas!
> The hair, the glances
> Darken the fragrance
> Of the poet's words

In futility.
Young women of going and coming
                        In the fog-covered valleys!
Young women of shame,
           Morning-dew
                  Humility
                         The flock!

The wounded heart of Aba'i
On the bosom of which of you
Has dripped blood?
Your breasts,
Which one of you,
Have blossomed
In the spring of his youth?
Your lips,
Which one of your
Lips, which one
           Tell me
Secretly planted
On his palate
The fragrance of a kiss?
In dim nights of
Drizzling rain
When nothing remains to be done
Now, which of you
Stays awake
In the violent bed of disappointment
In the tight bed of sorrow
In the painful bed of your secret thoughts
So that the memory of he
Who was anger and courage
                Burns late
The blaze of fire
In your open eyes?
Which one of you,
           Tell me!
Which of you
Is polishing
        Aba'i's rifle
For the day of revenge?[30]

A Semiotics of Defiance

The colonial deterritorialization of the land and its simultaneous constitution of an amorphous body ultimately sublate in Shamlu's poetry toward a semiotics of defiance. In Shamlu's poetry, an entire nation of ideas approximated itself to a whole new poetic semiology by way of a radical departure from its accustomed way of reading signs as signifiers, a fact that made the old-fashioned professoriate of Tehran University and its Orientalist cohorts entirely unaware of what was happening. In the body of Shamlu's poetry, an inner space was crafted to will a nation to resist power, not as much via a political head-on collision as through a poetic submersion into its own possibilities. Precisely through this immersion, emancipation from the condition of coloniality and repression was not reactive but provocative. Because of historical circumstances, we were never completely colonized. Because of our poets, we were never entirely postcolonial. We were put poetically outside the purview of a condition that the very project called Enlightenment Modernity had created. Through Shamlu's poetry, we broke through the trap that the colonial Enlightenment had set for us, as no matter how hard we tried we could not beat it on its own terms. In his poetry we played it our way, and we could not but win morally, even if our revolutions were repeatedly defeated politically. The fact that we could launch social protests and political revolutions one after the other over the last one hundred years is precisely because we have not been able to measure up in reality to the mental picture of ourselves, as poets like Shamlu imagined us. Shamlu and other poets have dreamt us in their poetry, and we keep trying to interpret that dream in reality. We have so far failed, a fact that makes the dream even more haunting, unrelenting and powerful.

Once all our signs collapsed, their communicative power and meaningful legitimacy, our poets became the prophetic visionaries of a new semiology that no one could learn or even inherit, and to which everyone had to earn admittance. The battle over the Nimaic revolution in poetry was fought over nothing more or less than the simple but disturbing fact that suddenly within a poetic culture the parental generation could not quite puzzle out what their youngsters were reading in the convoluted, disturbed, cacophonous countermelodies which defied the Persian poetic diction. Here Shamlu issued the manifesto of this new poetic insurrection in "The Poetry That Is Life" (1954):

The concern of the old poet
Was not life.
In the barren sky of his imagination he
Did not converse except with wine and women.
He fantasized day and night,
Caught ankle deep in the binds
Of the ridiculous hair of his beloved.
Meanwhile other poets,
In one hand a cup of wine
The other in the hair of their beloved,
Brayed drunkenly on God's Earth!
Since the concern of
The old poet was none
                      Other than this,
The impact of his poetry
                      Was none other than that:
One could not use it as a drill.
On the battleground,
With the weapon of poetry
No monstrous rock
Could be removed from people's path.
What I mean to say is
That it was completely useless,
No difference between its absence and existence.
One could not use it
Like a gallow.
Whereas I personally
                Once
With my own poetry
              Fought
Shoulder to shoulder
With my Korean comrade Shen-Cho
And once,
A few years ago,
I also hung
"Hamidi the Poet"
On the gallows of my poetry.
The subject of poetry
              Today
                  Is entirely different . . .

Today
> Poetry
>> Is the weapon of the masses

Since the poets themselves
Are like branches
Of the jungle of the people
And not the jasmine or the hyacinth
Of so-and-so's nursery.
The poet of today
Is not alien
To the shared suffering
Of the people.
He smiles with their lips
And he bears in his bones
Their pain and hope!
Today
> The poet
>> Has to wear a nice suit

And put on a clean pair of shining shoes
And then in the busiest parts of the city
Pick out the subject, rhythm, and rhyme
Of his poem
One after the other,
With a precision peculiar to him
And to no one else
Among the passersby:
"Would you please
Come with me
Fellow-citizen!
I have been looking for you
Desperately
> From door to door
>> Three days!"

"Looking for me?
> That is quite strange!
>> You must be mistaking me sir

For someone else!"
"No, my dear,
That is impossible:
I can tell the rhythm

Of my new poem
From miles away."
"What did you say?
      The rhythm of your new poem? . . ."[31]

The construction of this new semiotics of defiance was not always found in an innocuous walk through the open city in search of new rhythm and rhyme. It was also more violently achieved through an iconoclastic encounter with what the dormant culture considered sacred.[32] The erotics of the real in Shamlu's poetry is fused with a fiercely sacrilegious energy that is constitutional to his creation of an entirely fresh semiology. In "Damnation" (1957) we read the earliest eruptions of this signature revolt:

In all the night
There is no light
In the entire city
Not a cry.
You fearful Gods
Night-bound,
Comrades of darkness!
Lest I hang Satan's lantern
From the ceiling of every hidden torture chamber
Of this tyrannical paradise,
And lest I forever damn
These endless
Eternal
Magic-ridden nights
With the light of one hundred thousand suns
Do not open to me the gate
Of your dark, rotted heavens!
In all the night
There is no light
In all the day
Not a shout.
Like a starless night
My heart is alone.
Lest they know why I burn
I jealously guard
My tongue in my closed mouth.
My path is clear,

My feet are tired.
Like a tired hero,
I sing the old hymn of an ancient victory.
With his broken body,
        Alone.
A painful wound left behind by
A sword,
A heart-wrenching agony
        Of anger:
Tears boil up in bloodied eyes the violent story of suffering
The red wrath dries up the teary eyes.
In his dawn-less night
Alone.
Collapsed into himself
From within,
In a desert of fear
Waiting in every direction,
In rage and pain
From the torment
Of his wound and his own pride
He screams:
"In all the night
There is no light
In the entire valley
Not a cry...
You ecstatic Gods
Of darkness!
May we be denied forever
Your corrupt paradise!
Wait until I hang Satan's lantern
From the dome of every hidden torture chamber
Of this tyrannical paradise!
Wait until I forever damn
Your Magic-ridden nights
With the light of a hundred thousand suns!"[33]

In this semiotics of violence the visual and vocal constantly mutate into and inform each other, as they reach mutually for a new site of signification, at once seen and heard. Neither entirely vocal nor completely visual, trafficking between the two escapes from the trappings of one into the possibilities of the other, subverting the inhibitions that each separately sustains. It is thus not accidental that this simultaneous signing of visuality/vocality is construed, and the silent owl's voice is restored to the impeccable and extraordinary precision of his vision only after Shamlu's poetic persona leaves the painful dungeon of his solitude and enters the possibilities of the political scene out in the street. He proclaims an effective poetic manifesto in which perfect vision and vocality are claimed only after public engagement with the political act.

The whole semiotic of emancipation, though, ultimately hinges on a hope and rests suspended on the oscillating uncertainty of an aspiration. Shamlu's enduring legacy lies in giving the vision of our future a consistent elegance from which we cannot, and will not, turn away:

> I think
> That my heart has never been
>   So warm
>   and red.
>
> I feel
> That in the worst moments
> Of this deadly night
> The thousand fountains of a sun
> Spring with certainty
>   In my heart.
>
> I feel
> That in every nook and cranny
> Of this salt-desert of despair
> Thousands of fresh, joyous jungles
>   Suddenly sprout from the earth.
>
> Ah, you lost certainty,
> You slippery fish
> In the inlets of a mirror
> Winding into and into
> I am now a pure pond
> With the grace of love:
> From the inlets of the mirror
> Find your way to me!
>
> I think
>   That my hand has never been
>   So big and happy.
>
> I feel

That in my eyes,
   Under the crimson cascade of my tears,
The never-setting sun of a hymn
Now breathes.
I feel
That in every one of my veins
   With each beating of my heart
      Now the waking vigilance of a caravan
Sounds its drum.
She came to me
One night naked
   Like the soul of water:
Two fish in her bosom,
A mirror in her hand,
Her wet tresses smelling like sea-moss
Like sea-moss meshed together.
I burst from the threshold of despair:
"Oh lost certitude
I will never let you go!"[34]

Notes

1. From a letter written by Nima to Shamlu, 3 June 1951. See Nima Yushij, *Namehha-ye Nima Yushij* (The letters of Nima Yushij) (Tehran: Entesharat-e Abi, 1984), p. 171.

2. From a conversation with Naser Hariri. See Naser Hariri, *Honar va adabiyat-e emruz: goft-o-shonudi ba Ahmad Shamlu va Reza Baraheni* (Art and literature today: A conversation with Ahmad Shamlu and Reza Baraheni) (Tehran: Ketabsara-ye Babol, 1986), p. 41.

3. In a critical review of one of his contemporary poets, Rahi Mo'ayyeri, Shamlu praised Hafez for being true to his age and having his lyricism animated with his politics, a praise he denied his contemporaries. See Ahmad Shamlu's "The Shadow of What Life?" in *Az mahtabi beh kucheh* (On a moonlit street) (Tehran: Tus, 1977), pp. 9–19.

4. For a short biographical account of Shamlu, see Javad Mojabi, *Shenakht-nameh-ye Shamlu* (Knowing Shamlu) (Tehran: Entesharat-e Qatreh, 1998), pp. 8–13, 16–98. For a comprehensive study of his poetry, see Taqi Pur-Namdarian, *Ta'ammoli dar she'r-e Ahmad Shamlu* (Some reflection on the poetry of Ahmad Shamlu) (Tehran: Entesharat-e Aban, 1978).

5. For an excellent introduction to the formal and thematic aspects of Shamlu's

poetry, see Pur-Namdarian, *Ta'ammoli dar she'r-e Ahmad Shamlu*. Equally useful is Mohammad Hoquqi, *She'r-e zaman-e ma: Ahmad Shamlu* (The poetry of our time) (Tehran: Entesharat-e Zaman, 1982).

6. See Ahmad Shamlu, *Majmu'eh ash'ar* (Collection of poems), 2 vols. (Gißen: Bamdad Verlag, 1988), 1:19–20. Despite a number of valiant efforts, there is still no satisfactory English translation of Shamlu. We have opted for a fresh translation from the original of all the poems appearing in this essay.

7. We are reading this idea of "art as the will to resist power" against the grain of Heidegger's reading of Nietzsche as "the will to power as art." See Martin Heidegger, *Nietzsche: The Will to Power as Art,* vol. 1 (New York: Harper and Row, 1979). "The will to power as art" has no choice but to become "art as the will to resist power" when it is located on the colonial site of Shamlu's poetry. This reading against that power-basing grain is less suggested by Heidegger's reading of Nietzsche than necessitated by the colonial conditionings of our reading of Shamlu.

8. Shamlu, *Majmu'eh,* 1:422–6.

9. Ibid., p. 9. According to Shamlu, Nima had made certain revisions in this poem. See Shamlu, *Majmu'eh,* 1:594. For Nima's comments on Shamlu's poetry, see also Nima Yushij, *Namehha-ye Nima,* pp. 173–7.

10. Shamlu, *Majmu'eh,* 1:36–7.

11. Ibid., pp. 54–5.

12. See Shams al-Din Muhammad ibn Qays al-Razi, *al-Mu'jam fi ma'a'ir ash'ar al-'ajam* (The compendium on the principles of Persian poetry), ed. Muhammad 'Abd al-Vahab Qazvini (Tehran: n.p., 1909).

13. 'Ali al-Nezami al-Aruzi al-Samarqandi, *Koliyyat-e chahar maqaleh* (The four discourses), ed. Muhammad Abd al-Vahab Qazvini (Tehran: Entesharat-e Ashrafi, 1909), p. 26.

14. From an interview with Naser Hariri in Mojabi, *Shenakhtnameh,* p. 646.

15. In an interview with Naser Hariri in 1986, Shamlu identified two major components of his poetry as his repressed love for music and his brutal memory of having once in his childhood witnessed the terrorizing experience of a soldier being flogged. Melodic violence has thus been constitutional to his poetry. See Hariri, *Honar va adabiyat,* pp. 35–9.

16. Shamlu, *Majmu'eh,* 2:633.

17. Shamlu, *Majmu'eh,* 1:196.

18. Ibid., pp. 199–200.

19. Shamlu, *Majmu'eh,* 2:1137.

20. Shamlu, *Majmu'eh,* 1:243–5.

21. Ibid., pp. 281–3.

22. Ibid., pp. 246–7.

23. Ibid., pp. 64–5.

24. Ibid., p. 70.

25. Ibid., p. 112.

26. "Fereydun" refers to Fereydun Tavalloli, a contemporary poet whom Shamlu considered retrograde because he opted for "classical romanticism." "Vladimir" refers to Vladimir Mayakofsky, the Russian revolutionary poet who committed suicide by playing Russian roulette.

27. Alef Sobh or Alef Bamdad (A. Morning) is Shamlu's poetic nom de plume.

28. Mehdi Hamidi was a contemporary neoclassicist poet and the archnemesis of Shamlu.

29. Shamlu, *Majmu'eh,* 1:361–68.

30. Ibid., p. 119. For Shamlu's own reflections on this poem, see his letter to Aq Cheli in Mojabi, *Shenakhtnameh,* pp. 551–4.

31. Shamlu, *Majmu'eh,* 1:151–63.

32. In his nonpoetic polemic writings, Shamlu's most successful reversal of the Persian collective psyche came in 1990 when he launched a scathing attack against Ferdawsi and his version of the Iranian mythological history. See Shamlu, *Negaraniha-ye man* (New Jersey: Center for Iranian Research and Analysis, 1990).

33. Shamlu, *Majmu'eh,* 1:172–174.

34. "Fish" (1960), in Shamlu, *Majmu'eh,* 1:431–3.

4

The Discourse of "Authentic Culture" in Iran in the 1960s and 1970s

Negin Nabavi

In January 1974, in a trial broadcast on national television that captured the public imagination, Khosraw Golesorkhi, a Marxist poet and journalist, was charged along with eleven others for making an attempt on the lives of the shah, the empress and the crown prince.[1] In a defiant self-defense, Golesorkhi denounced the regime and paralleled Marxism with Islam, claiming that he who was a "Marxist-Leninist had first found social justice in the school of Islam, and then reached socialism."[2] He further likened himself to the third martyred Imam, Hoseyn, fighting the ruthless Yazid. Referring to 'Ali, the first Imam of the Shi'is, as the "first socialist of the world,"[3] he continued:

> [T]he life of Mawla Hoseyn is an example of our present days when, risking our life for the dispossessed of our country, we are tried in this court. He [Hoseyn] was in a minority, whereas Yazid had the royal court, the armies, authority, and power. [Hoseyn] resisted and was martyred. Yazid may have occupied a corner of history, but that which was emulated in history was the way of Mawla Hoseyn and his resistance, not the rule of Yazid. The [path] that nations have followed and continue to follow is the way of Mawla Hoseyn. It is in this way that in a Marxist society, real Islam can be justified as a superstructure, and we, too, approve of such an Islam, the Islam of Hoseyn and Mawla 'Ali.[4]

Following this trial the regime launched a campaign against what it called "Islamic Marxism."[5] Government propaganda in the form of articles or editorials in state-sponsored reviews disparaged the idea of Islamic Marxism, denouncing it as an insult to all Muslims. They pointed out the incompatibilities of Marxism and Islam, arguing that Islamic

Marxists were really Marxists who had put on the appearance of Muslims and that their claims to Islam were no more than a ruse to deceive and recruit people from the mosque.[6]

This episode is relevant to our purposes on two levels. First, it shows the confrontational approach adopted by the regime against the more radical activists. Second, and perhaps more important, it illustrates the significance of the notion of "authenticity" for both sides, that is, the trend of the intellectuals of the Left to authenticate themselves by means of Islam and the determination on the part of the state to deprive them of this claim to authenticity at any price. The question that comes to mind therefore is why authenticity should have gained such importance in the 1970s, for in the intellectual journals of this period both secular intellectuals and the state were preoccupied with defining an "authentic culture" or, in other words, of defining the characteristics of an Eastern as opposed to a Western culture. In this essay, we will look at how the discourse of "authentic culture" gained the foreground and examine the shape that it took in the 1970s.

Intellectuals and the Concept of Authentic Culture

Raymond Williams begins his definition of the concept of culture by referring to it as "one of the two or three most complicated words . . . partly because of its intricate historical development."[7] In his words, it is the "range and overlap of meanings" that make the term significant, and he identifies three categories of usage. He ascribes the noun to "a general process of intellectual, spiritual and aesthetic development; a particular way of life, whether of a people, or a period; and the works and practices of intellectual and especially artistic activity."[8] Although the word takes different meanings according to the contexts in which it is used, it is the fluidity and complexity of the term that makes the concept of culture defy any single definition. As will be discussed in the following pages, the discourse of authentic culture in Iran in the 1960s and 1970s was similarly affected by the lack of any single definition and by the different understandings that various parties had of the idea of culture.

The debate in Iran regarding authentic culture became prevalent among intellectuals—defined here as left-leaning essayists who considered it their primary task to question and challenge authority—because two factors, instrumental in its initial formulation, came together at this time. In the first place, the constraints imposed by the regime on political activity and freedom of expression in the mid-1960s had meant that the intellectuals who sought to challenge authority had to look for less direct avenues to express their opposition. And paradoxically enough, the enforcement of stricter censorship at this time (following the riots of June 1963) coincided with a proliferation of intellectual publications from 1964–65 onward, which in turn provided a forum for the discussion of ideas, even if under restrictions. Second, the triumph of third-world movements in defying Western powers served as an inspiration and provided the background for much of their writing in this period.

There were several aspects to this wave of third-worldism that enthused much of the intellectual circle in Iran in the 1960s. Whether it was the way in which burgeoning guerrilla movements were effectively challenging authority and powerful nations, as in the cases of the Algerian and Cuban revolutions or the impact and social turbulence that Vietnam had created for the United States, or the theories of "native culture" that had been put forward by third-world writers such as Aimé Césaire and Frantz Fanon, what was clear is that it enabled the disenchanted intellectuals to use third-world issues allegorically to refer to the state of affairs in Iran. In other words, by making parallels between the problems of the third world, which they were free to discuss, and those of their own country, which they could no longer address directly, they were able to attack the West and the imperialism that they thought responsible for having imposed and for supporting the Iranian regime.

Writers such as Fanon had expressed the importance of the role of culture in the struggle against imperialism and had asserted that venturing into the past in order to discover a sense of "dignity and glory" was a necessary stage in raising national consciousness and awakening the people.[9] These ideas inspired many secular intellectuals to acknowledge the need to take on the discourse of authentic or indigenous culture. The following extract by Manuchehr Hezarkhani, a translator and essayist, is an example of such reasoning:

> Although the issue of imperialism is not such a novel concern, and its political and economic aspects have been discussed several times, paying attention to its cultural aspect, however, is relatively recent. The imperialist culture is the manifestation of the ideological domination of imperialism in colonized societies. So no anti-imperialist struggle exists in which the cultural issue is not discussed.[10]

Thus, it was in the context of third-world discourse that culture became a loaded word and the idea of regaining an authentic culture became popular. There was of course a divergence of opinion concerning this issue. While there were the few exceptions who distinguished between an imperialist as opposed to a Western culture and suggested that Western culture could not be dismissed, a majority of intellectuals argued that it was necessary to regain an authentic culture that was theirs alone. In such an atmosphere, therefore, it was not surprising to find the following passage as part of the editorial of a popular intellectual magazine, *Ferdawsi*, in the late 1960s:

> We need our own Eastern culture. The very same which the Indians have preserved and the Japanese have safeguarded but which we have lost somewhere. In order to find it, we cannot cling to history. We have to reconstruct it.[11]

It was also in the pages of this same magazine that, from the summer of 1968 onward, a series titled "People's Culture" (Farhang-e mardom) began to be published. Its writers intended to collect and document indigenous customs, traditions, and folklore in an attempt to resist what they said were "the efforts of Westernized people *(farangi-ma'ab)* to eradicate them." Of course the fact that this period also coincided with the student rebellions in all the major Western cities, as well as the fact that Western thinkers were questioning their own civilization, only confirmed Iranian intellectuals in their stance. There was a general consensus that the West could no longer present a solution to their problems. Now that the West was experiencing a moral vacuum, intellectuals had to come up with a new alternative to the West, and many found this in the definition of an authentic Eastern culture. In short, the rhetoric of "authentic culture" was both a reaction to the West and what was thought to be a new imperialism, responsible for endorsing the regime in power, and vague enough to allow it to be interpreted in a variety of ways. But what was important was the oft-repeated idea that, provided an authentic culture was established, the East could both find a sense of dignity and identity for itself and avoid the mistaken ways of the West. This discourse became all-prevalent in the 1970s.[12] However, now it was no longer the exclusive domain of dissident secular intellectuals as the establishment too joined the debate.

The Establishment and the Concept of Authentic Culture

The 1970s have often been characterized as a time of heightened militancy. Incidents such as the Siahkal episode on 8 February 1971, which came to symbolize the first guerrilla activity that effectively challenged the regime and inspired many other radicals to take up arms, or the increasing number of student demonstrations against the shah, both within and beyond Iranian boundaries, did much to discredit and damage the image of the regime. In this context, therefore, it became all the more imperative for the establishment to co-opt the more moderate intellectuals.[13]

This co-optation was accomplished in a number of ways; on a practical level, an almost erratic assortment of magazines and journals were shut down without much explanation, and their publishers co-opted through financial reward or lucrative positions in the public sector.[14] On a more imaginative level, the establishment tried by several means to adopt the discourse that had characterized the left-leaning intellectuals of the 1960s. Thus, besides the founding of study groups and cultural institutions that shared the same objectives as intellectuals, namely, the preservation of an indigenous culture, perhaps the most important measure was the formulation of a cultural policy. For example, in a text drawn by the High Council of Culture and Art (Shawra-ye 'Ali-ye Farhang va Honar), a body founded several years earlier in 1967 that had become responsible for implementing the cultural policy, the importance of cultural authenticity from the point of view of the establishment is underlined:

> Paying attention to cultural authenticity *(esalat-e farhangi)* is the important element that reinforces the foundations of national unity . . . ; national unity will become more consolidated [only] if it is based on self-awareness *(khod-agahi)* of cultural heritage.[15]

"Cultural authenticity," in this context, therefore, was considered as a means of consolidating the foundations of national unity. Accordingly, the High Council of Culture and Art set its aim to be the promotion of Iranian culture and heritage, by which it meant making culture available to all, paying attention to cultural heritage, providing the means for intellectual and artistic creativity, and making Iranian culture known to outsiders while also making Iranians aware of other cultures.[16]

It was also in the context of this organization that an increasing number of cultural festivals came into being in the late 1960s and 1970s. They, too, claimed their aim to be the promotion of authentic culture by propagating Persian national cultural heritage on a wider scale. For example, the Festival of Culture and Art (Jashn-e Farhang va Honar), which first began in October–November 1967, was organized by the High Council of Culture and Art. It was held on an annual basis throughout the country. Each year, a particular theme was chosen, and, accordingly, exhibitions, films, plays, and discussions were organized.[17] Its launch was claimed to be in response to the need felt for a "search for authenticity,"[18] and it claimed to be an "important step in the way of familiarization *(ashna'i)* and reconciliation *(ashti)* with the forgotten face of our heritage."[19]

In addition to the Festival of Culture and Art, the other prominent festival was the Shiraz Arts Festival (Jashn-e Honar-e Shiraz), which first started in August–September 1967 and was held annually in Shiraz. In the 1970s, moreover, festivals were also held in celebration of folk culture. Among them were the Festival of Tus (Jashnvareh-ye Tus), which was first launched in June 1975 and held on an annual basis in Tus, Mashhad, to commemorate Ferdawsi and the Shahnameh, as well as the Festival of Popular Culture (Jashnvareh-ye Farhang-e 'Ammeh) and the Festival of Popular Traditions (Jashnvareh-ye Farhang-e Mardom), which were both inaugurated in October 1977.

There were slight differences of emphasis among the various festivals. Although the Shiraz Arts Festival became a "subject of controversy, because of the nature of some of its avant-garde performances"[20] and, in later years, came to be regarded as an important factor in mobilizing opposition against the regime, at the outset it was meant to have an international aspect. Its aim was initially announced as being that of assembling artists from all over the world in Shiraz in the hope of giving Iran prominence on the world stage as a center for cultural activities and encouraging the encounter *(barkhord)* of Eastern and Western civilizations. Other festivals placed emphasis on the celebration of aspects of Persian culture both on an artistic and a popular level. So the Festival of Tus, for example, had the aim of commemorating national epics, particularly that of Ferdawsi, and examining its role in people's everyday lives. The Festival of Popular Culture and the Festival of Popular Traditions were said to be held with the aim of celebrating Iranian folk culture and tradition.[21] However, the common aims of the festivals were to encourage the propagation *(shenasandan)* of Persian culture, develop a sense of familiarity and reconciliation with the past, and promote a sense of pride in Persia's cultural past; in other words, to propagate an authentic culture, precisely what the disenchanted intellectuals of the 1960s had written about.

In short, by the mid-1970s, the concept of authentic culture had become central to the national cultural policy. Similarly, the concept of the "onslaught of cultures" *(hojum-e farhangha)* from the outside, a threat that the country as a traditional nation had to beware of, was also articulated extensively in official statements as an irrefutable fact. At the same time, statements concerning the moral crisis in the West as an incentive in formulating a national culture also featured in official documents of cultural policy. So, for example, in the introductory section to the cultural program of the Fifth Development Plan (1973–77), the following argument was stressed:

> Now that the developed societies, entangled in cultural and moral crises, have begun to seek solutions ... we can endeavor to reinforce and consolidate the cultural and moral foundations of [our] society and to [refamiliarize ourselves with] *(bazshenasim)* and strengthen our national identity which is manifested in our national culture.[22]

As can be seen from the examples mentioned above, the establishment seemed to have adopted much of the discourse of the intellectual dissidents of the 1960s. Even though it was far from being a monolith,[23] as far as its cultural policy was concerned, the establishment had taken up the third-worldist notions of the "return to roots" and the "rediscovery of past culture and heritage." However, the two camps could still be distinguished from one another on two fronts. Whereas disenchanted intellectuals, by and large, included a degree of anti-Westernism as a manifestation of their third-worldism, for the establishment, promoting authentic culture did not necessarily equate with opposition to the West. In fact, there was an understanding that while the country was benefiting from a Western-style industrial civilization, an effort had to be made to maintain its traditions and national heritage in order to give a sense of identity to the nation. So traditions were useful in that they provided some continuity and a sense of identity vis-à-vis the outside world. Secondly, the way in which the establishment proposed to preserve the cultural heritage was not always acceptable to intellectuals. As part of this effort, the state encouraged the establishment of museums, as well as the restoration of architecture and decorative arts. The argument for this was that they enabled the preservation of a link between the people and their past authentic culture. For it was claimed that museums would provide an opportunity for cultural artifacts, as manifestations of authentic culture, to be collected, put on display, and made accessible to all, in an attempt to work toward a recognition of Iranian civilization and culture, which would then serve as protection against outside civilization:

> This compilation and study of cultural manifestations *(mazaher)* is not solely for the sake of diversion or self-glorification, but their preservation has a major role in the education of the young, for it will prevent foreign cultures from absorbing and overwhelming them.[24]

Therefore, central to the definition of the "return to authentic culture" used by the state was the element of recognition *(shenasa'i)* of past culture. Whether it was by means of the different festivals, the founding of museums and cultural institutions, or even perhaps the celebration of the 2,500th anniversary of monarchy,[25] the underlying notion was one of familiarization with and promotion of past traditions primarily through display, both to unite the nation and also to define an identity for the country, as an Eastern nation in the predominantly Western world. So the co-optation of the third-world discourse had ironically been used by the establishment to bring about reconciliation, a way of coming to terms with and not a confrontation with the outside world.

Recovering an Alternative "Authentic Past"

Intellectuals, by and large, found the state's stance unsatisfactory and could not approve of it for two reasons: first, because it was the proposition put forward by the state, and second, because it was far too conservative and elitist. In spite of the attempts at co-optation, as far as the intellectuals were concerned, the state had not gained any greater legitimacy in their eyes. Therefore, they sought to distinguish themselves from the establishment and so a debate began in the pages of many journals on how the past could be "truly" recovered.

In the early 1970s, when there was little openness, the objection that intellectuals made to the stance of the establishment with regard to culture had several facets. In the first place, there were general doubts concerning the wisdom of a cultural policy. That is, it was not clear to what degree the drawing of a cultural policy as part of a development program would sanction government interference in the task of the "creators of culture."[26] The other area of contention was the question of selection. Which elements of this cultural heritage were to be chosen and promoted as authentic? Which aspects of the past would be closer to the real past and more genuine? Which components were to be revived, which adapted, and which discarded? What were the criteria behind the selection? In other words, what purpose was to be served? Was the aim to display an identity to the outside world or was it to bring cultural and social change within the country itself? These questions became of central concern for all the parties involved; their standpoint on these questions often served to demarcate to which side they belonged. To those critical of the establishment, the selectivity involved in the course taken by the establishment seemed largely aimed at portraying a glorified image of the past, particularly of the pre-Islamic past, as a way of gaining recognition primarily from the outside world. What they seemed to emphasize in their writings on culture was the need for a reinterpretation of traditions that would result in some social change in the present.

Two very different aspects of this discourse are portrayed by two of the better-known essayists writing at this time, Daryush Ashuri[27] and Mehdi Parham.[28] Ashuri and Parham are best described as secular, liberal, and left-leaning essayists who, while not being activists in any way, questioned the attitude of the state/establishment toward culture. In a series of articles written in the early 1970s, Ashuri dismissed the efforts of the establishment to found museums, exhibit artifacts of the Iranian past, and hold festivals to glorify elements of Iranian folklore as different forms of "mummifying of culture."[29] None of these measures, he argued, had much connection with the past since they neither captured the spirit of the past nor stimulated any sense of history, which was now considered essential for bringing about some continuity. People needed a past to which they could refer in order to derive a sense of identity. Putting artifacts in museums was treating the past as if it were a dead object that had long ceased to exist. He wrote,

> Tradition is not heritage *(mordeh-rig)*[30] in the shape of an object independent from us, without any link to what we are. It is neither an antique vessel that we place on the shelf nor a manuscript that we keep in the library. The past is not a coffin that we take to the cemetery; tradition is that which gives ability and skill to man.[31]

In other words, preserving tradition or cultural heritage did not necessarily have to consist of "assembling fragments of the past into displays," and in any case, this did not make convincing history. This was no more than a history that existed in a "symbolic and decorative state."[32] It was of no consequence and merely an adornment that may have pleased the eye. Therefore, for Ashuri, the idea of "return," in the sense of recreating the past as entertained by the establishment, was no more than a fancy, and, furthermore, the manner in which this third-worldist concept had been coopted by the establishment reinforced its superficial aspect. He wrote in the same article, "What we do with the history, literature, art and all that has remained from the past . . . is archaeology. The task of the archaeologist is to search for the effects of the dead civilizations and forgotten ages and to preserve all that he finds, without evaluation or selection, and to give to museums."[33]

Ashuri was not alone in putting forth such an argument. What he, along with other progressive intellectuals, implied was that the culture promoted by the establishment was out of context; in other words, it was not representative of the indigenous life, since it lacked all social awareness. As another essayist wrote under a pseudonym a few years later:

> If the aim of the revival of indigenous Eastern thought by means of the reinvention *(dawbarehsazi)* and analysis *(tahlil)* of traditions, festivals, and ideas is to confront Western cultural attack, attention must be paid to the social essence of tradition *(jawhar-e ejtema'i-ye sonnat)*, which does not fit in the framework of official thought. It is for this reason that the "third-worldization" *(jahan-e sevvomi shodan)* of the festivals, celebrations, and customs is no more than a pseudointellectual claim and pretension. If third-world art does not stimulate social consciousness and effectiveness, then one cannot give it the attribute "third-worldist."[34]

Therefore, in order to recover the past, tradition had to be reintegrated into life. In other words, it had to be reinterpreted, brought in line with a "creative" present, and given new meaning. This was the task of writers, artists, and thinkers, and not that of the establishment. Furthermore, the efforts by the establishment to promote a glorified image of the East by means of exhibitions and displays were generally referred to as *"sharqzadegi"* or *"Eastoxication."* Just as *"gharbzadegi,"*[35] a phrase that had captured the public imagination, had come to signify an extensive threat and fast-spreading disease that encouraged a superficial emulation of the West without really appreciating its philosophy in depth, so was *sharqzadegi* likened to an epidemic.[36] It was regarded as a wave, an affliction that merely dealt with the surface of things, with little respect for the "real" traditions that were lived by the people. It was, thus, considered to be a Westernized idea of the East or an aspect of Westernization since it consisted of people discovering their roots in the manner of Western tourists, going and seeing artifacts in museums, instead of thinking about the true meaning of the East or feeling any commitment to an "Eastern authenticity." In other words, *sharqzadegi* was the mirror image of Westoxication. It was contrived, because it represented an imitation of the attitude perpetrated by Western Orientalism that preserved everything for its own sake. In Ashuri's words again,

> What is the meaning of the pandemonium *(hayahu)* that has arisen in recent years about the East and its cultural heritage? One must say clearly that a major part of the commotion that has arisen in the

name of opposing the West and glorifying the East has its roots in gharbzadegi. This means that while emphasizing the concepts of Western humanism . . . , we want to give a meaning to the East that is thoroughly alien to its essence.³⁷

In short, as far as Ashuri was concerned, the establishment's approach toward reviving the cultural heritage had not only been inspired by a Westernized mentality but it represented, moreover, the other side of the inferiority complex that had afflicted third-world nations in the nineteenth and twentieth centuries. More than any other factor, it was the dead nature of the history put on exhibition that appeared false to him. He considered all these efforts as no more than a form of "cultural tourism" aimed at the outside world.³⁸

While Ashuri merely outlined the problems with the establishment's understanding of authentic culture and only hinted vaguely at a solution in the way of reintegrating tradition into everyday life, others were more forthright and took the argument a step further. That is, they turned to the idea of mysticism and/or religion as representative of the authentic culture. In other words, since the method in which culture was being revived was little more than cultural tourism, it was argued, so the real authentic culture could only be found in the religion and myth of the society. One writer in whose essays this trend could be detected was Mehdi Parham. He wrote a series of articles in which he outlined the advantages of reviving some sort of spiritual life in the form of mysticism. He wrote:

> What today's far-sighted thinkers recommend as a way of escaping the alienation and confusion of the technological man *(ensan-e 'asr-e mashin)* is precisely what our mystic thinkers have expressed in the shape of beautiful and complex concepts to make the perfect man *(ensan-e kamel)*. Undoubtedly, if we refine these notions from the superstitious superfluities, then it will be in demand in the same way as our oil is in the chaotic West. But as I said before, our mysticism, like our oil, needs a refinery; otherwise, it is not a good worthy of supply.³⁹

Several points can be made at this stage. If mysticism had lost its dubious aspect for a left-leaning secular intellectual like Parham, it was primarily because it had been discussed by Western thinkers as an alternative to the technocratic society. In fact, the element of the Western need for some sort of spirituality was of utmost importance for intellectuals like Parham, hence his use of the metaphor, likening mysticism to "oil." After all, this article was written in 1974, in the midst of the oil crisis and the quadrupling of the price of oil, making this source of energy into a major point of concern in the Western world. Parham added, "Just as the civilized world has been and continues to be thirsty for our oil, now because of its continuous experiences and defeat from the ugly manifestations of capitalism, it has also become thirsty for our spirituality and mysticism."[40] In other words, mysticism had become of value because it seemed to be in demand in the West. At the same time, mysticism had the added advantage of serving as a counterdiscourse to the promotion of the authentic culture by the establishment.

However, this discussion of mysticism was more a means to an end than a matter of conviction. Articles had to be written to convince both the secularist himself and his readers that mysticism was feasible; mysticism would be acceptable once it was filtered and cleansed of its superstitious superfluities. This could be achieved in two ways; first, by describing its process of emergence, and, second, by outlining its potential function in bringing about a more equitable society. Invariably, the explanation given for its appearance was that it had come about either in order to confront and oppose the authoritarian clergy *(motesharre'an)* and the oppressive ruler, or that it had been a development resulting from man's aspiration for universalism *(jahan-vatani)*. In other words, the circumstances in which mysticism was said to have come about were portrayed as being similar to the concerns of the modern world and with which, consequently, the secular intellectual could identify and sympathize. So Parham wrote,

> If we look consciously, [we will see that] the reasons behind the emergence of positive mysticism *('erfan-e mosbat)* were approximately similar to those of the cooperative system. Just as the cooperative system removes the middlemen *(dalalan)* and brings the producer face to face with the consumer, so does mysticism cast aside the healers and false jurists *(motesharre'in)* who are really the middlemen of divine compassion and consider themselves as the mediators between the creator and the created.[41]

Secondly, mysticism was made acceptable by explaining its potentials in very practical terms. So, for example, once again according to Parham, mysticism represented the most remarkable system of liberation *(azadsazi)* and cooperation *(khodyari)*. By praising mysticism, he wrote in one of his articles, he did not want to compel people to go to sufi houses *(khanehqahs)* or *tekkiyeh*s in this age of science. But he wanted to present it as a possible alternative provided it was refined. In other words, this was a reinvented mysticism *('erfan-e bazafarini-shodeh)*. If mysticism had been viewed with suspicion in the past, it was because it had not been cherished and instead had been reduced to the rank of a narcotic. In short, what may have once been the cause of a movement had, by mistake, been used throughout the ages as a tranquilizer. A revision, therefore, was necessary. Once again, in Parham's words,

> Unfortunately, we do not have a correct impression of spirituality *(ma'naviyyat)* and usually think that spiritual people are those who categorically deny material things *(maddiyat)* and constantly recite poetry and love songs, or that they are constantly praying and have withdrawn from the world and all that is related to it. But this is not so. Real mystics used to do all sorts of things, only without exploiting anyone. . . . Mostly they would do manual work so as to break social classes and remove the gap between the theologian, the jurist, and the laborer. . . . This is exactly what the Chinese have become aware of today and so they oblige all professors, students, and high-ranking government employees to go to farms once or twice a year and do manual work.[42]

More than any other thinker, Parham seems to have been influenced by Roger Garaudy, the French philosopher,[43] who in the early 1970s wrote a series of books and articles exploring the potentials of religion as a revolutionary force and examining the idea of an alternative society where a combination of socialism and religion would be at work.[44] Garaudy, writing about Christianity, argued that religion need not be an opiate and engender resignation, provided it was reformed, and that once religion, together with socialism, addressed the problem of here and now, it became a militant and creative force. His argument was directly translated into Parham's argument:

> That which Garaudy means by a change of religion is not that a religion other than Christianity, for example, should emerge in Europe, but that there be a new interpretation of the fundamentals of religion, since the belief of a majority of people is still based in religion, and so it can have a role as a catalyst, to arouse them.[45]

As can be seen from the examples mentioned above, the language used in these articles was certainly not that of spirituality. The secularist had not suddenly become religious. Neither had he developed a more concrete understanding of religion. If Parham had written about religion *(mazhab)* and mysticism *('erfan)*, it was because he had arrived at the idea under the influence of Western thinkers who had become disillusioned with the technocratic state and were in search of a new alternative. But Parham was not alone in entertaining such ideas.[46] There was a general feeling among secular intellectuals at this time that being "progressive" no longer necessarily equated with being skeptical toward religion, especially since thinkers like Garaudy, after thirty-seven years of having been a member of the French Communist Party, had turned toward Christianity. Furthermore, it seemed that in most third-world struggles against imperialism, religion was taking on a more significant role. Whether it was Buddhism, which was generally considered to have played a major part in bringing about the victory of the Vietnamese against the United States,[47] or Islam, in the case of the Arab world, this appeared to be the trend of the second half of the twentieth century. It was in this context that religion and/or mysticism became important. They gained significance inasmuch as they had the potential of being a catalyst for bringing about change, provided they were interpreted afresh and made relevant to the times.

Conclusion

In conclusion, as has been argued, the discourse of "authentic culture" gained prevalence in response to a combination of third-worldism and the movement of counterculture predominant in the West. While initially adopted by disenchanted intellectuals as a means of voicing opposition against all that the regime represented in their eyes, by the late 1960s it had gained sufficient importance that the establishment could not remain indifferent to it. However, once the establishment joined in the discourse, secular, left-leaning intellectuals, in their capacity as critics of power, reacted and sought an alternative approach to authentic culture. As shown above, the trend toward mysticism and/or religion was one alternative. It was useful insomuch as it was ostensibly traditional. However, its significance lay in the fact that it was different from the society exported by the West as well as that which the regime promoted as authentic culture. So if mysticism and religion became prevalent in the 1970s, it was for their worldly potentials. Religion and mysticism were old notions that, if interpreted in a new light, could bring about the change that other ideologies had failed to achieve. It is no wonder then that once the first manifestations of a religious opposition to the regime began, advocating the cause of authentic culture, secular progressive intellectuals did not question the meaning of this rhetoric. Instead, they gave it their full backing.

Notes

A version of this essay has been published in Persian in *Iran Nameh: Majalleh-ye Tahqiqat-e Iranshenasi* 19, no. 3 (spring 2001), pp. 263–77.

1. Apart from Golesorkhi, the eleven others who were put on trial included Karamatollah Daneshiyan, Mohammad Reza 'Allamehzadeh, Teyfur Batha'i, 'Abbas 'Ali Samakar, Manuchehr Moqaddam-Salimi, Morteza Siyahpush, Farhad Qeysari, Ebrahim Farhang-razi, Rahmatollah Jamshidi, Shokuh Farhang-razi (Mirzadegi), and Maryam Ettehadiyeh. See Baqer 'Aqeli, *Ruzshomar-e tarikh-e Iran* (The chronology of Iranian history), vol. 2 (Tehran: Nashr-e Goftar, 1991), p. 281.

2. "Defa'iyyat-e Khosraw Golesorkhi" (The defense proceedings of Khosraw Golesorkhi). Reprinted in *Nazm-e Novin,* vol. 7 (August–September 1985), cover page.

3. Ibid.

4. Ibid.

5. Of the twelve, five, including Golesorkhi, were sentenced to death, and the remaining seven were sentenced to prison terms ranging from three years to life sentences. 'Aqeli, *Ruzshomar,* p. 281.

6. An example of such an argument can be seen in the following government-sponsored report on the subject of the trial: "These [people] who have never set foot in a mosque in their life and have not become familiar with the eternal rites and the deep meaning of Islam and the word of God, have obviously insulted the rightful religion and the prophet. . . . They have tried to attach a creed whose main aim is to attack religious beliefs and godliness . . . onto the rightful religion." "Niru-ye enqelabi-ye Iran, mardom-e mosalman-e ma, har guneh talash-e mazbuhaneh ra mahkum mikonand" (The revolutionary force of Iran, our Muslim people, condemn all sorts of futile attempts), *Ferdawsi* 25 (2 February 1974), p. 6. Many such articles were also published in a series titled "Bargha-ye andisheh" (Leaves of thought) in the weekly *Tamasha.* For example, see "Terorism: hasel-e marxism-e eslami" (Terrorism: The product of Islamic Marxism), *Tamasha,* vol. 5 (16 August 1975), pp. 8–9.

7. Raymond Williams, *Keywords: A Vocabulary of Culture and Society* (London: Fontana, 1988), p. 87.

8. Ibid., p. 90.

9. Frantz Fanon, *The Wretched of the Earth,* trans. Constance Farrington (Harmondsworth: Penguin, 1985), pp. 169–70.

10. Manuchehr Hezarkhani, "Mas'aleh-ye farhangi dar mobarezeh-ye este'mari" (The cultural question in the colonial struggle), *Ferdawsi,* no. 871 (5 August 1968), p. 11.

11. *Ferdawsi,* no. 895 (20 January 1969), p. 3.

12. This discourse has also been broadly referred to elsewhere as "nativist." See

Mehrzad Boroujerdi, *Iranian Intellectuals and the West: The Tormented Triumph of Nativism* (Syracuse, N.Y.: Syracuse University Press, 1996), p. 14.

13. This was not the first attempt at co-optation. Contrary to popular perceptions, the shah was not indifferent to the intellectuals' opinion; rather, he longed for their approval. For a discussion of the shah's attitude toward intellectuals, as well as attempts on the part of his longest-serving prime minister, Amir Abbas Hoveyda, to mediate between dissident intellectuals and the regime, see Abbas Milani, *The Persian Sphinx: Amir Abbas Hoveyda and the Riddle of the Iranian Revolution* (Washington, D.C.: Mage Publishers, 2000).

14. For a detailed account of these series of closures, see "Yaddasht" (Notes), *Andisheh va Honar* (January–February 1979), pp. 1–3.

15. Changiz Pahlavan, "Barnamehrizi-ye farhangi dar Iran" (Cultural planning in Iran), *Farhang va Zendegi,* no. 15 (summer 1974), p. 54.

16. Ibid., pp. 52–71.

17. For more on the components of the second Festival of Culture and Art, see "Dovvomin jashn-e farhang va honar" (The second Festival of Culture and Art), *Farhang va Zendegi,* no. 2 (January 1970), pp. 70–79.

18. Ibid., p. 77.

19. Ibid., p. 78.

20. Anthony Parsons, *The Pride and the Fall: Iran, 1974–1979* (London: Jonathan Cape, 1984), p. 54. Parsons, in fact, considers the Shiraz Arts Festival and its "avant-garde absurdities" to have had political repercussions in provoking some of the Islamic backlash at the time of the revolution in 1978–79.

21. See "Ehya-ye jashn-e farhang-e mardom: harfha-i dar hashiyeh-ye bargozari-ye farhang-e mardom" (The revival of the Festival of Popular Traditions: Some words around the convening of the Festival of Popular Traditions), *Tamasha,* vol. 7 (1 October 1977), p. 88.

22. Pahlavan, "Barnamehrizi-ye farhangi dar Iran," p. 55.

23. For a portrayal of the various factions within the establishment, see Asadollah Alam, *The Shah and I: The Confidential Diary of Iran's Royal Court, 1967–1977,* ed. Alinaghi Alikhani (London and New York: I. B. Tauris, 1991).

24. "Gozareshi az jashn-e farhang va honar" (A report from the Festival of Culture and Art), *Farhang va Zendegi,* vol. 7 (January 1972), p. 125.

25. At least a similar argument was put forth for the celebrations marking the 2,500th anniversary of the monarchy. According to one article, the celebrations "aim primarily to address the past cultural and scientific glories of Iran, [which] in themselves will provide an opportunity for our nation to assess its cultural treasury." See "Jashnha-ye dawhezar-o pansad saleh-ye bonyad-e shahanshahi-ye Iran: yadavari-ye farhang va melliyat" (The celebrations of the 2,500th anniversary of the foundation of the Iranian monarchy: A reminder of culture and nationhood), *Ferdawsi,* vol. 21 (4 June 1971), p. 5.

26. Hamid 'Enayat (1932–1982), political scientist and writer, for example, questioned the independence of the "culture" that was produced as a result of a

"cultural policy." He argued that culture was distinct from ideology in that it was fluid and not organized and developed according to exchanges of ideas in a free environment, whereas a cultural policy, with its inherent set of aims and objectives determined by official expectations, necessarily imposed an orientation on the course of culture and thus prevented it from being an independent effort. See Hamid ʿEnayat, "Rabeteh-ye ekhtelafat-e farhangi ba ekhtelafat-e beyn al-melali" (The relationship between cultural and international differences), *Negin*, vol. 10 (22 July 1974), p. 5.

27. Daryush Ashuri (b. 1938), a prolific writer, translator, and essayist, had been a member of the youth organization of the Tudeh Party. Following the invasion of Hungary in 1956, he lost faith in Communism and joined Khalil Maleki's League of Socialists in 1960. Once all political activity became impossible, he concentrated on his study of literature and philosophy. See "Goftogu ba Daryush Ashuri" (In conversation with Daryush Ashuri), *Kelk*, no. 37 (March–April 1993), pp. 187–253.

28. Mehdi Parham (b. 1919), an economist with a doctorate in economics from the University of Paris, was active as an essayist. Although some twenty years older than Ashuri, Parham seems to have experienced some of the same stages in his political thinking. He had been a member of the Tudeh Party in 1943 but seceded alongside Khalil Maleki in 1948 and founded *Sharq-e miyaneh*, a newspaper, in defense of Maleki and the secession. This, however, did not prove to be a lasting venture, and so he turned away from politics to his professional life. According to his own account, upon retirement in 1977 he resumed his full-time writing for several journals, including *Negin*. Personal correspondence with the author, January 1995.

29. Daryush Ashuri, "Sonnat va pishraft" (Tradition and progress), *Farhang va Zendegi*, no. 1 (January 1970), p. 72.

30. *Mordeh-rig* has the sense both of heritage and useless and inconsequential matter.

31. Ashuri, "Sonnat va pishraft," p. 72.

32. Ibid.

33. Ibid., p. 71.

34. Farhad [pseud.], "Ehya-ye tafakkor-e bumi-ye sharq ba dawbarehsazi va tahlil-e sonnan, marasem va ʿaqayed" (The revival of Eastern indigenous thought with the reinvention and analysis of traditions, customs, and beliefs), *Ferdawsi*, vol. 25 (21 September 1973), p. 22.

35. *Gharbzadegi*, translated as "Westoxication" or "Weststruckness," was an expression that became identified with Jalal Al-e Ahmad (1923–1969), who politicized and popularized it. Broadly speaking, it came to mean all aspects of Westernization that infringed on the Iranian way of life and prevented Iranians from preserving their cultural identity.

36. Others, too, shared Ashuri's point of view. See, for example, Farhad Qabusi, "Sima-ye tamaddon-e shahri dar javameʿ-e dar hal-e roshd" (The expres-

sion of urban civilization in developing societies), *Ferdawsi*, vol. 21 (21 June 1971), p. 12.

37. Ashuri, "Sharq va gharb" (East and West), *Farhang va Zendegi*, no. 15 (Summer 1974), p. 27.

38. See also Ashuri, "Iranshenasi chist?" (What is Iranology?), *Majalleh-ye rahnama-ye ketab*, vol. 14 (June– September 1971), pp. 218–26.

39. Mehdi Parham, "Azadi-ye bardegan-e enerji" (The liberation of the slaves of energy), *Negin*, vol. 9 (April 1974), p. 7.

40. Ibid., p. 60.

41. Parham, "Farhang-e taʿavon" (The culture of cooperation), *Negin*, vol. 11 (March 1976), p. 72.

42. Parham, "Naqdi az jameʿeh-ye naw" (A critique of the new society), *Negin*, vol. 12 (August 1976), p. 51.

43. Roger Garaudy (b. 1913) had been a member of the French Communist Party and a representative in the French Parliament, but following his objection to the Soviet invasion of Czechoslovakia in 1968, he was expelled from the party. Although this led to his rejection of Soviet Communism, he maintained his belief in Marxism and advocated a system in which Marxism with a "human face" could prevail. In 1982, he converted to Islam.

44. In conveying the ideas of Garaudy, Parham refers to three of his books on the subject of the "alternative society" more specifically. They are *L'Alternative* (Paris, 1972); *Parole d'homme* (Paris, 1975); and *Le projet ésperance* (Paris, 1976).

45. Parham, "Naqdi az jameʿeh-ye naw," p. 52.

46. See, among others, M. E. [pseud.], "Pazhuheshi dar farhang-e sharq: janbehha-ye motaraqqi-ye ʿerfan va tasavvof-e Iran" (An examination of the culture of the East: The progressive aspects of the Iranian sufism), *Negin*, vol. 8 (October–November 1972); Farhad Qabusi, "Sima-ye tamaddon-e shahri dar javameʿ-e dar hal-e roshd" (The expression of urban civilization in developing societies), *Ferdawsi*, vol. 21 (21 June 1971); Farhad Qabusi, "Rang bakhtan-e esalat dar hojum-e dar hal-e tawseʿehgi" (Losing the color of authenticity in the assault of development), *Ferdawsi*, vol. 23 (24 April 1972); Reza Baraheni, "Poli beyn-e sosialism va eslam" (A bridge between socialism and Islam), *Ferdawsi*, vol. 21 (19 June 1971).

47. Parham, "Farhang-e taʿavon," p. 9.

Part II

Intellectual Expressions and Dynamics in Postrevolutionary Iran

5

Crossing the Desert

Iranian Intellectuals after the Islamic Revolution

Morad Saghafi

Entering the post-1979 revolution period as the weak ally of the strong Islamist forces, Iranian intellectuals had to face, during two decades, several important challenges that could be classified as "external" and "internal." On the external side, the first challenge was experiencing a political scene dominated by populist acts and discourses. The next challenge was facing a war that they neither had the permission to participate in, nor the right to ignore. Third was confronting a rivalry with the emerging "religious intellectuals," who by distancing themselves from their secular colleagues in fact contributed to their marginalization. Last but not least was the most durable challenge of living and working in an environment in which the only predictable rule was the political and cultural persecution of intellectuals.

From the internal point of view, foremost were the differences that occurred in quite an aggressive way between the intellectuals who criticized the emerging Islamic Republic and those who supported it in the name of anti-imperialism. For those intellectuals who sympathized with leftist political groups, the shattering of the "Communist dream" confronted them with the challenge of a break in ideology. This happened partly because of the fall of the Soviet empire but partly also because of the tangible experience of the Islamic Republic. Especially during the Iran-Iraq war (1980–88), the Islamic Republic resembled in many ways the ideological political system they had praised, with the difference that they did not run it.

Needless to say, with the challenges, pressures, self-doubts, loss of ideals, and persecution they experienced, Iranian intellectuals went through a long period of crisis. A large number of them moved out of or fled the country. Those who stayed took a low profile, at least until the end of the war, when press freedom began to be established slowly. Some were killed, while others never emerged again as intellectuals. Among the ones who left the country, only a few could continue their intellectual life. Others—if they were lucky—turned either to an academic life or to business; the unluckiest lived a life of depression before dying in exile.

Nevertheless, at the end of the war with Iraq, when the press and, after a while, public space slowly opened up, Iran experienced a shy return of intellectuals to the social and cultural scene. Later, with the shortcomings of the experience of "religious intellectualism" and then the evidence of widespread social and cultural crisis in Iranian society, intellectuals became more visible. It is not an exaggeration to say that at the level of discourse—and not only with regard to social and cultural areas, but also politically speaking—intellectuals obtained a hegemonic situation in society, particularly since the 1997 presidential election that brought Mohammad Khatami to office. It is important to stress that this hegemonic situation has no parallel in contemporary Iranian history.

In this chapter, it is not possible to explore in depth each and every one of these experiences and the role that they played in the maturation process of intellectualism in Iran. Yet, an overview can help one to appreciate the long desert so many of them tried to cross. Only a few of them achieved acceptance, if not by all, at least by those Iranians who desired to accomplish something for the country.

Entering the Islamic Era

Iranian intellectuals entered the Islamic era in a very odd—if not paradoxical—situation. From 12 February 1979, the day after the victory of the revolution, until 4 June 1980, the day that all universities throughout the country were closed and the "cultural revolution" began, the life of intellectuals in Iran could be summarized as a "chronicle of an announced defeat." The majority of Iranian intellectuals had good reason to consider the victory of revolution as their own. In fact, they were among the forces that had shaken, since the middle of the 1960s, the pillars of legitimacy of the Pahlavi regime. They were more leftist than right wing, more or less political, and in some ways involved with Mohammad Reza Shah Pahlavi's dream of building a modern Iran. Nevertheless, they collectively shared a critical attitude toward the Pahlavi regime, an attitude that finally paved the road to revolution. The less political and more involved intellectuals were critical of the regime for its use of technology and for its Westernized approach.¹ The less involved and more political ones blamed the monarch for serving the Western countries' interests and thus neglecting his own people. Despite their differences in approach and attitude, the two groups shared a common belief: that the Pahlavi regime had created a situation of collective depression. This societal depression prevented Iran—despite its 2,500 years of history, its centuries-long domination of Asia and parts of Europe, its extraordinary cultural heritage from both Islam and ancient Persia, and its significant past contributions to world civilization through its prominent scientists and creators of beautiful art and architecture—from producing any products of high standards.² And if this was the situation with regard to industrial products, it was a sign of illness when it came to intellectual production, which was related directly to culture and not to technology. The disease finally was recognized by Ahmad Fardid (the promoter of Heidegger's ideas in Iran) and launched publicly by the most influential Iranian intellectual, Jalal Al-e Ahmad, who named it *gharbzadegi* (Westoxication) to stress its infectious and poisonous nature.³

Al-e Ahmad did much more than publicly announce the prevalence of the disease of *gharbzadegi*. By bringing together a multitude of anti-intellectual arguments that before him had existed only as fragments of other discourses, he constructed for the first time in Iran a holistic anti-intellectual discourse.⁴ Indeed, before Al-e Ahmad, Iran had had no wide experience of deep anti-intellectualism, as one could find in other cultures. Of course, after the secular and democratic consequences of the constitutional revolution (1906) became evident to clerics and conservative social and political forces, anti-intellectual arguments were advanced as part of anti-Western or antimodernist discourses. The most common such critique was *farangi bazi* (acting like Westerners), developed by some conservative writers in the early 1900s.⁵ The other very common discourse was the pro-Islamist and then anticonstitutional discourse developed by eminent clerics in the same period.⁶ Later, when the Iranian Communist movement's discourse superseded the antiforeigner economic discourse of nationalists and Islamic forces, a new type of anti-intellectual argument that had much in common with populism developed. This took the form of denouncing aristocrats and wealthy merchants, considered as the local allies of imperialists. As previously noted, however, these arguments were neither directly anti-intellectual nor autonomous discourses. Al-e Ahmad made an explosive mix of them all, putting the intellectual at the center of his argument.

In a very paradoxical argumentation, Al-e Ahmad thought of intellectuals as being the only group that could take the country out of infertility. Yet, while he believed that intellectuals could be of service to the country, what in fact they had done since the constitutional revolution was nothing but "treason." He wrote that those intellectuals "who represent the minimum of intellectualism as well as those who represent the maximum have the same characteristics." And he described five of these common characteristics as being negative. First, in continuity with the inappropriate learning of the era of the constitutional revolution, intellectuals propagated the values of the "Metropol" countries, ideas and behaviors that were not appropriate to colonized countries like Iran. Second (and following from the first), Iranian intellectuals were alienated from the people, not in touch with them, and inevitably lacked any concern for them; hence, they thought not about local problems but imported ones. Third, Iranian intellectuals wished to be the tool of democracy, like their Western intellectual role models, but since they lived in an undemocratic environment and lacked access to readers and people who could be affected by their ideas, they at best served the censorship system of the state. Fourth, the Iranian intellectual was still a dependent person, without roots, who easily could be kept away from politics. And finally, this combination of characteristics was why the intellectual finally becomes "melancholic," "a heroin addict," "mad," or "Westoxicated." Whatever he became, he was a consumer, not a producer; and he forgot his ideals and became "infertile."[7]

Al-e Ahmad was not entirely negative. For example, he stated that most Iranian intellectuals were educated in the social sciences and thus were unlikely to lead the country to "technocracy." A second positive attribute was that despite the fact that they were all dependent on a foreign culture, this culture was not monolithic; some were French-toxicated, others English-toxicated, and still others poisoned by American or Russian values. This situation created a kind of pluralism that prevented total dependency. This is why Al-e Ahmad thought Iranian intellectuals would be able to "fulfill their historical duty." To do so, however, several things had to happen. First, intellectuals had to understand that the primary responsibility of their education was to take a position against the colonizers; second, they had to become familiar with indigenous and local problems and essentially try to solve them; and third, they had to clarify precisely their place between the people and the government.[8] For a local historical model of this kind of attitude, Al-e Ahmad refers to the Shi'i clergy who, "by virtue of their defense of tradition, are a type of resistance force against the encroachments of colonialism whose primary target for pillage is cultural and traditional. Thus, the clergy are a bulwark against the Westoxication of the intellectuals and the absolute submission of the government toward the West and its imperialism."⁹

In this way Al-e Ahmad gave Iran's contemporary sociocultural debates the first holistic anti-intellectual discourse. At the same time, he assigned intellectuals a central role in society, taking them out of anonymity, giving them advice on how to fulfill their duty, and letting them choose between being in the service of their country and being traitors. For nearly two decades, this viewpoint and conceptualization not only dominated any analysis about the role of intellectuals in society but also served as a directive for most intellectual behavior with regard to cultural, social, and, of course, political issues. This is why on the eve of the Islamic revolution an anticolonialist, anti-imperialist, antitechnocratic, and, of course, populist discourse dominated Iranian intellectualism. This discourse was accompanied by a positive outlook toward Islamism and was reflected in the use of Islamic symbolism in all intellectual productions.

When the revolutionary movement began in 1978 and Islamist groups appeared to be its central forces, it was hard to find any intellectual who doubted Al-e Ahmad's sociological and political analysis of Iranian society and the role of intellectuals. With the victory of the revolution, it became clear that with regard to every single one of those dominant concepts, it was the Islamist forces, and not the intellectuals, who had a hegemonic position in society. This was because the Islamists were much more genuinely populist and naturally more antitechnocratic and anticolonialist. With the occupation of the American embassy in November 1979, the Islamist forces also caught up with their delay in engaging the anti-imperialist issue. Thus, the intellectuals clearly appeared to be the weak ally of the strong Islamist faction, which used this weakness to drive the intellectuals out of the political scene.

The less radical and less political intellectuals who had adopted a much more democratic and tolerant discourse were among the first to be expelled from the public sphere, primarily because they failed to get the backing of their more radical colleagues. Two very significant examples were Shahrokh Meskub and Changiz Pahlavan, both of whom angered Islamists by their articles in the newspaper *Ayandegan* during the spring and summer of 1979. Meskub was declared persona non grata when he criticized proposals before the assembly drafting the new constitution to grant unlimited power to the Leader of the Revolution. Pahlavan's criticism of the initial postrevolutionary purges in the universities resulted in his being banned from publishing for many years. Yet, within less than two years' time, the more radical and more political intellectuals faced the same fate as the first group. Having accepted the three above-mentioned concepts as the ultimate criteria for intellectualism and their political awareness, the intellectuals were asked by Islamist forces either to join the Islamist ranks and accept their leadership if they were sincere in their declaration or to close down. Of course, the intellectuals rejected this offer, and on 4 June 1980, Islamist mobs attacked Tehran University, the last bastion of leftist groups and their intellectual allies in the capital. The eviction of leftist faculty and students from campuses in Tehran and other important cities such as Tabriz and Shiraz did not take place without injuries. Later, leftist groups talked about this event as a coup d'état against the real revolutionary forces. But during the days and months that followed the event, the degree of stupefaction was inversely proportional to the capacity for analyzing what had happened.

The Iranian Writers Association, which could be considered the voice of Iranian intellectuals, dedicated an entire issue of its magazine to the university problem. With the exception of one article that recognized the attackers as being "lumpen," this special issue was silent about the composition, class affiliation, or nature of the "forces who attacked the united rank of collegians, students, and workers" and pushed them out of the universities.[10] The writers were sure that the attackers had not invaded the universities to carry out a "cultural revolution":

> If the problem is the cultural revolution, we were the first to ask for it. We were the first who started doing purges at the university. We wanted to put the Savaki [members of the shah's secret police] out of the university. We wrote and wrote to get their list. . . . We asked to purge teachers who were dependent on the old regime, and we purged some of them by the decision of our council. Do you know what was the main reason for creating the university councils? The reason was exactly these purges.[11]

The groups and intellectuals in the universities had another good reason not to understand why, in the name of revolutionary acts, the attackers wanted them to leave academia. In fact, they themselves had projects for curriculum change. By reading the aim of these projects, one can see how much Al-e Ahmad's point of view had been adopted by Iranian intellectuals and their affiliated political groups:

> The curriculum of universities in an exploited country is such that the engineering department educates engineers who only know how

to mount pieces [versus designing machines]. The social sciences department treats issues that are alien to the objective problems of the country. In literature, they teach old texts and feudal cultures, and in the arts, they propagate trendy and "chic" art.[12]

Given such viewpoints, it was inevitable for the Writers Association to conclude that the attackers were sent by the "imperialist-oriented faction of the government," which, in return for aid from its master, had promised to "do away with revolutionary forces at the universities and elsewhere."[13] And while doing this, the local allies of imperialism did not care about the most basic rights of the oppressed people and millions of poor workers in the country. Despite this analysis, it was clear to objective observers that the people who attacked universities were the very same oppressed people whose rights the intellectuals claimed to be defending. These people were not moved to act by the direct or indirect orders of any imperialist force but by their belief that their revolutionary dream could be realized if Iran were "cleansed" of leftists, democrats, and other secular forces. The reality was that the situation had changed, and Al-e Ahmad's paradigm of the intellectual serving his country was no longer valid. This changed situation actually had been the subject of discussion between some intellectuals less than four months before the cultural revolution, when Esma'il Kho'i, in an article written in the form of a letter to a friend, stated, "We can't deny that, in the past, finding the road was easier for our association [Iranian Writers Association], . . . but now in the period of the establishment of a revolutionary state and due to the complex nature of contradictory forces and actors involved with the revolution, any decision making . . . has become like a hard problem."[14]

Mohsen Yalfani, a member of the Writers Association executive board, gave a similar analysis during the extraordinary assembly held a few months before the cultural revolution:

> In the past, during Aryamehr [a designation for the shah], one could distinguish between "good" and "bad" at the first look. "Good" was what the oppressive monarchic system considered "bad," and "bad" was what that diabolic system considered as "good." Everything was simple and the fronts were recognizable one from the other. You were either from this side or the other side. On this side you had the people . . . and on the other side you had the system, . . . [but] today we have a situation in this country in which one finds, beyond its popular layers, diverse and multifaceted textures and domains.[15]

While this same view emerged among more intellectuals in subsequent months, the problem for those who were aware of the limitations of Al-e Ahmad's paradigm of intellectualism was that they had no other paradigm to replace it with. As a result of the cultural revolution, they, along with their leftist colleagues, were pushed out of the universities. Soon thereafter, their association and their newsletter were shut down with the help of the same people whom they had dreamed, à la Al-e Ahmad, of serving.

The War

The election of Mohammad Khatami as president of the Islamic Republic in May 1997 made it possible to have a public debate on some sensitive issues. One such issue was the attitude of various social or political groups during the war with Iraq. Prominent writer Mahmud Dawlatabadi, when asked in an interview about the reasons for the nonparticipation of intellectuals in the national effort to defend the country against the Iraqi attack, responded frankly:

> This is an unfair judgment. When the war started, I was then in charge of the theater union. We published an appeal in the *Ettela'at* newspaper, saying that we had prepared twelve plays and were ready to perform them at the war fronts. We said that we wanted nothing more than to be able to go to the fronts. . . . . No answer. Thus, it is not true that intellectuals did not partake in the efforts. They were pushed out. The dominant political current considers intellectuals as nonreligious. It builds a wall and says intellectuals are on the other side of the wall. Reality, however, is more complex. During the years before the revolution, our intellectuals became revolutionary in a way that did not fit in with the Islamic revolution. Many intellectuals were among the groups in which the system not only lacked any confidence but even considered as opponents. . . . Intellectuals were not trusted politically by the Islamic Republic and were put aside as opponents.[16]

Dawlatabadi is right in saying that the Islamic Republic put aside the intellectuals as opponents before the war started. He is also right in saying that, despite this, most intellectuals, together with the political groups with which they were affiliated, supported the state in its effort against the enemy. Finally, he is right in saying that in spite of this support, the intellectuals never gained the confidence of the regime and were marginalized during the whole duration of the war. In fact, by reviewing briefly the most important political confrontations between the victory of the revolution and the beginning of the war, one can appreciate how the different political groups were pushed out of the political scene. The taking of hostages at the American embassy in November 1979 pushed the most moderate revolutionary factions, namely the Iran Liberation Movement and the National Front, out of political power. The cultural revolution in June 1980 created a bloody gap between the leftist, secular political groups and the government. The civil war that started a few months after the victory of the revolution in Kurdistan pushed the powerful Iranian-Kurdish political parties (the Kurdistan Democratic Party and the Komeleh) into military opposition against the regime. By taking positions in favor of Kurdish political demands, some non-Kurdish and leftist political parties found themselves in opposition to the regime. A similar development occurred in the Turkman Sahra region to the east of the Caspian Sea. There, peasant demands for land reform turned into armed struggle between farmers and the nascent Revolutionary Guards. One also may add to this long list the underground rivalry between different revolutionary forces to take control of the army and the less traditional Revolutionary Guards.[17]

Nevertheless, when Iraqi forces invaded Iran in September 1980, only a few extreme leftist political groups declared that "the war [was] one between two reactionary regimes with the aim of serving imperialist countries and world capitalism to keep their domination over the people of Iran and Iraq" and appealed to the people of both countries to "transform the war to an internal" struggle.[18] The most important groups issued very clear statements in favor of mobilization against the enemy. At the top of the list was the Tudeh Party, which had a positive attitude toward the government.[19] But the more critical groups followed suit as well. Even the Mojahedin, which nine months later would enter into armed struggle against the regime and subsequently ally itself with Iraq, issued a statement in support of the government.[20]

The solidarity with the government went deeper than merely launching appeals to supporters and the general population to defend the country against the aggressor. For example, after the first ten days of fighting, when it became evident that Iraq's plan for a quick victory was not going to succeed, Iraqi president Saddam Hussein proposed peace talks. The Iranian government rejected the proposition on grounds that the last Iraqi soldier had to evacuate Iranian territory, and this decision received the backing of the leftist, secular political groups.[21] In fact, the war provided the Islamic Republic with the possibility of bridging the gaps created during the first year and a half since its establishment. However, the regime not only failed to use this opportunity but on the contrary tried to formulate a totalitarian approach to politics that lasted at least as long as the war with Iraq continued.

While the war still was ravaging western Iran and every single speech was an appeal for maintaining national unity against the enemy, the government issued a very odd communiqué that aimed to define the political attitude of the regime toward the various political groups. The communiqué stated:

> The political parties and groups are divided into four categories: the ones that back the Islamic revolution; the ones that agree with it; the ones that are against it; and the ones that fight against it. We have clarified our stand toward each category. . . . The state will benefit from the good ideas of the first group and even ask their help for executive tasks. The second category sometimes will be put to cooperation. The groups that are against us but do not fight us (that means they have not taken arms against us, or they have but we have not discovered it yet) have permission to be active, but there will not be any compromise, alliance, engagements, or cooperation between us. The Tudeh Party and the Cherikha-ye Fedayi-ye Khalgh Aksariyat are among these groups. We consider their ideas to be in opposition to the revolution and the Islamic Republic, and we think that their acts are based along these ideas. Their actions could not be in support of the Islamic revolution, and even if so, we consider them as limited, tactical, and dictated by political reason.[22]

This text merits attention for showing the thinking of the leaders of the Islamic Republic and also the degree to which the pushing out of political groups and their affiliated intellectuals was programmed and applied by the government. The situation with regard to the Tudeh Party and Fedayi organization, both of which had the same favorable political position toward the Islamic Republic, is revealing. They were regarded with high suspicion and never called on for cooperation. Thus, one can imagine the situation of the more critical leftist groups and their affiliated intellectuals. In fact, considering that the war from its very beginning was against the Islamic revolution, the intellectuals whom Islamic forces deemed as being secular were kept aside from any kind of participation in the war or any intervention related to it.

The reactions of intellectuals to this attitude were diverse. Some intellectuals just kept silent; others chose more social and cultural subjects as their field of interest; and a few decided to talk—when they could—about peace. Consequently, the war took place—and still remains—outside the intellectuals' sphere of interest. As a result of this phenomenon, the war suffered and continues to suffer from a lack of intellectual analysis or commentary. Even the literature of war or the cinema of war is still regarded mainly as a political field, dominated by Islamist forces who continue to use it for recalling or deepening the gap that exists between themselves and intellectuals. Even as late as 2000–2001, it was very common for groups of young people—who, considering their age, had never participated in the war—to be mobilized in the name of defending the values of the war and then to attack, both verbally and physically, gatherings of intellectuals, sometimes killing people. At the same time, intellectuals also benefited from popular discontent over the war. The discontent began to surface by 1986 due to a growing perception that the war had lasted too long and changed its nature from a patriotic struggle to a war of aggression, and ended with extensive human and material losses but without victory for either side. Because they were not involved with the war, intellectuals were considered exempt from any responsibility for its outcome.

Rivalry and Internal Dispute

The third challenge that Iranian intellectuals have had to face since 1979 came from within their own ranks. In fact, following the end of the war with Iraq and the death of Khomeini, some Islamist thinkers became increasingly critical of the cultural point of view and the social and political forces that dominated the Islamic Republic society, thus de facto joining their secular colleagues. Aware of the risk of being marginalized by the political power, as their secular colleagues had been, or perhaps just wishing to differentiate themselves religiously, these thinkers chose to enter their critical phase under the name of "religious intellectuals." The public appearance of these newcomers weakened in two ways the already fragile situation of the secular intellectuals. The religious intellectuals not only created one more fissure within the intelligentsia, which already suffered from chronic dispersion, but also, by insisting on their Islamism, they placed their secular colleagues in an even more delicate and unprotected position. Throughout their experience as societal critics, religious intellectuals encountered the same political difficulties (for example, censorship and hooligan attacks) as did their secular colleagues. Despite the situation, the secular intellectuals not only failed to show any enthusiasm for inviting religious intellectuals to join their ranks but also adopted a repellent attitude toward them. As justification for this attitude, secular intellectuals pointed to the role played by religious intellectuals at the beginning of the revolution as supporters and even ideologues of the Islamic regime. While this attitude, along with the discourse that accompanied it, could be analyzed on its own merits, the experience is more understandable in view of other major disputes that occurred in the Iranian intellectual body during the half-century existence of the Writers Association.

The intellectuals' attitude toward the issue of freedom of speech is instructive. For example, less than a year after the victory of the revolution, on 31 December 1979, a group of 137 writers, poets, and essayists gathered to decide on the dismissal of five members of the Writers Association, some of whom were among its eldest members.[23] The reason given for this unusual action was that "the association wants to be faithful to its program, which was signed by all members."[24] The reference here is to the "Mawzeʿ-e Kanun" (The association's position), which had been ratified in the general assembly of the association in April 1979 and later was integrated into the introduction to the association's statute. The five people being considered for dismissal had opposed the paragraph of the statute that emphasized "freedom of speech and thought for every person and group without any limitation and restriction"; and also the entire article that denounced "any censorship of freedom of thought or any form of diffusion of intellectual products." Their expulsion was approved, with 81 votes for expulsion, 42 votes against, and 4 abstentions.

The fact that the dismissed writers were members of or closely affiliated with the Tudeh Party—which at the time held that the prerogatives of the revolution were as important as those of free speech—was important. They had said that freedom without any limitation and restriction could be damaging to the revolution: "If we don't define 'revolutionary patience' in a proper way, we could betray the revolution."[25] In an historical irony, the very people who were reluctant to support "freedom without limitation and restriction" in 1979 were the same ones who ten years earlier had insisted on including this phrase in the statutes of the Writers Association.[26] At that time the sentence had been added to avoid a split in the association.

Despite the debate over the clause "freedom without limitation and restriction," the real issue was not free speech. In both 1969 and 1979, the most important reason why some intellectuals adopted an intransigent position was to prevent others from having anything to do with the government of the time. For example, during the 1960s, the orthodox communists of the Tudeh Party feared that the less politicized writers would cast them aside while dealing with the monarchic government to obtain legal recognition of the Writers Association. During 1979–80, the now more radical intellectuals feared that the Tudeh members would prevent the association from taking a radical position against the Islamic revolutionary government on the ground that it was an anti-imperialist regime. In another historical irony, the anti-imperialism of the regime did not prevent it from attacking other anti-imperialist forces—leftist political groups and their affiliated intellectuals—after 1981.[27]

In fact, during both periods, the social reality and the dominant ideology of intellectuals had little to do with unlimited and unrestricted freedom of speech for everyone in the society. In addition, during both periods, this unrealistic and irrelevant discourse was one factor that prevented the Writers Association and intellectuals from playing a more effective role in the society. These experiences and intellectual dilemmas are not necessarily limited to the Iranian case, as theorists of intellectual behavior have demonstrated. For example, the high degree of affinity between the majority of Iranian intellectuals and the political leftist parties, as well as their desire to be recognized as the voice of workers (as reflected in their discourse), could recommend Antonio Gramsci's model of "organic intellectuals" for analyzing intellectuals' attitudes during the postrevolutionary period of Iran.[28] But given the weakness of these leftist political parties and the not-yet-clear functions of intellectuals in society generally and in the labor movement in particular, a looser model may be more appropriate.

Julien Benda's moral vision of intellectuals describes them as "people whose work does not basically follow a functional aim" and holds that "the realm of intellectuals is not of this world."[29] This view, however does not prevent Benda from praising intellectuals who, from Jesus Christ to Nietzsche, took positions against the powerful authorities and beliefs of their own times. The unworldly realm of Benda's intellectuals concerns the truth, knowledge, and the light to which these intellectuals are answerable; it does not apply to society, their own actions, or political reality. Although Benda's intellectuals are pure and believe in unchangeable values, they are moral and should be conscious—and prepared—that at any time they could be "burned," "crucified," or "exiled." In one phrase, they are ideal intellectuals. As Régis Debray noted about Benda's description of intellectuals: "The idealization of intellectuals by intellectuals necessitates the reduction of political power to a purely pragmatic management of immediate and national interests. Hence he [the intellectual] keeps under his license the monopoly of values."[30]

It was the tendency to represent this monopoly that pushed the first

Writers Association, ten years before the revolution, to include the famous sentence about unlimited and unrestricted freedom in its statutes and thus prevented it from becoming officially established. It was the same belief in having a monopoly on values that pushed Iranian intellectuals to solve their internal disputes by expelling some members from the Writers Association. And finally, it was the same belief that determined and still determines the strategy adopted by "secular intellectuals" with respect to the rivalry generated by the rise of "religious intellectuals."

The rise and fall of religious intellectuals can be followed through the career of the best known among them: ʿAbdolkarim Sorush.[31] Although he was part of the establishment of the Islamic Republic at the beginning of the revolution, Sorush entered into his critical role at the end of the war with Iraq by publishing an article, "The Theoretical Contraction and Expansion of the Shariʿa."[32] His main idea was that while unchanging religious truths exist, our understanding of them remains contingent on our knowledge of other fields, particularly science and philosophy. The article elicited strong reaction from traditionalists, who accused Sorush of being a relativist; soon after, *Keyhan-e Farhangi,* where Sorush published his articles, was closed down. Thus, de facto, Sorush and other religious intellectuals with similar ideas joined the ranks of the secular intellectuals. Partly because of this political reaction and partly because of the needs of society, which was seeking a new political discourse, Sorush turned to more political writing. "Hokumat-e demokratik-e dini" (The democratic religious state) was the first of a series of articles in which Sorush debated the relation between democracy and religion, and later that of politics and religion.

In "Hokumat-e demokratik-e dini," Sorush discusses the possibility of an Islamic democracy by introducing the concept of collective reason.[33] Arguing that collective reason in an Islamic society would choose an Islamic government, he stresses the democratic shaping of such a government. While Sorush's position on democracy is clear, his general argument regarding the nature of collective reason and the foundation of democracy was subject to critique among intellectuals.[34] Although Sorush revised his approach a few times, in none of these revisions did he retreat from his democratic position. On the contrary, by restraining the realm of religion, he allows increasing autonomy for politics and democracy. He not only admits that "some of the sides of political debates are outside the realm of religion,"[35] but in talking about the legitimacy of the government—the exact word used by Sorush is "governmental responsibility"—he stresses that it is "driven by the nonreligious rights of religious people."[36] Further,

Sorush explains that "democracy means a form of government where the people's regulation of their rulers' performance is a human and nonreligious right."[37] Thus, after long and controversial debates regarding the creation of an "Islamic democracy," the whole project leads to secularism.

For anyone who followed these discussions and witnessed the difficulties religious intellectuals faced in society, it was clear that the end of the dream for creating an "Islamic democracy" only could be the strengthening of secularism and democratic ideas in society. And these debates prepared the grounds for reactivating the Writers Association with the participation of a large number of intellectuals who came to the association to defend freedom of thought, opinion, speech, writing, publishing, and all other individual and social freedoms. It was clear that the joining of religious intellectuals to the ranks of defenders of freedom could give strength to the position of intellectuals in society. However, the reaction among the majority of intellectuals not only was once again totally unrealistic but also lacked any tolerance. When the idea of rebuilding the Writers Association was launched in 1996, the more active members added to the statutes one more paragraph that directly targeted the religious intellectuals. This paragraph stated that "a writer could become a member of the association as long as he/she had never been involved in, justified, or helped directly or indirectly the censorship system."[38] Julien Benda's intellectualism was once again at work.

It is obvious that the attitude of some Islamist thinkers who later became religious intellectuals is less than defendable. One very significant example is Sorush himself. During the first months following the revolution, Sorush appeared as the ideologue of the Islamic regime. He was part of all the public debates that defended Islamic thought and the Islamic regime against any of its secular rivals, but especially against Marxists.[39] Thus, Sorush was in charge not only of helping to establish a regime that he now criticizes but also of assisting a regime that even at the time was showing clear antifreedom tendencies. Another accusation against Sorush concerned his membership in the High Council of the Cultural Revolution, the organization deeply involved with the aforementioned cultural revolution during and after which many students and teachers were purged or even killed. More generally, many figures who came to adopt an increasingly democratic discourse after the beginning of the 1990s had been part of the Ministry of Culture and Islamic Guidance (the ministry responsible for giving permission to publish materials), or even members of the Revolutionary Guards, which had many internal security and intelligence responsibilities.

It is also obvious that during the first part of their critical phase, religious intellectuals tried to protect themselves by insisting on their nonsecular approach, justifying de facto the attack their secular colleagues were experiencing. This attitude of religious intellectuals and their followers therefore is also a point of criticism. For more than six years, contend secular intellectuals, the religious intellectuals' fight for freedom of speech concerned only their own freedom and not that of anyone else. For them, the hooligans' attacks were wrong because they were attacking their religious brothers.[40] In defending their cases before the Special Court for the Press, the religious intellectuals argue that they have been and continue to be Islamic, before and after the revolution; they have no aim other than to reinforce religion, and what they publish is only in the service of religion.[41] Finally, when religious intellectuals faced harassment from conservative pressure groups, the latter was reminded that the only aim of religious intellectualism was the modernizing of Islamic discourse, not the taking of further steps.[42]

The essence of all these "defensive discourses" was to say that the attackers had been given wrong directions, not that they were wrong in general. By adopting this discourse they created a gap among intellectuals and legitimized the attack on "secular intellectuals."[43] The most radical faction among conservative forces took advantage of this gap in 1998 when its members decided to reclarify frontiers between "secular" and "religious" forces behind Khatami's election to the presidency. The serial killing of intellectuals (all of them secular) could be read as a warning to religious intellectuals and intellectualism to demonstrate the differences they had insisted on for more than six years.

This warning remained without a response or, more precisely, received unexpected reactions. The intellectuals, both religious and secular and backed by governmental political figures, reacted in unison against these savage acts. In fact, the killers did not realize that after the failure of the project for creating "Islamic democracy," the discourse of religious intellectuals had changed. In their new discourse, concepts like "civil society" and "democracy" replaced "religious society" and "religious democracy." This meant that they had adopted a much more tolerant discourse and had accepted that freedom of speech and thought applied to everyone.

Nevertheless, given the experiences of secular intellectuals since 1979—difficulty publishing their books, staging their scripts as plays, and generally making a living by selling their cultural productions—it perhaps is understandable that they could not simply forgive those whom they held accountable for having created such a situation. Yet, this attitude can be counterproductive when one recalls the genuine acceptance of the principle of democratic and tolerant discourse by religious intellectuals. And it needs to be noted that the behavior of many secular intellectuals during the first years following the revolution with respect to such issues as freedom of speech, university purges, and expulsions from associations exhibited the antidemocratic attitude of Sorush and the other "regime ideologues." The whole story of Iranian intellectuals facing an unfair rivalry shows the lack of any sociological and political analysis among them. This absence could be explained by the ideological way of thinking that dominates their approach and the frame of thought that could be recognized as Benda's paradigm of intellectualism.

Shattering of the Communist Dream?

The emergence of religious intellectuals and the gradual opening up of the political system coincided with a major international event with repercussions for Iran, namely, the dissolution of the Soviet Union. It perhaps was inevitable that the collapse of the Soviet empire would have a much wider political impact in third-world countries such as Iran than in Western countries. The reason is that, in third-world countries, intellectuals are politically affiliated more with the Left than with the Right. The fall of the Soviet empire and the release of internal information about the nature of Soviet society seems to have broken the dreams of some leftist intellectuals about the concept of the "dictatorship of the proletariat" and the ideal government they had envisioned for Iran. It seems that the Iranian intellectual experience of the collapse of the Soviet dream had two other characteristics that differentiated it from other third-world-country experiences. First, the daily living experience of intellectuals in the Islamic Republic, especially during the war when the Islamist leftists had an upper hand, resembled that of Soviet society. Second, there was a wide range of leftist parties in Iran, but only a minority among them were pro-Soviet. In addition, the forced migration of many intellectuals and the scant possibility of debating such issues in Iran need to be considered to obtain a full picture of the real impact of the collapse of the Soviet empire on Iranian intellectuals.

The most common and pronounced tendency observable among Iranian intellectuals has been the appearance of democratic ideas and concepts in their discourse. From the more militant to the less politically involved, there is active discussion and reevaluation of concepts such as freedom, civil society, democracy, and liberalism. It seems, however, that the leftist and anticolonialist tendency that dominated Iranian intellectualism during the 1970s has remained valid. Thus, the integration of democratic concepts into Iranian intellectual debates has resulted in a visible social-democratic tendency among intellectuals. While "democratization" is the dominant current, some of the "old leftist" discourse also has survived. This is because the collapse of the Soviet Union did not necessarily mean the shattering of the communist dream for all Iranian intellectuals but rather the collapse of one Marxist solution; other such solutions continue to spark interest as alternatives to capitalism.[44]

Integrating democratic concepts into the discourse of Iranian intellectuals cannot be considered only in relation to the political program they are defending or the political system they wish to see in Iran. This democratization also has to be measured by the way they analyze their past attitude, especially with respect to the first months and years after the victory of the revolution. In this regard two tendencies are observable, one that tries to be critical and one that seems to forget that period and places all responsibility for Iran's political confinement on the Islamist movement.

An example of this emerging critical perspective is "In the Purgatory of Fear and Hope," a 1990 article written by the same Mohsen Yalfani who in 1979 as a member of the executive board of the Writers Association had asked for the dismissal of the five Tudeh members.[45] In this article, Yalfani argues that the deep roots of the collapse of the Soviet empire lay in the inability of the socialist regimes to create a new set of "ethical values." He debates the shortcomings of the leftist movement in Iran during the initial years of the Islamic Republic, contending that the Iranian leftist movement was virtually dead before entering this new era. This was because the old Left was "practically and mentally dependent on the Soviet Union, from which it could not liberate itself due to a lack of self-confidence. This dependency lethally affected society."[46] The new and independent leftist movement, in contrast, "was a defeated and terminated" political force at the dawn of the revolution because, as a guerrilla movement, it experienced massive arrests during the 1970s. For Yalfani, the new Left experienced a rapid rise in popularity due to the revalorization of armed struggle during the revolution. In other words, the independent leftist movement benefited from a situation that it had had no role in creating. In this way the leftist movement became the second force behind radical Islamic forces that used the leftists for establishing their own domination. Yalfani concludes his historical revision:

> If the Islamic regime is to be considered responsible for the physical elimination of the leftist movement, the elimination of their credibility and dignity was the result of their own politics and acts. Honesty and human consciousness, in addition to common sense, would dictate to the leaders of this movement to become conscious about their faults by seeing their defeat . . . , to request pardon from the people to whom they had done irreversible damage, to close their shops, and look for other jobs.[47]

Yalfani, who, like the majority of his intellectual colleagues has remained a leftist, ends his article with a note about what could be the future of Iranian intellectualism:

> We could consider the downfall of the [Marxist-Leninist] castle as the beginning of a new era, an era in which we will be more nude and more without shelter; but we will be more free and more conscious before the totalitarianism of money, which is in fact the most well-equipped and competent totalitarian regime in the world. The future will show how humanity will take a stand in this battle.[48]

Not all Iranian intellectuals are as critical of their past as is Yalfani, nor are they as committed to the future. As previously stated, numerous texts published outside Iran by intellectuals who sought refuge in Western countries defend democratic values and the Iranian civil society's political struggle and denounce what they call the Islamic Republic's authoritarianism. Very few of these intellectuals, however, are critical of their own past attitude.

The situation inside Iran is different. While civil society has gained much space since 1997 and expressing criticism of social and political conditions has become much more possible, nevertheless, complete freedom of speech still has not been achieved. Thus, it perhaps is not unusual that, in assessing the first years of the revolution, more intellectuals engage in self-criticism than in criticizing the actions of the government. Nevertheless, the nature of these self-critiques is interesting. For example, in a roundtable discussion about the attempt to reactivate the Writers Association, when the question of the past was raised, it became evident that Iranian intellectuals had not spent their time during the last decade thinking about their past attitude as heroic. The most common comments and critiques were directed toward the "exaggerated political orientation of the Writers Association" during the first months after the revolution.[49]

Nevertheless, some other serious issues also were mentioned. Mohammad Mokhtari, for example, proposed that the discussion starts with the "past faults." He insisted that not only "they," meaning those who had stayed at the association after the famous "purge," but also "the ones who had left the association or those who had been made to leave . . . should be invited to the discussions."[50] Baqer Parham, a member of the board of the last association, insisted that "the article concerning the rights of ethnic groups (meaning Kurds, Turks, and so on) should be revised."[51] When some participants proposed a clause forbidding membership to those who had been involved with censorship, others protested by saying that there was no "clear definition of what could be called censorship."[52] When the question of "freedom without limitation and restriction" was raised, no one insisted on retaining it. Although this roundtable was followed by a few more, ending in a series of conditions for membership, overall the experience had shown that things had changed for intellectuals, although perhaps not enough to enable them to cross every bridge. Perhaps Iranian intellectuals are not yet as ready to be without shelter as Yalfani had predicted or as free as he perceived them to be.

Conclusion

It is difficult to draw any final judgments about the long and difficult road Iranian intellectuals have crossed since 1979 because the process of change in ideas and attitudes is still evolving. One can see genuine tendencies toward democratic concepts, but at the same time it seems that tolerance is not necessarily close at hand. While it may be difficult to come to any conclusions as to the new dominant values accepted by Iranian intellectuals, their ascending social and political role is evident. There is no single newspaper published since Khatami's election (and there have been many) that does not include at least one interview with intellectuals on a systematic basis. The more conservative newspapers focus on the more specialized intellectuals, while reformist papers choose their interviewees from among the more political. There is no social category that can compete with the presence and hegemony that intellectuals have achieved in society. Even the clergy—including President Khatami himself—owe part of their popularity to the intellectualism of their discourse. The same interest is evident in the large number of books and articles published about Iranian intellectualism. Such publications receive more than the average attention Iranians give to other social science issues. This phenomenon certainly needs much more attention; hopefully, it will receive the analysis it merits.

One explanation for this phenomenon could be that after a century of existence, Iranian intellectuals finally have become "public intellectuals," as defined by Russell Jacoby.[53] He claims that the enrollment of American intellectuals into the academic world, where culture is produced, diminished intellectual life by transforming intellectuals into academic specialists. While respecting all the differences between the two experiences, it seems possible to use the Jacoby concept to understand the increase in intellectual life in Iran during these last years. By chasing intellectuals out of universities, by preventing them from participating in important events and the debates they generated, and, finally, by avoiding them for more than a decade, the Islamic Republic pushed Iranian intellectuals into becoming public intellectuals. Thus the more the public turned against the state, the more the public looked toward intellectuals, who, in the absence of political organizations, seemed to be the only group capable of having a sociopolitical discourse. Every loss of legitimacy for the state benefited the only social group that, despite all difficulties, seems to have crossed the desert. What is unknown at this stage is whether intellectuals will be able to handle this new challenge.

By looking at both their capacity for self-criticism and their weaknesses in appreciating that they now have new allies in society, namely, the "religious intellectuals," it seems that the success of intellectuals in handling the challenge successfully will be related directly to their ability to provide an account of their experiences during the 1980s and 1990s. This account, however, should not be explained as the "right of everyone to make mistakes." Nor should it fall into a "historical denial of responsibilities." Rather, it has to be done in the way Paul Ricoeur calls "curing the memories with history." This effort will be possible if—and only if—we are able, as Ricoeur said, to "transform personal experience into public knowledge, meaning into history."[54]

Notes

An earlier version of this essay has been published in *Critique: Journal for Critical Studies of the Middle East*, no. 18 (spring 2001).

1. For a fair but critical account of this attitude, see Omid Farhang, "Az cheshm-e gharb" (From the Western viewpoint), *Goft-o-gu*, no. 6 (winter 1995), pp. 43–54; this article discusses the cases of Ehsan Naraqi and Daryush Shayegan and the fundamentals of critical thought.

2. For a more detailed discussion of this point, see my interview with Gholamreza Kadji, "Setarvan budan: daghdagheh-ye rawshanfekran-e Iran qabl az

enqelab" (Being infertile: The problematic of Iranian intellectuals before the revolution), parts 1–3, *Entekhab* (9–11 July 2000).

3. See Jalal Al-e Ahmad, *Gharbzadegi* (Tehran: Ravaq, 1978).

4. Much has been written about Al-e Ahmad since the 1979 revolution, both lauding and criticizing him and his notion of *gharbzadegi;* few studies, however, provide an objective overview of his work. One of the more successful analyses is Farzin Vahdat, "Return to Which Self? Jalal Al-e Ahmad and the Discourse of Modernity," *Journal of Iranian Research and Analysis* 16, no. 2 (November 2000), pp. 55–71.

5. See, for example, Mo'tazed al-Molk, *Hadiqat al-Adab* (The garden of norms) (Tehran, 1905); Jaberi Ansari, *Resaleh-ye Nuchdaru* (Essay on counterpoison) (Tehran, 1902); and Moshir al-Atebba, *Resaleh-ye Madaniyyeh* (Essay on civility) (n.d., but likely to have been published in the same period).

6. A good collection of these essays is Gholam Hoseyn Zargarinejad, ed., *Resaleh-ye Mashrutiyat: hejdah resaleh va layehheh darbareh-ye mashrutiyat* (Essays on constitutionalism: Eighteen essays about constitutionalism) (Tehran: Kavir, 1995).

7. Jalal Al-e Ahmad, *Dar khedmat va khiyanat-e rawshanfekran* (On the service and betrayal of intellectuals), 2d ed. (Tehran: Ravaq, 1981), pp. 407–9; Al-e Ahmad wrote this book between February 1964 and September 1968.

8. Ibid.

9. Ibid., p. 255.

10. On the role of the lumpen, see 'Ali Akbar Akbari, "Lompanha: pishahang-e sarkub va koshtar" (The lumpen: Vanguard of repression and massacre), in *Andisheh-ye Azad* (Free thought), special issue on the universities, no. 16 (June 1980), pp. 46–8; more typical of articles in this issue is that of M. Farda, "Moqavemat, mohafezat" (Resistance, conservation), whose quoted phrase is on p. 14.

11. Akbar Sarduzani, "Khiyaban-e moqavemat" (The street of resistance), in *Andisheh-ye Azad*, special issue, p. 16.

12. 'Alireza Afsharniya, "Amuzesh-e bourgeoisie: daneshgah-e vabasteh va amuzesh-e novin dar jame'eh-ye nawkhasteh" (Bourgeoisie learning: The dependent university and new learning in a new society), in *Andisheh-ye Azad*, special issue, p. 30.

13. Bozorg Purja'far, "Bara-ye tashkil-e jebheh-ye moqavemat bar zedd-e erteja' va imperialism, farda kheyli dir ast" (Tomorrow is too late to set up a resistance front against reaction and imperialism), in *Andisheh-ye Azad*, special issue, p. 35.

14. Esma'il Kho'i, "Gozareshi vizheh beh yek dust" (A special report to a friend), *Ketab-e Jom'eh* (Friday book) 1, no. 26 (7 February 1980), p. 15.

15. Mohsen Yalfani, "Gozaresh-e majma'-e fawq al-'addeh-ye Kanun-e Nevisandegan-e Iran" (Report of the Extraordinary Assembly of the Iranian Writers

Association), *Khabarnameh-ye Kanun-e Nevisandegan-e Iran* (Newsletter of the Iranian Writers Association), no. 4 (January 1980), pp. 4–5.

16. Mahmud Javanbakht, "Discussion with Mahmud Dawlatabadi" (in Persian), *Salam,* 3, 17, and 22 February 1998.

17. For more detailed accounts of these political developments, see Morad Saghafi, "Enqelab, jang va jabeja'i-ye nokhbegan dar jame'eh" (Revolution, war, and the elite turnover in society), *Goft-o-gu,* no. 23 (spring 1999), pp. 35–55.

18. "Ettela'iyeh-ye Sazman-e Peykar dar Rah-e Azadi-ye Tabagheh-ye Kargar, darbareh-e jang (The communiqué of the Organization of Struggle for the Liberation of the Working Class regarding the war), *Peykar* (22 September 1980).

19. See further *Nameh-ye Mardom* (21 September 1980).

20. See, for example, *Mojahed* (25 September 1980).

21. See, for example, *Nameh-ye Mardom* (6 October 1980); and *Kar* (30 September 1980).

22. Behzad Nabavi, spokesman for the government, *Jomhuri-ye Eslami* (21 December 1980).

23. The five members were Mahmud E'temadzadeh (who used the pen name of Beh Azin), Siyavosh Kasra'i, Hushang Ebtehaj (pen name, Sayeh), Fereydun Tonokaboni, and Mohammad Taqi Borumand (B. Keyvan).

24. Yalfani, "Gozaresh-e majma'-e fawq al-'addeh-ye Kanun-e Nevisandegan-e Iran," p. 4.

25. Beh Azin, "Azadi va enqelab" (Freedom and revolution), *Shawra-ye Nevisandegan va Honarmandan* (The writers and artists' council), no. 3 (spring 1981), p. 26.

26. Mohammad 'Ali Sepanlu, "Khaterati az fasl-e avval-e Kanun-e Nevisandegan-e Iran, 1346–1349" (Reminiscences of the first session of the Iranian Writers Association, 1967–70), *Kelk,* no. 4 (June 1980), pp. 101–111.

27. For more details on these disputes and their political roots during the 1960s and 1980s, see Morad Saghafi, "Nim qarn talash: Moruri bar 'amalkard-e kanunha-ye nevisandegan-e Iran" (Half-century of effort: Survey of functionality of Iran's writers' associations), *Goft-o-gu,* no. 7 (spring 1995), pp. 8–33.

28. For Gramsci's definition of "organic intellectuals," see Antonio Gramsci, *Selections from the Prison Notebooks* (New York: International Publishers, 1985), p. 15.

29. Julien Benda, *La trahison des clercs,* 5th ed. (Paris: Grasset, 1975).

30. Régis Debray, *Le scribe* (Paris: Editions Grasset et Fasquelle, 1980), p. 81.

31. For a good summary of Sorush's intellectual production, see Afshin Matin-Asgari, "Abdolkarim Sorush and the Secularization of Islamic Thought in Iran," *Iranian Studies* 30, nos. 1–2 (winter/spring 1997), pp. 95–115; for a summary of Sorush's political ideas, see Valla Vakili, *Debating Religion and Politics in Iran: The Political Thought of Abdolkarim Sorush* (New York: Council on Foreign Relations, 1996).

32. 'Abdolkarim Sorush, "Qabz va bast-e te'orik-e Shari'at" (The theoretical contraction and expansion of the Shari'a), *Keyhan-e Farhangi* 7, no. 73 (1990), pp. 12–9.

33. 'Abdolkarim Sorush, "Hokumat-e demokratik-e dini," *Kiyan*, no. 11 (March–April 1993), pp. 12–5.

34. For a critique of Sorush's use of "collective reason," see Morad Saghafi, "Mardom va farhang-e mardom dar andisheh-ye siyasi-ye Shari'ati va Sorush" (The masses and mass culture in the political thought of Shari'ati and Sorush), *Goft-o-gu*, no. 2 (winter 1993), pp. 25–39; for a critique of his use of the concept of the "foundation of democracy," see Bijan Hekmat, "Mardom-salari va din-salari: piramun-e mobaheseh darbareh-ye hokumat-e demokratik-e dini" (Democracy and religiocracy: On discussions over the democratic religious state), *Kiyan*, no. 21 (1994).

35. 'Abdolkarim Sorush, "Din va azadi" (Religion and freedom), *Kiyan*, no. 33 (1996).

36. Sorush, "Tahlil-e mafhum-e hokumat-e dini" (Analyzing the meaning of the religious state), *Kiyan*, no. 32 (1996), pp. 2–13.

37. Ibid.

38. The draft text for this new condition of membership was first published in *Takapu*, no. 13 (November–December 1994).

39. Sorush's early writings, published and distributed during the first months following the revolution, include *Tazadd-e dialektiki* (Dialectical contradiction) (Tehran: Hekmat, 1979); *'Elm chist, falsafeh chist?* (What is science, what is philosophy?) (Tehran: Serat, 1979); and *Ide'olozhi-ye sheytani* (Satanic ideology) (Tehran: Yaran, 1980).

40. Editor's note, "Be ja-ye sokut" (Instead of silence), *Kiyan*, no. 12 (1993), p. 2.

41. Reza Tehrani, "Mashruh-e dadgah-e Kiyan" (The complete text of Kiyan's defense in court), *Kiyan*, no. 33 (November–December 1996), pp. 62–6.

42. Editor's note, "Najva-ye pa'izi" (Autumn's lament), *Kiyan*, no. 26 (August–September 1995), p. 2.

43. For a critique of this discourse, see Morad Saghafi, "Bi panahi-ye rawshanfekran" (No hiding place for intellectuals), *Kiyan*, no. 11 (March–April 1993), pp. 21–5.

44. A study prepared by the intellectual journal *Cheshmandaz* (Perspective), published in Paris, raised the question of the Left's future in Iran after the collapse of the Soviet Union and the "defeat" of the Islamic revolution. Among twelve leftist intellectuals, only three exhibited social-democratic tendencies; the nine others insisted on the possibility of creating a radical alternative to capitalism. See "Nazar-azma'i-ye ayandeh-ye niruha-ye chap va taraqqikhah dar Iran va jahan" (Poll regarding the future of the leftist and progressive movement in Iran and the world), *Cheshmandaz*, no. 10 (spring 1992), pp. 2–51.

45. Mohsen Yalfani, "Dar barzakh-e bim va omid" (In the purgatory of fear and hope), *Cheshmandaz,* no. 7 (spring 1990), pp. 84–93.

46. Ibid., p. 90.

47. Ibid., p. 92.

48. Ibid., p. 93.

49. "Zarurat-e tarh va shenakht-e nazarha dar nakhostin-e miz-e gerd-e Kanun-e Nevisandegan" (The necessity of knowing the points of view in the first roundtable of the Writers Association), *Takapu,* no. 6 (December 1993).

50. Ibid., p. 29.

51. Ibid., p. 31.

52. Ibid., p. 28.

53. Russell Jacoby, *The Last Intellectuals: American Culture in the Age of Academe* (New York: Basic Books, 1987).

54. Paul Ricoeur, "Tarikh, khatereh, faramushi" (History, memory, forgetfulness), *Goft-o-gu,* no. 8 (summer 1995), pp. 47–59.

6

Religious Intellectuals and Political Action in the Reform Movement

Hamidreza Jalaeipour

Introduction

On the face of it and within the context of contemporary Iranian politics, the category of the "religious intellectual" seems ambiguous and even paradoxical. On the one hand, there is still no consensus among the Iranian educated strata as to who falls into this category. There is even no agreement about whether religious intellectuals constitute a cultural or a political force. On the other hand, despite this ambivalence, the leading and influential role of religious intellectuals in what has come to be known as the Dovvom-e Khordad reform movement is acknowledged by most observers and analysts. This essay will offer examples of religious intellectuals in different arenas and discuss their role in and their relationship to the reform movement. The category of religious intellectuals is not an undifferentiated category, and the analysis of the differences that exist within the category is important for understanding the more prominent role some sections of religious intellectuals have come to play in the reform movement.

Religious Intellectuals and the Reform Movement

The first question to ask is how religious intellectuals manifest themselves in the reform movement. It will be easier to answer this question if a distinction is made between the general understanding of the term and its more specific sense. In the general sense, all Muslim individuals (cleric or noncleric) who are interested in and reflective about the ideas of thinkers such as Mehdi Bazargan, Ayatollah Mahmud Taleqani, ʻAli Shariʻati, and Ayatollah Morteza Motahhari can be considered religious intellectuals. Since these leading Muslim personalities offered a critical reading of religious, social, and political institutions and were intent on solving cultural, political, social, and economic problems through the realization of an Islamic revolution, the Islamic revolutionary discourse of 1979 is in important ways indebted to their intellectual activities (which in that era offered an ideological interpretation of modernity). Furthermore, after the Islamic revolution, despite increasing differentiation and disagreements in perspective, the category of the "religious intellectual," in the general sense of the term, has continued to be of relevance until the present day. All intellectuals who are defenders of the authenticity of Ayatollah Motahhari's intellectual works, as well as those who are insistent on the lasting and momentous role of ʻAli Shariʻati or who are interested in the works of ʻAbdolkarim Sorush, can be included in this broad category. However, the category of the religious intellectual, broadly understood, is not the subject of this essay. It should be realized that not all religious intellectuals are supporters and promoters of the Dovvom-e Khordad movement. Some have been passive and indifferent toward the movement, while others have even opposed it. In fact, many of the conservatives opposing the reform movement do not have any problems with the category of the religious intellectual in the general sense and indeed consider themselves to be religious intellectuals par excellence. As such, it is necessary to pay attention to the more specific meaning of the category and its manifestation among the most persistent promoters of the reform movement in Iran.

If we decide to identify the two types of intellectuals mentioned above on the basis of important events, we can consider the religious intellectuals of 1979 to be the *leading* intellectuals, as opposed to those who have engaged in intellectual activities alongside the reform movement and who can be regarded as the *late* ones (emphasizing a nonideological interpretation of modernity). Rather than rallying around prominent personalities, these "late" religious intellectuals are centered around three intellectual focal groups or circles. The first circle is made up of individuals who tend to identify with the radical "Students Following the Line of the Imam" *(Daneshjuyan-e khatt-e Emam)* and with the intellectual-political works published in the journal *Kiyan*. The second circle engages in intellectual-political activities as a national-religious force, and its works are represented in the journal *Iran-e Farda*. And the third focal group includes the intellectual activities of clerics and writers of the monthly *Naqd va Nazar* published in Qom. Although there is, of course, diversity and lack of consensus within each circle, there are also certain characteristics that differentiate these circles from each other (see table 6.1).

All these circles not only have religious concerns but also attempt to critique the performance of cultural, religious, political, and economic institutions from the point of view of modernity (and modern society). Instead of calling for a revolution, they all aim at reform and the improvement of the current conditions.[1] It can be said that the reformist discourse that picked up momentum after the election of Mohammad Khatami in 1997 is the result of intellectual interaction among these focal circles (as well as with other intellectuals).[2] At the same time, despite the presence of a variety of intellectual voices, it can be said that the members of the first circle have played the more prominent role in the reform movement and have, therefore, been put under greater pressure.

The more influential role of the first circle can be shown in reference to three episodes. First, in the stunning elections of 23 May 1997 (when 20 out of 30 million ballots were cast in favor of Khatami), these intellectuals had a decisive role in convincing the electorate to vote for Khatami and in organizing his media campaign. The second focal group, on the other hand, was rather passive in the presidential elections and encouraged its supporters to cast a "white ballot." Meanwhile, the third group, not believing in political activity, did not explicitly support Khatami in the elections.

The second instance was the emergence of the reformist press following the elections, which resulted in their carrying much of the burden of the Dovvom-e Khordad movement. The activities of most of the influential newspapers (which reached a circulation of more than a million), such as *Salam, Jame'eh, Tus, Khordad, Sobh-e Emruz, Neshat, Mosharekat, 'Asr-e Azadegan,* and *Bahar,* depended on the role and presence of these first-circle intellectuals. During this time, due to various factors, including limitations imposed on them by the conservatives, the level of activities of the second circle never went beyond the readers of *Iran-e Farda* (with a circulation of less than 50,000). Similarly, the newspaper *Entekhab,* which was closer to the third circle, was likewise never able to sell more than 50,000 copies a day, in spite of the fact that it received financial support from the government and as a result enjoyed absolute security.

The third case in point involved the elections for the Sixth Parliament, in which intellectuals of the first circle played an important role. In these elections, which led to the loss of the absolute majority on the part of the conservatives in favor of reformist candidates, the list of candidates for Tehran's slots that was supported by the reformist press was widely approved by the voters. This was despite the fact that the Council of Guardians had already disqualified many of the well-known candidates close to the religious intellectual circles. In short, all three episodes suggest the more influential role of the first circle of religious intellectuals. And perhaps it is because of this influential role that the conservatives have imposed the most extreme pressure on this group, closing down their papers, arresting many of their most effective communicators, and preparing "judicial files" for most of their members.[3]

Cultural or Political Force?

After establishing the political importance of the first circle of religious intellectuals, another key question arises. Does this prominent political role undermine the importance of religious intellectuals as a cultural force and turn them into a political force or party? If we refer to the writings of these religious intellectuals, we notice that not only do they not perceive themselves as a political force but, in fact, they emphasize the cultural aspect of their role. In a society of religious people, they understand themselves to be carriers of the project of modernity. Rather than pursuing political and governmental positions, their aim is to strengthen and institutionalize the public sphere. This is the sphere in which institutions, such as the press and independent associations, have come under extreme pressure from the conservatives, under the guise of religion, revolution, and martyrdom. From the perspective of religious intellectuals, however, the defense of religion is not possible in a society devoid of a public sphere for critique and analysis. They consider the implementation of religious values and codes through governmental power and force as detrimental to the influence and spread of religious and pious action. Instead, they promote civil institutions as more effective vehicles for the support of religious values.

Despite this stated preference for cultural activities, the following conditions have, nonetheless, led to political action on the part of the religious intellectuals. In the first place, the institutions necessary for the livelihood of the public sphere are weak, and without minimum guarantees and security in this arena, intellectual activity essentially cannot thrive, interact, correct, and reform itself. Secondly, the policies of the conservatives in the past years have deprived the polity of a multiparty and competitive system to the point that before the elections on 23 May, even the progressive political groups and tendencies were unable to defend the public sphere and the need for intellectual activity in any meaningful way. Accordingly, pressure groups benefiting from the silence of the conservatives could attack various elements constituting the public sphere, such as meetings at the offices of publications and intellectuals, in broad daylight and with impunity. Finally, those perpetrating political violence and engaging in the killing of secular intellectuals and the threatening of many religious intellectuals as a means to create a chill in the public sphere have also played a role. The combination of these factors has forced religious intellectuals into political action in order to protect and strengthen both the public sphere and intellectual life. In other words, it is in the face of massive conservative pressure that religious intellectuals have been forced to defend political groups, the press, and reformist politicians and candidates. In short, even though their activities may not have appeared cultural on the surface, when they were pursued at all it was to protect self-expression and society, and as such they had important cultural implications as well.

Continued Importance of Religious Intellectuals

Having explained the reasons why religious intellectuals became politically active, another question that arises concerns the reasons for their continued importance on the Iranian political scene. In other words, why do religious intellectuals continue to be of significance, despite the serious opposition that is exhibited by the conservatives? As is well known, following their defeat on 23 May, the conservatives, rather than attempt to reconstitute themselves as a powerful political force within the context of a law-abiding, progressive, forward-looking, conservative political party, have tried to thwart the political power of Khatami's government through methods based on "rights of monopoly."[4] The pressures increased further after their defeat in the Sixth Parliamentary elections to the point that some extremist sections of the conservatives accused religious intellectuals of "silently engaging in the overthrow of the system" or being "new hypocrites"! During that same period, more than twenty newspapers were closed en masse, writers were sent to prison, and Saʿid Hajjarian, one of the most prominent religious intellectuals, was shot (he is still in a wheelchair and has not returned to his daily activities). Despite these pressures, three factors can partially explain the continued success of religious intellectuals in the Dovvom-e Khordad movement.

The first factor is social. Iran, with a population of 60 million, is now more than 70 percent urban. Most of this population is young and educated, with more than 5 million holding at least a college degree. Such a society can no longer be molded by conservatives into any shape or discourse. In fact, for such a society, particularly its educated strata, the reformist discourse and the objectives of religious intellectuals are much more appealing. Second, in their critiques and analyses, intellectuals in the first circle are not seeking macroprescriptions for the creation of an imagined utopia on earth. Even more than engaging in the critique and analysis of the prevalent discourses, they are interested in the analysis of discourses that were prevalent during their youth. Unlike the conservatives, they are not intent on propagating a teacher-disciple model of relationship. They do not even hesitate to critique their own preeminent teachers and scholars. Such a discourse is naturally appealing to the educated and influential strata that are witness to societal problems (many of which are related to the utopianism of the official propaganda).

The third factor goes back to the background of the first circle of religious intellectuals. The average age for this group is around forty, which is about ten years younger than the second circle. During the Islamic revolution the religious intellectuals of the first circle were mostly dedicated youth and students who made many sacrifices both for the establishment of the Islamic Republic and later during the Iran-Iraq war. As such, the conservatives cannot easily use the weapon and the label *"gheyr-e khodi"* (outsider) to eliminate the first-circle religious intellectuals as they have done rather effectively against secular intellectuals and religious intellectuals of the second circle.[5]

Because of the above factors, religious intellectuals, despite intense conservative opposition, have been able to defend the reformist discourse of the Dovvom-e Khordad movement, making its objectives appealing to an overwhelming majority of Iranians. This is why they received the vote of confidence of the electorate in both the city council and the parliamentary elections.[6] The victory of the majority of the reformist candidates clearly showed that the Dovvom-e Khordad movement has been successful in deepening its discourse and objectives.[7]

Table 6.1. Characteristics of the three religious intellectual circles

Circles and subcircles	Names of publication	Personalities and writers	Approaches to the political system	Political orientation	Influence in universities	Influence in seminaries	Financial source
The first circle							
Subcircle around *Kiyan* and *Dovvom-e Khordaad* publications	*Kiyan, Sobh-e-Emruz, Jame'eh, Tus, Nesbat, 'Asr-e Azadegan, Bahar*	Sorush, Mojtahed Shabestari, Malekian, Shamsolva'ezin, Tehrani, Alavitabar, Naraghi, Soltani, Mohammadi, Mardiha, Jalaeipour, Ganji, Akbari, Ghazian, Kashi, Reza'i, Mozaffar, Noruzi, Baqi	Reformist	Social Democrat, Liberal	High	Low	Nongovernmental
Subcircle around *Salam* and *'Asr-e Ma*	*Salam, 'Asr-e Ma, Mosharekat*	Armin, Aghajari, Hajjarian, 'Abdi, Mazru'i, Arghandeh-pur, Mirdamadi	Reformist	Social Democrat	High	Medium	Nongovernmental

Group	Publication	People					
Association of Qom, Hawzeh-ye 'Elmiyyeh Teachers		Meybodi, Aba'i, Ayazi, Musavi Tabrizi	Reformist	Not clear	Medium	Medium	Nongovernmental
Writers in Khordad	*Khordad*	Nuri, Kadivar, Hekmat, Farastkhah	Reformist	Social Democrat, Liberal	High	Medium	Nongovernmental
The second circle							
Subcircle around *Iran-e Farda*	*Iran-e Farda* (biweekly)	'Ezzat ollah Sahabi, Eshkevari, 'Alijani, Rahmani, Zeidabadi, Saber, Raja'i	Reformist	Social Democrat	Medium	Low	Nongovernmental
Peyman subcircle	Bulletins	Habibollah Peyman	Reformist	Social Democrat	Low	Low	Nongovernmental
Freedom Movement subcircle	Bulletins	Yazdi, 'Abdol 'ali Bazargan	Reformist	Liberal	Medium	Low	Nongovernmental
The third circle							
Circle around *Naqd va Nazar*	*Naqd va Nazar*	Qanbari, Faqihi	Reformist	Not clear	Low	Medium	Governmental
Circle around *Entekhab*	*Entekhab*	Taha Hashemi	Reformist	Not clear	Very low	Medium	Governmental

The objectives that have now taken root in the society can be summarized in the following manner:

- On a general level, there is a belief in objective secularism—that is, the separation of religion and state—and a corresponding lack of belief in subjective secularism, in the sense that people no longer believe that secularism can be extended to the domains of culture and meaning.
- In the governmental sphere, all institutions must become responsible and accountable on the basis of the Constitution;
- At the level of polity, a transparent multiparty and competitive system must be instituted as soon as possible;
- In the economic sphere, special monopolies should be dismantled, large economic institutions should become responsive, and investments should develop institutionalized security;
- In the political and cultural spheres, the patriarchal model of behavior should be transformed into a democratic one;
- In the scholarly domain, conditions should be created in which research can be pursued freely and with security, and offered to the public (hence strengthening the public sphere);
- In the religious sphere, the buttressing of religious behavior should not be based on force;
- In the individual sphere, more guarantees for the pursuit of individual rights and prevention of interference in the private lives of people should be instituted.[8]

Let me end by suggesting that, despite the achievements of the religious intellectuals on the level of discourse, there is very little that can be considered settled. It seems that religious intellectuals will continue to operate under abnormal conditions until Iran experiences the multifaceted and institutionalized strengthening of the public sphere, the establishment of a multiparty system in a transparent arena of politics, and the emergence of a legal and forward-looking conservative party that does not remain silent in the face of pressure group violence. In short, they will continue to operate under these abnormal conditions until it becomes possible to rethink the current dual nature of the Iranian Constitution (which recognizes the sovereignty of both the clerics and the people) in a peaceful and tolerant manner. These conditions will continue to necessitate political action from this essentially cultural force as a means to protect the public sphere.[9] As such, it is not the activities of religious intellectuals that must be seen as paradoxical but rather the conditions and characteristics of the Iranian polity itself.

Notes

1. It is important to point out that in the writings of these three focal groups there is also a difference in the choice of term that is used to convey the idea of the "religious intellectual." The first circle uses the term *rawshanfekr-e dini* (religious intellectual) repeatedly and explicitly. The second group seems to prefer the term *naw-garayan-e dini* (religious modernists), since it appears more often than *rawshanfekr-e dini* (religious intellectual). Finally, in the writings of the third group, prominence is given to *naw-andishi-ye dini* or "new religious thinking."

2. Note that the reformist discourse is not only the product of interaction among these three focal groups of religious intellectuals. It is also the result of engagement with the works of other intellectuals. Thinkers and intellectuals such as 'Ezzatollah Fuladvand, Hoseyn Bashiriyeh, Baqer Parham, Daryush Ashuri, Homa(yun) Katouzian, Daryush Shayegan, Javad Tabataba'i, Ramin Jahanbeglu, and Morad Saghafi have played an important role in shaping the discourse of reform.

3. A close look at the number and composition of prisoners in the past few years also suggests that pressure on the first circle has been more intense. During this period, intellectuals from the third group have essentially not had any prisoners. From the second circle, 'Ezzatollah Sahabi, Yousefi Eshkevari, and 'Ali Zeidabadi have gone to prison. But from the first circle, 'Abbas 'Abdi, Ma'shallah Shamsolva'ezin, Hamidreza Jalaeipour, Mohsen Kadivar, 'Abdollah Nuri, Akbar Ganji, 'Emadeddin Baqi, and others have gone to prison (and have had their newspapers closed down).

4. For a list of activities and events against the reform movement since the election of Khatami, refer to Hamidreza Jalaeipour, *Dawlat-e penhan* (Hidden government) (Tehran: Tarh-e Naw, 2000), pp. 339–74.

5. Of course, it would be more precise to say that the conservatives have so far not been able to eliminate them, since it is difficult to make any predictions about the future. This is particularly a concern these days when, through the use of public media, religious intellectuals are accused of being new hypocrites and silently engaging in the overthrow of the regime. The surprising aspect of all this is that the more rational conservatives have also chosen silence. The sad implication of this silence lies in its meaning. It suggests that the outcome of the twenty-year conservative management of the society has been the "production of new hypocrites"! Apparently, the extremists see the continued livelihood of the Islamic Republic to lie in the complete suppression of religious intellectuals. The words of Ayatollah Mesbah Yazdi serve as a case in point: "We have reached a point where some, using the term 'national-religious intellectual,' claim that freedom must come first, and these things are published in newspapers. . . . If people accompany us they will

go to a place where '*Arab ney mizanad,*' where their fellow-travelers went during the first years of the revolution." *Iran* (3 October 2000).

6. Despite financial and organizational weakness, the reformists have been able to influence the 5 million educated people with their reform discourse and aims. This large educated group has been able to overcome the weaknesses of the Dovvom-e Khordad political organizations and spontaneously shape the vote of the larger public.

7. Of course the extent to which these objectives can become actualized via the Sixth Parliament, reformist parties, or Khatami's government is another discussion outside the scope of this essay.

8. See Jalaeipour, *Dawlat-e penhan,* pp. 167–97.

9. Despite this conclusion, I do not agree with the use of "religious intellectuals" as a political category for the analysis of the political sphere under normal conditions. For my more elaborate discussion of this issue refer to *Dawlat-e penhan,* pp. 137–44.

7

Improvising in Public

Transgressive Politics of the Reformist Press
in Postrevolutionary Iran

Farideh Farhi

> The press does not create anything. At most its power lies in the reflection of the society's hidden angles.
> **Akbar Ganji**[1]

Introduction

The Iranian reformist print media has been the subject of much interest in the past few years, not simply as a reflection of reformist politics but as one of the main forces influencing the course of events in Iran.[2] In other words, in contrast to Akbar Ganji's rather humble assertion stated above, the press has been the subject of reflection as an institution itself, making or creating news. Indeed, familiar scenes throughout the two years leading to the 2000 Sixth Parliamentary elections consisted of daily congregations around newsstands throughout the country of increasing numbers of readers scanning available reformist dailies to digest the news the dailies were "creating." To be sure, readers were interested in reportage or new information revealed about the "hidden angles" of the day, ranging from tidbits about the serial killings of intellectuals and political activists by members of the Information Ministry to behind-the-scene maneuverings about the candidacy of various political figures. But another interesting dynamic related to the way news spread was the extent to which a particular daily was willing to be more revelatory or bold on any given day. People did not expect a set formula in the way a public speech uttered in the newspapers crossed red lines or political taboos. But they were indeed fishing for transgressions, whether it was through the so-called straight news about political conflicts of the day, through interviews with prominent intellectuals and political figures, including journalists, through opinion polls, readers' call-in statements, political satire, and cartoons, or by means of analytical articles or op-ed pieces written by well-known journalists/intellectuals such as Akbar Ganji or 'Emadeddin Baqi, who were by now expected to perform as public stars by revealing their genius in expository writing and public argumentation. No matter what, the news spread fast. Even the politically uninspired could be moved to look all over town for the "newspaper of the day" with the realization that a particular newspaper might already have become scarce in the morning hours.

In this chapter I will attempt to make sense of the pandemonium created around the reformist press as a way to shed light on the dynamics of the public sphere in contemporary Iran. The idea is not to give a chronology or genealogy of the Iranian print media as a way to recount the manner of its development.[3] Rather, my intention is to put forward an argument about the improvisational nature of the public dynamics during the unusual spurt of activities that took place in Iran in the two years between the initial publication of *Jame'eh*, a newspaper billed as the first civil-society daily in Iran, in spring 1998 and the closure of many reformist papers and journals that came about in April 2000.

Before jumping into the main corpus of this essay, however, a couple of caveats are in order. First of all, the focus on the two-year period mentioned above should not be seen as an attempt to denigrate analyses of roots and causes of what came before. Certainly, the foundations for what culminated in the explosive or almost manic activities of the printed press between 1998 and 2000 were laid before.[4] In the pages that follow I will take a cursory look at two dailies, *Salam* and *Hamshahri*, that began publication well before 1998, as a means to shed light on the forces that shaped the media explosion in the Khatami era. But in general my endeavor here is less about foundations (or how things built up to the manic phase) and more about the public production and interactions of this particularly intense period. I am interested in the dynamics of the democratic public conversation that the print media, as represented in such postelection newspapers as *Jame'eh* (and its various reincarnations, *Tus*, *Neshat*, and *'Asr-e Azadegan*), *Khordad*, *Sobh-e Emruz*, *Fath*, *Mosharekat*, *Arya*, *Azad*, and so on, helped engender and fashion. The idea is to lay bare the improvisational as well as the transgressive aspects of this democratic conversation, while offering some tentative ideas about contemporary Iranian politics.

The second caveat relates to the opposite end. The wholesale closure of many reformist newspapers and journals in April 2000 and subsequent extralegal attacks by the judiciary against a variety of print media and journalists can certainly give observers of Iranian politics a tangible benchmark for declaring the death of what has come to be known as the reformist press in Iran. But this is not my intention.[5] Indeed, if the arguments of this chapter are to be taken seriously, the impact of the outburst of activity that took place between 1998 and 2000, which included the publication of up to thirty dailies in the city of Tehran alone, is going to be felt in Iran for years to come.[6] But precisely because this two-year period was so intense, making blatant dynamics not clearly seen before, it can give us important clues about the shape of things as they were developing before the outburst and as they may unfold in the future. In many ways, it can be argued that this period helped fashion the perception of interests and hence the development of dynamics that are going to be in currency for years. As such, it can be seen as a period in which the press behaved like a *revolutionary* press.[7] As pointed out by some students of revolutions, revolutionary "feeling" will not spread unless people come to the conclusion either that it is possible (as well as necessary and desirable) to change the shape of power itself or that it is impossible to prevent the upcoming change.[8] Much of this conclusion, it is argued, is dependent upon the perceived weakening of the existing power relationships. But the revolutionary experience is not merely a reaction. The envisioning of change in the shape of power is an active reading of the context of politics and requires a public togetherness based on a new language and set of symbols.[9] And this, I maintain, is precisely the way the reformist press perceived its role during this very active phase.

The press became the medium through which symbolic practices, particularly language and imagery, were transformed into an instrument of political and social change, not conceived as a mechanical change of political regime but experienced as an ultimate moment of political choice.[10] Performing as the country's only real public space and serving as its national forum for political debate, the print media's call was for the suspension of the givens of social existence and status hierarchies, with the only power being the power of imagination in making the Iranian political landscape anew.[11] More important, for the sake of the print media as a medium, this intense period helped solidify a process that had already begun to recreate or establish the press in terms more in tune with standards of professional journalism.

All this, I maintain, helped a different conception of politics, already brewing, to exhibit itself clearly, even if not in a hegemonic fashion; one that eschewed conspiracies and understood politics to be about making claims.[12] Politics was represented as the activity through which individuals and groups in any society articulate, negotiate, implement, and enforce the competing claims they make upon another and upon the whole. As such the reformist press and the people who produced it sought to become an indispensable link between the government and the public. They attempted to lodge themselves at the heart of an emerging political culture of publicity and openness that was meant to ensure that the rulers ought truly to reflect the will of the people.

The claims made were in some ways astonishingly simple and familiar. Highlighting the democratic, even if admittedly ambiguous, aspect of the Iranian Islamic Constitution, the print media operated on the basis that, first, the sole foundation upon which a government can claim legitimacy was popular consent. Second, it insisted that all or at least most of politics had to be carried out in public in order to be legitimate. It saw its role and professional responsibility as one of making the operation of power and its "hidden angles" as transparent as possible. But, in order to make its own enterprise seem legitimate and popular, it had to traverse a very dangerous territory created by the constant pull between the existing political taboos and the increasing public appetite for breaking them. This is why friends and foes repeatedly warned or worried about the possibility of the reformist press going too fast and undermining the reform and democratic processes it was presumably spearheading. The newspapers opposing reform, such as *Keyhan* and *Resalat,* were understandably replete with threats implicit in their argument that the reformist papers were agents of "sinister foreign forces." But warnings came from friends as well.[13] The possibility of going too fast was in fact a constant preoccupation for the press itself. Expressions such as "crossing the red lines," the need to "apply brakes," and so on became part of common discussion. Hamidreza Jalaeipour, the managing editor of *Jame'eh,* for instance, in his interview with *Payam-e Hajar* after his release from prison, critically reflects upon the conscious and unconscious efforts of his newspaper to cross some presumed red lines.[14] In general, being avowed reformists made the idea of not going too fast and applying brakes a natural consensus for many well-known journalists. But political conditions and dynamics made it hard to figure out when the brakes should actually be applied and whether there was any way to apply them. Later, when the controversial article by Akbar Ganji came out regarding the possible culpability of the former president, 'Ali Akbar Hashemi Rafsanjani, in the illegal activities of the Intelligence

Ministry, Jalaeipour even attempted to come up with some sort of criteria to use in deciding whether the public argument had gone too far and was in danger of undercutting the reform movement.[15]

Newspapers ended up having a greater social impact than other media because people of all social backgrounds read them. Moreover, they reached their audiences every day, at the same time in all public places, and thus became the almost obligatory diet of daily conversation. As such they acted more powerfully than any other form of writing, and, as said above, they themselves became the subject of news.

But newspapers became important not merely because of the actual number of their readers, which reportedly tripled with the advent of the reformist press,[16] but also because of the kind of impact that they had on society. Alone among the array of media present in postrevolutionary Iran, they served as a symbol and stand-in for "the public," which by now was no longer an undifferentiated lot in whose name all political acts were carried out, but a voting and discriminating public whose allegiance had to be wooed actively even by the members of the press. Of course, according to both versions of the postrevolutionary Constitution (as written in 1979 and amended in 1989), the people were to choose representatives and confer on them the power to make laws, which would be binding on the electorate because they were the outcome of the people's own expression of its will. But the national elections held in the 1980s and early 1990s were hardly convincing expressions of the public will.[17] Participation was either relatively low or not significant in light of the lack of choices offered. In the absence of organized political parties, the position of candidates and their allegiances were never clear; and the postrevolutionary circumstances changed so quickly that the representatives found themselves dealing with issues that had not even been dreamed of at the time of their election.

Under these conditions, the political press seized the moment to become an indispensable symbol of the public opinion of a people searching for varied means to speak. Public opinion ceased to be an abstract conceptual entity or a mere rhetorical figure. It became a source of authority that even the proponents of absolutism were compelled to appeal to, in their call for the continuance of revolutionary zeal. It became something definite, tangible, discriminating, and manifested on a daily basis in the newspapers. "People with views" *(saheb-nazaran)* now had opinions about everything ranging from the relationship between Islam and democracy to the dynamics of elite competition, the bills debated in parliament, the way the investigation of the serial murders of intellectuals was being conducted, and foreign policy. Opinion polls became legitimate and oft-reported news. And the press became the vehicle through which differentiated opinions were made public, not merely as a means to inform but also as a claim to power. As such the press acted as a very important vehicle for making competitive and differentiated politics public and therefore legitimate. But this was not centrally planned or done smoothly; it was a process carried through by almost daily improvisation and transgression. Before talking about improvisation and transgression, however, a few words are in order about the politics of contestation that made the pandemonium created by the press possible.

The Politics of Contestation and a Different Kind of Journalism

A relatively free press is not an unprecedented phenomenon in the post-constitutional period in Iran.[18] The use of the journalistic venue as a means to propagate ideas about the need to reform the political system is also not new. In fact, newspapers have historically served more as a venue for intellectuals intent on making their voices heard than as an arena for professional journalists to engage in the business of reporting news. But the two-year period under discussion here exhibited characteristics that made it different if not unique in comparison to the other periods of relatively free expression in the twentieth century.[19] As pointed out by Mas'ud Behnud, a veteran journalist and student of Iranian history, the other periods all suffered from a scarcity of literate or interested people to read newspapers, lack of professional journalists, and balance.[20] An interested readership, the development of a professional cadre of journalists trained in the revolutionary and postrevolutionary years, and a clearer sense of responsibility and balance that has come with increased professionalism were the properties that to Behnud created the unique conditions under which a relatively large number of Iranians came to abandon their reliance on other media (ranging from gossip to foreign radio broadcasts) in favor of domestic news. More important, according to Behnud, despite occasional setbacks these characteristics are precisely the ones that will make the impact of this most active phase lasting.

Of course, the point about increased readership is relatively straightforward. Iranian society is basically a very different society than even the one that existed during the 1979 revolution. At that time, which was a real transition period, everything seemed to hover around midpoints. Half of the male population was literate, half was not (for females, the percentages were more skewed). Half was urban, half lived in the countryside.

Contemporary Iran, on the other hand, has moved beyond a transition point sociologically, with different literacy numbers and urban/countryside ratio. Well over 80 percent of the urban population (both male and female) is literate, and nearly 70 percent of the population is urban, with increasingly fewer ties to the countryside. As such a straightforward sociological analysis can go a long way in analyzing the novelty of the surge in the readership and also an increase in the number of trained journalists. But it is not enough.

For a fuller understanding of this novelty a political analysis is also needed. There is no doubt that competition at the top of the political pyramid has been an important catalyst for the spread of a competitive, if not fully autonomous, press in Iran. In fact, the recent public spurt of competitive politics seems to have had a direct impact on the number of publications. Setting aside the burst of energy unleashed during the revolutionary period, the trials of the postrevolutionary press can be divided into three distinct periods. The first can be linked to the war and the period of emergency, extending from fall 1980 to summer 1988. This period of national and unified mobilization solidified closures that were already well under way even before the war started, reducing the number of all publications to sixty-two.[21] But this period is important because of the precedent it established in terms of governmental subsidies to the press. During this period of heavy import restrictions the press essentially became dependent on the government for the supply of paper and most other basic materials. Some public-sector newspapers, such as *Keyhan* and *Ettela'at*, became totally dependent on governmental disbursement of foreign currency while others benefited from partial subsidies. A combination of factors—such as the understanding that people would not include newspapers in their daily expenditures unless they were made cheap through heavy subsidies, and the will to use the press as an instrument for revolutionary propaganda and/or furthering government policies—can be considered to be the root causes of governmental support for the press during the war period.

After the end of the war, with the reemergence of competitive politics as well as the establishment of an office for press affairs in the Ministry of Culture and Islamic Guidance, a new era began that increased the number of publications to 550 by 1994.[22] The end of the war economy should have led to some sort of reevaluation of policies instituted in terms of subsidies of basic necessities, especially since the postwar government's avowed direction was toward the reduction of subsidies in general, and toward privatization in particular.[23] However, a lack of consensus led to an on-the-spot approach to problems as they arose regarding the import and distribution of basic materials. The result was the effective continuation of the war policy of financial support for the press, despite increasing criticism of the haphazard way the policy was being implemented.

With the election of Mohammad Khatami, which itself was a reflection of the highest level of elite competition the Islamic Republic had seen since its inception, an open press season was set loose. In a span of less than one year the number of publications throughout the whole country reached 850.[24] The first professional organization pursuing the interests of journalists, the Association of Iranian Journalists (Anjoman-e Senfi-ye Ruznamehnegaran-e Iran) also began operating in fall 1997.[25]

Competitive politics influenced the rise of the competitive press in three fundamental ways. First, it gave rise to a number of publications that wanted to maintain a voice for those who were in danger of losing their public say. In the process of doing this, it also created space for some of those who had lost their right to be heard once the Islamic state had become consolidated at the beginning of the revolutionary period. Second, it created conditions under which the idea of wooing readers on the basis of services or ideas offered became an increasingly acceptable proposition. Last but not least, it created conditions under which a cadre of able political analysts, rejected by a state controlled by the political opposition, increasingly turned toward writing as a means of economic survival as well as self-expression.[26] The last point is particularly important as it suggests a talented pool of resources looking for something to do both politically and economically. The state bureaucracy could no longer absorb this talent, and the wielders of political power were still too afraid to allow direct political activities through the establishment of political parties. The print media offered itself as an untapped possibility.[27]

As mentioned above, the interaction of these dynamics became highly explosive after Khatami's election, when the Ministry of Culture and Islamic Guidance, now controlled by the pro-reform faction, began giving licenses to an increasing number of dailies, weeklies, and monthlies throughout the country. But in order to understand fully the interaction among the three factors mentioned above and the new kind of journalism to which it gave rise, a short foray into the history of two postrevolutionary newspapers—*Salam* and *Hamshahri*—that became important inspirations for post-Khatami newspapers could be instructive.

The birth of *Salam* was perhaps the most visible manifestation of elite competition in Iran. It came onto the political scene precisely at a moment when an elite faction known as the Association of Combatant Clerics

(Majmaʿ-e Rawhaniyun-e Mobarez) perceived itself as endangered in the arena of direct political competition. According to its own "storytellers," the direct motive for the publication of *Salam* came to life in the election for the Second Assembly of Experts. During this election, for the first time, use of the vetting process against leading clerics led to the elimination of some candidates from what was also known as the left faction, leading to the withdrawal of some others in protest. The idea of publishing a newspaper of their own was born when the association was "astonished" to find out that all the print media had been banned from publishing their public statement regarding the vetting process.[28] According to the "storytellers," the idea of publishing a newspaper naturally followed from this politics of exclusion.[29]

Published by Seyyed Mohammad Musavi Khoeiniha, an influential cleric in the association and a former revolutionary prosecutor general, *Salam* was to become the platform replacing that which had been taken away from the Association of Combatant Clerics through the vetting process. But the nature of the platform also meant a reassessment of the means of appeal. In its nine years of existence, *Salam* received quite a bit of government assistance in the form of foreign currency at a favorable exchange rate, as well as governmental advertisements, subsidies, printing paper, and equipment. The amount received in each of the categories was considerably less than the amount of assistance given to such large news conglomerates as *Keyhan* and *Ettelaʿat* but also less than the amount given to comparable papers from the opposite political camp, such as *Resalat*.[30] Nevertheless, governmental support was critical and yet another reflection of how competitive politics within the government helped the rise of the nongovernmental competitive press.

Despite direct and indirect government help, *Salam* could not be a mouthpiece for the government because of the competition in the political field. In order to remain politically viable, it had to find a way to distinguish itself as a new enterprise. And *Salam* did this by identifying several themes that tested well and gained the interest of a readership that was not very large but was significant.[31] During its almost nine years of publication of 2,339 issues, beginning in 1991 and including two short forced closures, *Salam* identified its mission as one of "defending the sovereignty of law [which included the rejection of the institution of *velayat-e faqih* as being above the law]: defending people's rights, disclosing administrative corruption, struggling against violence, rationally defending the revolution and Islam, and offering in-depth analyses of events as well as establishing effective communication with people and readers."[32]

Such a mission differentiated *Salam* from other dailies published at that time. Whether improvised as a means to attract readers or deliberately thought out as a result of being out of power, *Salam*'s understanding of print media as a means to sell certain ideas to readers, no matter how selective, was very different from the understanding of news as revolutionary propaganda, as practiced by dailies such as *Keyhan*, or news as a means to promote government policies, as practiced by more sedate dailies such as *Ettela'at*. The "politics of persuasion,"[33] as I like to call it, was hence deemed necessary as a means to appeal to a larger pool of readers than the ones already committed through their allegiance to the Association of Combatant Clerics.

Competitive politics also caused *Salam* to become a model in areas that were previously considered taboo. As a sounding board for a faction facing elimination in the political arena, it became a platform for the critique of economic and social policies as well as policies intended to tighten the ruling circles. It did so by engaging in what can be considered selective investigative journalism that revealed pockets of corruption and cronyism through the use of governmental resources. To be sure, *Salam* did not have a monopoly on selective investigative journalism that focused on revealing the improper economic activities of political opponents. Highly partisan publications such as *Keyhan, Shalamcheh, Sobh,* and others from the other side of the political spectrum also practiced it, but *Salam*'s deliberately professional language of investigative journalism, as opposed to the more flamboyant rhetorical denunciations of others, began to give the paper an additional nonpartisan readership that was not available to others.[34] *Salam*'s "Report" page, rather than being a fill-in page as in many other papers, also dealt with real social problems such as drug addiction.

In promoting the idea of professional journalism, *Salam* relied on a diverse group of journalists. They differed greatly in the degree of their involvement in the profession and the kind of journalism that they engaged in. The "stars" were the great editorialists, like 'Abbas 'Abdi, who had already distinguished himself before his arrest by being both a member of *Salam*'s editorial board as well as the mentor of budding journalists. These editorial writers were less collectors of news than commentators, political essayists working on a daily or weekly schedule. But the more numerous rank-and-file staff was made up of distinctly less glamorous "news workers" who were mostly drawn from recent university graduates.[35]

Salam also became a platform for the expression of what can be considered differentiated public opinion. The daily "Hello Salam" column became a stage for unidentified readers to ruminate on the issues of the day, with the newspaper dutifully responding to their questions. *Salam* also made a point of soliciting the opinion of "experts" or "those with views" about the concerns of the day. It also increasingly relied on the use of opinion polls on a variety of issues.[36] These practices later became standard for all newspapers.

Finally, by establishing its own printing factory, again made possible by favorable foreign currency credits given by the government, the *Salam* enterprise managed to assure its survival economically even if not politically. Later on, after its closure, the printing facilities were put to use for the publication of other dailies.[37]

Economic success was even more a key to the operation of *Hamshahri*, which began with the resources available to Gholamhoseyn Karbaschi, the mayor of Tehran. Again, competitive politics necessitated the rise of this particular paper as it effectively became a platform for the mayor's agenda, which was part and parcel of the programs of a strand within the ruling circles later identified as Kargozaran-e Sazandegi (Servants of Construction). And again professionalism, or at least the appearance of professionalism, was deemed a plus in promoting a message that emphasized economic development and rationality and environmental awareness for city-centered living.[38] Using smaller and denser colored pages as well as low prices, this paper quickly managed to lodge itself, despite its focus on Tehran, as the highest-circulation paper in Iran, displacing the more traditional nationwide dailies such as *Keyhan*, which, despite their flamboyant and conspiratorial approach to news, were still bought because of the advertisements and obituaries they carried.[39] Where *Salam* used selective investigative reporting and direct interaction with the readers over political issues, *Hamshahri*'s forte was its focus on reporting on the events and news of the city, together with its entertaining style. Its classified advertisements and listings of all social and cultural events made it a city paper par excellence even if quite a few of its sections contained translations of philosophical or theoretical pieces and fillers that did not really fit the newspaper format. *Hamshahri* also ultimately proved more resilient than other papers, managing to become more political during certain periods and less so when its survival was at stake. It even managed to weather the arrest of its managing editor, Gholamhoseyn Karbaschi, the mayor of Tehran, who was the first victim of intense factional conflicts that ensued following Khatami's election. It continues to operate as one of the most important dailies in Iran.

Understanding the needs of the readers, as represented in the success of newspapers such as *Salam* and *Hamshahri,* became a key in the formula envisioned by the architects of *Jame'eh,* loudly advertised on giant bulletin boards throughout Tehran as Iran's first civil-society newspaper. In fact, *Jame'eh*'s prepublication advertisement about itself suggested that *Hamshahri*'s success in luring readership on the basis of advertisement and entertaining style had already been digested by the new newspaper. Like *Hamshahri,* the paper was presented in a colorful format, with beautiful and uplifting pictures and sections that dealt with events in the city. *Jame'eh* was presumably not merely a political enterprise; it was intended to be successful as an independent economic enterprise, as well. But like *Salam,* it was also a hard-hitting tabloid filled with political news and commentary. Its star editorial writers, who were not all journalists and later wrote for other papers as well, not only deliberated on the issues of the day but also engaged and critiqued each other and opened a space for civil conversation that was simply too attractive to resist. Readers followed debates that more often than not invited outside writers' commentary as well. In-depth interviews with political pundits and intellectuals dealt with topics as varied as the relationship between modernity and tradition and the dynamics of contemporary political conflicts.

Jame'eh also did something else. Taking the lead from another publication, the weekly *Gol Aqa,* which had become popular in the postwar years, as well as feeding on a long-standing tradition, it relied on satire and political cartoons to attract readers. Like writers of *Gol Aqa* in general, and its chief editor, Kiyumars Saberi, in particular, *Jame'eh*'s main satirist, Ebrahim Nabavi, used detailed knowledge of behind-the-scenes conflicts and competitions at the top to offer a fairly accurate and biting representation of conditions in Iranian society and politics. Along with political cartoons, Nabavi's columns became *Jame'eh*'s first "must read," developing a following of loyal daily readers.

Jame'eh was closed after 120 issues, but its impact proved more lasting. Not only did the same editorial team continue to publish a succession of papers, but also the format of hard-hitting and interactive political commentary combined with more entertaining news and satire struck a chord among the readers. The impact was such that almost all the papers that followed, not only in Tehran but also other cities, had something of *Jame'eh* in them. In fact, the success of *Jame'eh* was so astounding and quick in terms of readership that one is tempted to think of it as being the brainchild of a visionary editorial team that foresaw society's demand for a democratic conversation. To be sure, such a demand and yearning existed, and the founders of *Jame'eh,* under the guidance of veteran editor

Mashallah Shamsolvaʿezin, understood that demand well.[40] At the same time, it is important to understand that, by the very nature of the enterprise, which was to engage more and more people in a democratic conversation, *Jameʿeh* and the other newspapers that followed during the turbulent two years constituted an interactive media, and as such they relied on feedback to produce commentary and news. Feedback came in the form of fired-up responses from opposing factions on the political spectrum, both from the people who felt threatened by this new experiment with press freedom and from those who generally constituted a growing readership.[41] The dynamic was simple: the reformist papers wanted more readers, and the readers wanted more news about the operation of the Iranian political system. Revealing more and more was the only way to sustain a readership in a highly competitive marketplace for the trade of "state secrets."[42] Revealing more and more was also a natural outcome of public exchanges among writers and editors who were now not only well-known journalists but also figures who carried the weight of being former or even current public officials. The addition of newspapers such as *Sobh-e Emruz* and *Khordad*, run by political heavyweights such as Saʿid Hajjarian and ʿAbdollah Nuri, who had been key players in the establishment of various postrevolutionary political institutions, gave the process the necessary stamina to satisfy the ever-increasing public thirst for information. *Sobh-e Emruz*, in particular, proved relentless as the public rewarded it with a high circulation.[43] The result of all this was a highly dynamic process of improvisation and selective transgression. It was improvised because what was publicly produced was not predetermined and resulted from the conversational dynamics. It was transgressive because the language used to talk about politics was so open and plain. However, it continued to be selective because not everything was put on the table, at least not as yet.

On Improvisation and Transgression

Improvisation is about composing on the spur of the moment; making, inventing, or arranging offhand. It is generally done in the midst of an audience, a public, with their mood and reaction very much in mind. The idea is to play together with the greatest possible freedom—which, far from meaning without constraint, actually means to play together with sufficient skill and communication in order to be able to select proper constraints in the course of the piece, rather than being dependent upon predetermined ones. According to the musician Ann Farber, "In the most successful improvisational art, the give and take of conversation functions as a model of democratic interaction: No single instrumentalist or structure establishes dominance. Instead the voice and structures keep weaving in and out, modifying and reshaping one another."[44]

The application of the idea of improvisation to a period avowedly identified as reformist then seems like an odd choice of words. Improvisation is a process that eschews dominance or control on the part of any of the players. It suggests a conversation between the players and a wider field with open-ended and unpredictable results. The idea is not about playing uncontrollably or with total license, but about constraints revealing themselves in the process of the act and not beforehand. Reform, at least in its ideal sense, on the other hand, is all about predetermined controls. As Morteza Mardiha points out in his critique of Akbar Ganji's attempt to lay bare the hidden angles of power as wielded by the former president Rafsanjani, "Unlike revolution, reform is a movement accompanied with a plan and a design."[45] Reform conceived in this way not only has built-in limits but operates on the presumption of the leadership and dominance of certain key players and structures.

Following this understanding of reform as designed from the top, one could argue that the use of the term for the kind of movement for change that has occurred in Iran might be a misnomer. The so-called reform movement in Iran did not emanate from a robust process of reflection about the speed and direction of change in an essentially ideology-based political system.[46] Rather, as mentioned above, the idea came into vogue when sections of the revolutionary elite felt increasingly isolated from centers of power and became fearful of becoming completely eliminated. As such, ideas such as reform or civil society, as a constellation of interest-based and social organizations that could pressure the state, essentially got a political boost as a strategy for survival but did not have much theoretical depth. Indeed, even after the election, the discussions regarding how to go about deepening reform or enlarging the civil society did not go further than the desire to set up nongovernmental organizations. To be sure, quite a bit of theoretical debate did occur about the meaning of reform or civil society, but these discussions at least initially had a borrowed quality, relying heavily on the experiences and discussions in Eastern and Central Europe as well as Latin America.

It is of course true that elite competition itself has given the movement for change in Iran a top-down quality. Yet, within the Iranian context it is also important to remember that in this latest round of elite competition and conflict,[47] the idea of limited competition was hampered from the beginning. First of all, unlike prior rounds of elite competition, it was not set up as competition among groups coalescing around dominant personalities. Groups or factions competing for power each had certain internal dynamics of their own not necessarily controlled by any one individual or set of individuals. Second, limited elite competition was hampered by the fact that sections of the elite, because they did not have sufficient resources within the elite circles, were forced to look for support outside the closed ruling cliques. In fact, they had to look for support among the population, and as such the limited game of elites competing against each other had to be always on the verge of transgressing or, in other words, of going beyond the predetermined boundaries.

Added to this chaotic context was the reality that there were no long-standing and well-developed political structures that could oversee this experiment in elite competition, manage popular demands, and in time play a pacifying role. Accordingly the "reform" game that was begun had no set rules by which all parties could abide or arbiters who could assure all rules were applied in an equitable fashion.[48]

Meanwhile, the key players had to maneuver under the eyes of a diverse public that was intensely watching this very fluid and delicate political game, while consistently siding with the forces that were, granted perhaps only for the moment, on the side of political and cultural opening. To be sure, this "public" did not include the whole population of Iran, but it was large enough to make a difference in terms of the number of newspaper readers. In an ironic fashion, one could say that this public was not very interested in civil society as an arena for organizing interests and institution building, at least as yet. It was as though it intuitively knew that the fate of an enlarged and politically significant "public" rested in the continuation and ultimate institutionalization of elite competition to the point where no political force would be in fear of political elimination and no force would be powerful enough to eliminate others. Its time and energy were mostly consumed watching as well as engaging with the political society. Through the print media this public repeatedly stated its desire for the state to pull back and let the society live. But it also did something more essential. It established itself as a player, or more accurately a set of players, that competitors for power could no longer take for granted as either being mute or rendered mute. They made clear that whatever the political or ideological positioning at the top, the complex politics of the society had to be taken into consideration.

For the so-called reformist print media, operating in the midst of an intense elite conflict while, at the same time, being a reflection of it, the political fluidity of any given moment then became the condition of its existence. On the one hand, the media attempted to build legitimacy for the movement for which it had become a lightning rod. On the other hand, because of the political fluidity of the moment, it had to keep up with rapidly shifting public opinion, since in that environment it is public opinion that lays the basis for legitimacy—even if the latter be replete with instability and in constant need of reaffirmation.

In order to maintain its legitimacy as an enterprise "reflecting the opinion of the people," the print media constantly had to keep the interest of the readers by transgressing/violating old and no longer acceptable lines and taboos. The readers had to be regularly reminded, explicitly or implicitly, of the high stakes involved and the risks taken.[49] And the writers had to improvise the next piece of writing based on the conversation generated in response to the earlier pieces. In this process the print media was aided by the fact that the societal dynamic of the moment was toward crystallizing a fundamental question around which opinion was being formed.[50] Indeed for the reformist print media, as well as the public as a whole, the fundamental question around which opinion was being formulated and reformulated was increasingly simple: how to reconcile civil society with religion after the choice had been made by the religious establishment to abandon the companionship of civil society and become not only a political player, but also a monopolizer of political power. The ultimate question was (and of course continues to be) how to return religion to civil society as a voice of conscience, drawer of limits, and articulator of sentiments in ways that would allow the smooth running of a modern state. Another face of the same question is how to reconcile the continued role of the clergy in politics—and here I use the term clergy as a metaphor for a relatively closed circle of revolutionary elite who now had sons and daughters who also wanted to be in politics—with the aspiration of others interested in enlarging the decision-making circle.

The reformist print media, in its manic phase, was not able to generate answers to these very fundamental questions, at least at the practical level. Matter-of-fact answers never reveal themselves as a whole, or in a top-down manner. Of course, the political realities of the moment and the fact that there is still a body of power wielders in Iran that is not willing to abide by the rules, not always under their control, also thwarted attempts at finding answers. However, by posing these questions in a variety of ways and engaging in conversations about them, the print media opened up space for a specific kind of discursive interaction about the desirability as well as the necessity of rationalizing political domination by rendering states accountable at least to some of their citizenry. A clear sense was created that the discussants in the public sphere were deliberating as peers irrespective of the inequalities of status, and the result of their open-ended discussion was "public opinion" in the strong sense of a consensus about the common good of reform. Momentarily, at least, public debate about the common good replaced street demonstrations and brokered backroom compromises as sources of change. To be sure, student riots that gripped the nation for a few days in the summer of 1999 when *Salam* was ordered closed were an important exception that cannot be overlooked. At the same time, the fact that they occurred over the closure of a newspaper was itself a reflection of the interactive dynamic between the print media and the public mood. It was also significant that the closure and the riots themselves provided further food for thought and public engagement. And in the process, among other things, a new and much more refined conception of what was deemed an acceptable role for the mass media crystallized. The result was a questioning and even a rejection of the idea of the unidirectional control of the public sphere by means of propaganda, and gaining an understanding of the role of mass media as being based on a more open-ended and improvisational interaction of forces and voices that exist in the public sphere.[51]

The valorization of public debate made possible by the domestic news and media also entailed a turn toward internal solutions for the problems of Islamic Iran. No longer was the public debate centered on which model of development to follow. To be sure the initial debate over whether political development or economic development should be a priority was somewhat influenced by the experiences of other countries such as China that had engaged in controlled reform. But this conversation never really did get off the ground beyond generalities about economic versus political reform. Rather, the conversation shifted to the desirability and necessity of reform as a new form of relationship between society and the state in light of domestic constraints and possibilities. As such, reform, defined as a necessity for the creation of "rational" political authority, became the marker of changed or frustrated aspirations and turned into a criterion and symbol through which anyone standing against public opinion could be identified and accorded a loss in political status. Nowhere was this dynamic more evident than the unusual public debate that took place over the candidacy of 'Ali Akbar Hashemi Rafsanjani for the Sixth Parliament.

As most observers of Iranian politics readily admit, the debate over the candidacy of Hashemi Rafsanjani was unusual both for its unexpected and bold nature and for the transparency it brought to the Iranian political arena. The lasting impact of the debate, however, must be found in the way crystallized public opinion concerning the need to reform the structure of governance led to the loss of legitimacy of the kind of political authority wielded by Hashemi Rafsanjani. In order to appreciate this point, a short foray into recent history is necessary.

At the risk of gross generalization, I think it is fair to say that when all the ideological and religious defenses of notions such as *velayat-e faqih* or the institutional inventions such as the Council of Guardians are stripped to their essence, the most important political innovation of the Islamic Republic rests on the clerics' claim to *direct* rule. This of course does not mean that no one else can become part of the leadership and the decision-making processes. It also does not mean that no diversity is allowed in opinions or actions. It simply means that, using a variety of rhetorical as well as institutional instruments, the "clerics" are posited as the final decision makers as well as "king" makers. This assures that, like the previous monarchical system, governance continues to be primarily based on acquiescence to superior force rather than on consent supplemented with some measure of repression.

The term clerics should of course be used delicately here. The idea of clerical guardianship was not intended to connote that all clerics should be politically involved or that it was through their unanimity that clerical rule was made possible. Rather, it simply suggested that, first of all, there was a "will" to rule, no matter at what cost, and second, there existed certain interpersonal and nontransparent dynamics among the revolutionary clerics that would allow them to negotiate their way out of political crisis. In short, the notion of clerical guardianship portrayed the revolutionary clerics as deliberate, determined, and flexible in their claim to power, and this has been an important source of political legitimacy in a society in search of stability.

Ayatollah Khomeini was of course the most important figure in the construction of the idea of clerical guardianship. He not only resurrected the idea as a purely political formulation but also epitomized the idea in flesh. He *was* deliberate, determined, and flexible. He was a political man who could also rise above it all and be the final arbiter among political men. Yet, Ayatollah Khomeini's dominant presence should not overshadow the ideological dimension of clerical rule. Even without Ayatollah Khomeini, the Iranian revolutionary leadership always strove to derive legitimacy by relying on the existence of de jure or de facto authorities, be they individuals, institutions, or behind-the-scenes negotiation processes, that could rise above the everyday scenes of partisan politics and define the parameters of accepted public speech and actions. The media was deemed important insofar as they could project these parameters to a public perceived as generally malleable, on the one hand, and ready to be mobilized, on the other, whenever there was truly a need for unity and harmony.

Here it is important to note again that, given the diversity as well as the sheer number of centers of power, the idea of clerical guardianship in Iran never took the form of complete control over the public sphere. Indeed, by the end of the war there were serious disagreements over a number of substantive issues related to the running of a modern political economy. Clerical guardianship was also never intent on undermining the multiple centers of power. The idea, as said before, was that a nontransparent, nontangible tacit agreement among the clerics would always prevent policy disagreements and, more importantly, power struggles from getting out of control.

Understood in this way, after a revolution explicitly made in the name of rejecting monarchy, the only remaining and principal justification for absolute authority was its fundamental responsibility to contain the ideological potential of religious or political disputes to disturb the political order. Flexibility, backroom negotiations, shifting ideological positions, political opportunism, lack of clarity, and so on were all legitimate resources in the clerics' arsenal in preventing factional disputes from getting out of control. And these resources were presumably put to good use in Hashemi Rafsanjani's eight-year tenure as president. But the fact that there was no longer an absolute authority that could keep things from going out of control had already become a fact of everyday politics after Khomeini's death. Certainly the election of Khatami reflected that reality in important ways, but it was the debate staged in the print media over Hashemi Rafsanjani's candidacy that robbed absolute authority of all its ideological justification, and for the purposes of this essay, it is important to see how.

Hashemi Rafsanjani was pulled into the political fray presumably on a call of duty to save the nation from political breakdown. To be sure, much was made of the pressure on him by one section of the political elite to enter the parliamentary race, but he registered as an independent candidate while saying that he was willing to allow any political group, irrespective of political view, to place him on its slate of candidates.[52] The nation-state as a unified entity needed him to serve and of course he had to oblige as the "man of crises" to moderate the increasing immoderation of political factions. And the votes of the "noble people of Tehran" were expected to provide him with a "national license" to bring "national harmony" to the country once again and "open the way to the future for all."⁵³

Hashemi Rafsanjani's candidacy for the Sixth Majles was not unexpected and came after intense public discussions in publications of all political orientations about the wisdom of the decision. What was unexpected was the directness of the political language and questions regarding his public record and behavior. Rather than giving him a national license to create harmony, his candidacy gave the print media unbridled license for public scrutiny and acrimony. This did not happen immediately, but the process gained steam through an interactive dynamic. Initially the interaction came in the form of a conversation between "defenders" of Hashemi's candidacy, some of whom were members of his family, and others who were reacting to his answers to particular questions regarding his role in the arrest and murder of the leading opposition members and writers. The conversation was complicated by the fact that some of the people or factions that had previously criticized Hashemi's policies were now publicly forced to explain their change of position. Some "people with views" even objected to the fact that Hashemi's interview was shown on national television, a presumably nonpartisan venue not to be used for the promotion of one candidate over others.⁵⁴ As such, from the beginning, his claim to be above factions was challenged and undercut.

Others deliberated on the nature of the political equation now unsettled by Hashemi Rafsanjani and the high likelihood that he would become the next speaker of the Majles.⁵⁵ Still others found his move an opportunity to appraise his political behavior and policies critically. In general, five sets of interrelated but distinct conversations could be detected regarding Hashemi's candidacy. The first one centered on the meaning of his candidacy and precisely why he felt compelled to enter into the political fray. The second one focused on the implications of his political move for his own supporters, particularly the Servants of Construction Party, and some of the members of that party who were now part of Khatami's cabinet. The third set of conversations entered the much more dangerous territory of who Hashemi Rafsanjani really was and how he had behaved politically since the revolution. The fourth set of conversations was more policy oriented and was put forth as a means to discuss his position within the fluid spectrum of contending political forces. And, finally, the fifth set of conversations centered on the wisdom of discussing Hashemi Rafsanjani and his record in such direct ways. A variety of arguments developed. Some saw his entry as helpful in deepening what by now had become identified as the reform project, while others worried about his potential to derail the same project. Some affirmed his moderation while others bemoaned the lack of political transparency that he had exhibited throughout his years in office. Still others compared his style of governance to the shah's style whereas others lamented the unfairness of the critiques that did not take into account the political field in which Hashemi was operating.[56]

The debates about the candidacy of Hashemi Rafsanjani were multifaceted and included independent voices that supported him as a man on the side of reform.[57] However, the language he used to fend off his critics undercut his claim to either moderation or reform and hence exposed him as a candidate who was against reform. Not understanding the obsolescence of the language of political unity, he and his supporters continued to describe him as the man whom the nation needed based on his record of "construction" and/or "moderation." Public opinion, on the other hand, was demanding something else from him and everyone else: an interrogation or critical reflection of that record as a means to make up its mind about his candidacy. Whether Hashemi Rafsanjani could have gotten better results through engagement with public opinion is something we will never know. The point is that his refusal to engage with the public about his record became the most important reason for his identification as an opponent of reform. As such, every move he made to make himself look like a reformist was interpreted as a reflection of his opportunistic politics of the past.

Meanwhile the print media, pushed by the public hunger to know more and more, relied on public records to identify inconsistencies in Hashemi Rafsanjani's public positions and statements. This in turn fed the demand for Hashemi to enter the fray to clear his presumed public record of inconsistencies. And the demand for clarity could not stop at Hashemi's tenure at the helm as president. The operation of the Intelligence Ministry during his tenure was no longer the only issue under scrutiny. Journalists wanted to know about his role in the continuation of the Iran-Iraq war as well.[58] This demand for clarity was so direct that it culminated in a rather odd call by a journalist for a public debate, not public interview, with him. By now, the journalist, Akbar Ganji, who had exposed many of the inconsistencies in Hashemi Rafsanjani's public statements, was making a direct claim as a stand-in for the public.[59] The debate of course never happened, and the journalist who called for the debate is now in prison, but very few outside Hashemi's close family circles suggested that the call for debate between a journalist and a politician was odd. In other words, Ganji's claim to political power, based on his command of the printed word, made perfect sense within the context of the politics of the moment. Meanwhile Hashemi continued to respond in the old language replete with threats and warnings about hidden and foreign-guided enemies. His refusal or inability to engage in a conversation about his public record further undermined his own claim to any absolute political authority. It also suggested that, in general, any claim to legitimate political authority that did not engage with public opinion under the new terms was considered suspect. Of course this does not mean that from now on those intent on holding on to power have to heed public opinion. They could easily, as they have done, ignore public opinion or willfully go against it as a means of making a statement about their will to power.[60] But given the existence of "public opinion" so dutifully chronicled by the print media, they are no less publicly faced with the singularly urgent political question of how to govern Iran than the reformist president and current parliament, whose attempts to build a basis for "rational dominion" are being thwarted.

Conclusion

Let me conclude by placing the very modest claims of this chapter into the context of the contemporary debates about politics in Iran. It seems to me that some of the debates that have been occurring about the pace and even genuineness of the reform movement in Iran may be underestimating the improvisational nature of what has been happening. The reform movement and its lightning rod, the press, are represented as a movement either with or without a well-thought-out plan of action. In either case, the door is opened for a constant and dominant conversation about the failure or success of the reform movement. Is Khatami doing enough? Did the press go too far and invite reaction? Has the reform movement run out of steam or has it been blocked? Is the reformist ideology, whatever that is, sufficiently coherent to lead to intended results, whatever they are? These are questions that essentially consume the minds of political observers. Meanwhile, democracy is implicitly presented as an *end,* repeatedly thwarted. The point of this essay has been to emphasize the open-ended and interactive dynamics that continue to make the Iranian political landscape so hard to figure out in terms of the immediate power balance and end results. Irrespective of the final results of the political jockeying at the top, fundamental changes have occurred in the way politics are conceived and conducted in Iran. As such, these changes must be seen as part and parcel of a democratic process that has been going on for a while, but clearly exhibiting itself by means of the press activities during the past few years.

What seems to be the most interesting aspect of contemporary Iranian politics is the juxtaposition of postrevolutionary dynamics and democratic processes generated out of a political stalemate or gridlock. Democratic theorists of course have long postulated the potential of stalemates over long-standing political conflicts in paving the way for the acceptance of democratic rules by competing factions.[61] Adam Przeworski posits persistent stalemate as a precondition for enduring democracy. To be more precise, he argues that enduring democratic checks and balances will emerge only if the future balance of forces under democratic rule is unknown at the time when the institutions are being designed.[62]

But besides the importance of elite competition or conflict in creating a democratic space, there is also something in the proximity of revolutionary upheavals that makes the focus on the dynamic processes by which Iranian elite do or do not reach agreement on democratic rules even more interesting and fluid. Notwithstanding disclaimers about their not creating blank slates, revolutions do turn some things upside down or at least sideways. The least they do is to create momentary uncertainty and fluidity because of the participation of a variety of social forces in the political arena. In the Iranian case, that political uncertainty and fluidity was temporarily put on hold by ideologically determined clerics/revolutionaries and a war, and yet it is back in full force during a time span in which many of the first-generation revolutionaries are still around. This gives the Iranian dynamics a tinge of a polity still in the making rather than of one in the process of being remade after a collapse, as, for instance, in the case of the Soviet Union. As such, there seems to be more room for all the societal forces that came to play a prominent role during the revolution to stake a claim in the overall direction of the political society. Lack of an entrenched political institution or party also enhances the possibility of this process remaining open-ended for a longer period.

To be sure, the initial agitation for a change in the rules of the game did not emanate from a robust process of reflection about the need for and nature of change in an essentially closed political system. It was pursued as a strategy for survival. Nevertheless, and perhaps because of this strategic predicament, the dynamic process unleashed was not "owned" by any one group or faction. And precisely because the process was not owned, the conversation that was carried through the print media ended up being both improvised as well as relatively unfettered, feeding as well as being fed by a renewed public interest in politics. The print media could not merely call for a new form of politics on the basis of the rejection of old politics. It had to offer new forms of argumentation, new kinds of information, and, most important, new political possibilities embedded in the language and format it used to report on contemporary politics. As such it remains, even when gagged, uniquely dangerous to the political order it said it merely wanted to reform.

Notes

1. Akbar Ganji, "Hey'at monsefeh va dadgah-e matbu'at" (The jury and the Special Court for the Press), *Sobh-e Emruz* (26 October 1999). Reprinted in *'Alijenab-e sorkhpush va 'alijenaban-e khakestari* (The red eminence and the gray eminences) (Tehran: Tarh-e Naw, 1999).

2. This research is part of a larger project on the expansion of the public sphere in Iran funded by a grant from the United States Institute of Peace. I would also like to thank Hamidreza Jalaeipour for useful comments on an earlier draft and Nargess Khatoun Barahoui for research help.

3. This does not mean that the story of how and why the reformist press came to be and the role it played in the reform movement is not a worthy enterprise. In fact, much work needs to be done in that area. For a preliminary attempt see Hamidreza Jalaeipour, "Seh sal jonbesh-e eslahi bar shaneh-ye matbu'at" (Three years of the reform movement on the shoulders of the press), *Gunagun* (29 June 2000).

4. If we understand the history of the printed press in Iran as part and parcel of the struggle to promote a shift from a repressive mode of domination to a hegemonic one, that is, from a rule based primarily on acquiescence to superior force to a rule based primarily on consent supplemented with some measure of repression, then the story of the print media in Iran is indeed a long one. It clearly goes back to the agitation for a constitutionally based system at the beginning of the twentieth century, with episodic outbursts of activity for at least a hundred years. Even a more immediate analysis of roots and origins must go back to the end of the Iran-Iraq war, the relative opening of the political atmosphere, changes in the implementation of the press laws between 1988 and 1989, the tenure of Mohammad Khatami as the minister of culture and Islamic guidance, and the establishment of newspapers, weeklies, and monthlies such as *Salam, Gol Aqa, Adineh, Donya-ye Sokhan, Iran-e Farda, San'at-e Haml-o-Naql,* and *Kiyan*.

5. The difficulty and confusion of writing about a situation that continues to be unsettled should be abundantly clear. The problem is even present at the more mundane grammatical level of choosing verb tenses. The choice of limiting the essay to the two-year period makes the past tense a logical choice. But the reality of continuing fluidity in the Iranian political conditions leads to occasional slippage, which I hope the reader will forgive.

6. This is of course not to underestimate the sustained attacks that have been staged by the Iranian judiciary, in its various guises (Special Court for the Press, revolutionary court, special clergy court, and so on), against the press. Exact numbers are difficult to access, but according to the newspaper *Seda-ye 'Edalat* (17 April 2001), between spring 1999 and spring 2001, about 50 journalists were arrested, 20 received sentences, and more than 150 were issued warnings. During the same period this newspaper reports, quoting Shaban Shahidi, a deputy minister at the Ministry of Culture and Islamic Guidance, the ministry completed applications for 1,396 new publications. Shahidi does not say how many were approved, but the sheer number of applications suggests a determination on the part of those involved in the print media to continue their activities despite adversity. For a reporting of the openings and closures that have taken place since Mohammad Khatami was elected president, see William Samii, "A Snail Crawling along a Razor: The Press in Iran, 1997–2001," *RFE/RL Iran Report* 4, no. 15 (19 April 2001).

7. For a succinct discussion of a revolutionary press, see Jeremy D. Popkin, *Revolutionary News: The Press in France 1789–1799* (Durham, N.C.: Duke University Press, 1990).

8. See, for instance, Francois Furet, *Interpreting the French Revolution* (Cambridge: Cambridge University Press, 1981); and Lynn Hunt, *Politics, Culture, and Class in the French Revolution* (Berkeley: University of California Press, 1988).

9. By "togetherness," I do not necessarily mean agreement without conflict, dispute, or struggle. I mean a new basis for the negotiation of meanings.

10. A revolution here is not merely considered an event; it is also an idea and an attitude, "a way of thinking and feeling," "a mode of relating to contemporary reality." Borrowing from Hannah Arendt, revolutions occur when there is a sense that the course of history "suddenly begins anew, that an entirely new story never known or told before, is about to unfold." Hannah Arendt, *On Revolution* (New York: Viking Press, 1965). People believe that they are agents in a process that spells the end of an old order and brings the birth of a new world. My point here is about a sense of making something new, even if the newness, in this case, was perceived to be in the form of a reformist politics previously shunned in Iran.

11. On the concept of "public" and "public sphere," I am influenced by Habermas's notion of public sphere and its critiques. According to Habermas, a body of private persons assembled to discuss matters of public concern or common interest constitutes a public sphere. As a counterweight to absolutist states of early modern Europe, these publics initially aimed to mediate between society and the state by holding the state accountable and by making state activities subject to scrutiny via the force of public opinion. Later, of course, the general interests of the society were presumably transmitted to the state through such features as legally guaranteed speech, free press, and free assembly, and ultimately through the parliamentary institutions of representative government. From this point of view the idea of public sphere means at least two things. One provides for some sort of institutional

mechanism for "rationalizing" political domination by rendering states accountable to at least some of the citizenry. The second sees the public sphere as an arena for unrestricted and rational discussion of public matters. It is in this latter arena, in which discussants deliberate as peers irrespective of inequality of social status, that public opinion in the strong sense of a consensus about the common good is generated. As Habermas's critics, such as Nancy Fraser, have pointed out, such an ideal understanding of the liberal public sphere neglects the fact that a "discourse of publicity touting accessibility, rationality and the suspension of status hierarchies is itself deployed as a strategy of distinction," leaving out multiple ways of contributing in public. But for the purposes of this essay, the focus is on the way the reformist press perceived itself as creating a public sphere as a place for dialogue regardless of distinctions and hierarchies. On "public sphere" see Jürgen Habermas, *The Structural Transformation of the Public Sphere: An Inquiry into a Category of Bourgeois Society*, trans. Thomas Burger with Frederick Lawrence (Cambridge, Mass.: MIT Press, 1989). For discussions and critiques of Habermas's notion of public sphere, see Craig Calhoun, ed., *Habermas and the Public Sphere* (Cambridge, Mass.: MIT Press, 1991). Fraser's critiques can be found in this volume.

12. The Iranian political landscape and language has remained filled with a conspiratorial understanding of politics. This understanding is exhibited in political writings and oratories (as in, for example, Friday prayers). The point here is that a different understanding of politics, again already brewing, clearly exhibited itself, making the conspiratorial approach look outdated and out of place. The contest was not simply about the content of the political arguments but the form as well. This new form of writing relied on "public records" to report as well as analyze and as such insisted on making records public. A good example of the insistence on the use of public records can be found in the work of journalist 'Emadeddin Baqi on what has come to be known in Iran as the serial killings of political activists and intellectuals. Baqi's analysis of these killings, initially published in the newspaper *Khordad* in fall 1999, is reproduced in his book, a collection of articles, *Trazhedi-ye demokrasi dar Iran* (The tragedy of democracy in Iran) (Tehran: Nashr-e Ney, 1999).

13. For instance see Mas'ud Behnud, "Pasdari-i az in zarif-e naw-pa" (Protecting this delicate newcomer), *'Asr-e Azadegan*, 23 January 2000; "Shahrag-e demokrasi kojast?" (Where is democracy's jugular?), *'Asr-e Azadegan*, 29 January 2000, reproduced in *'Alijenab-e sorkhpush*.

14. Reproduced in Hamidreza Jalaeipour, "Pas az dovvom-e Khordad" (After the second of Khordad) (Tehran: Kavir, 1999).

15. See "Shahrag-e demokrasi kojast?" For more on the debate concerning the attack on Rafsanjani, see below.

16. *Bahar*, 22 June 2000.

17. Signs of change were evident in the 1996 parliamentary elections and of course the 1997 presidential elections. The 1999 city and village council elections

and the 2000 parliamentary elections are further obvious examples. For a discussion and critique of past elections, see Akbar Ganji, "Hashemi Rafsanjani va demokrasi" (Hashemi Rafsanjani and democracy), *Fath*, 7 February 2000, reprinted in *'Alijenab-e sorkhpush*.

18. The first Iranian press law, based on the 1881 French press law, was approved by parliament in February 1908. Stressing general press freedom and prohibition of censorship, this law also abolished the requirement for publishers to obtain permission for the publication of newspapers, and delimited press offenses. Later the requirement for obtaining permission was reinstated and reiterated at several historical junctures, including in the postrevolutionary period.

19. Short periods of relatively free press included a few years during the interlude of the constitutional revolution, the stretch between 1942 and 1953, and a short period following the 1979 revolution.

20. Interview with Behnud in the daily *Iran*, 5 July 2000.

21. This is the official figure given in the publications of the Ministry of Culture and Islamic Guidance, as reported in the special issue of the monthly *Daricheh*, 20 June 2000.

22. Ibid.

23. For an in-depth analysis of the change in policy directions and the competitive dynamics of this era, see Anoushiravan Ehteshami, *After Khomeini: The Iranian Second Republic* (London: Routledge, 1995).

24. *Daricheh*. According to the data given to the Association of Iranian Journalists by the Ministry of Culture and Islamic Guidance, the ministry gave licenses to 571 new publications between May–June 1997 (Khordad 1376) and October–November 1999 (Aban 1378). I am thankful to Nargess Khatoun Barahoui, an Iranian journalist, for digging this out for me.

25. Information about the activities of this association in providing better working conditions for journalists can be found at the association's website, www.aoij.org.

26. In a very interesting analysis in *Gunagun*, 29 June 2000, Hamidreza Jalaeipour argues that there were three circles of intellectuals who were influential in the rise of both the reform movement and the reformist press. The first circle, according to Jalaeipour, was formed around the ideas and personality of 'Abdolkarim Sorush, leading to the publication of journals such as *Kiyan*. The second circle revolved around the Center for Strategic Studies, which was first headed by Seyyed Mohammad Mousavi Khoeiniha, with many members who crisscrossed between dailies such as *Salam* and other periodical publications such as *'Asr-e Ma* and *Rahbord*. Finally, the third circle included close to 2,500 students who were sent to Europe, Australia, and Canada during the presidency of 'Ali Akbar Hashemi Rafsanjani. Some of these, including Jalaeipour himself, became important forces in the push for an independent press. Neglected by Jalaeipour, I think, are some important institutional factors. For instance, an important trend during Hashemi Rafsanjani's presidency, and even before, was the move by many minis-

tries to create their own universities through which the cadres of these particular ministries were trained. Important ministries that pursued this approach included the Ministry of the Interior and the Ministry of Foreign Affairs. The result was the effective shutting out of many of the finest students who studied in Iran's best universities from gaining access to positions in government. While no concrete study has been done on the background of reform journalists, I would not be surprised if a large number had been drawn from this highly talented pool. There are also no reliable figures on the number of people who work as journalists or identify themselves as such. The only concrete figure available is the number of people who belong to the Association of Iranian Journalists, which stood at 1,626 (286 of whom were women) as of fall 2000.

27. The existence of this pool should also give clues about why it is hard to block the reform movement completely, even with such acts as the wholesale closure of the reformist papers. The pool is there searching for ways to express itself. In the words of Hamidreza Jalaeipour, "It was easier to get a license to open a newspaper than a license to open a [political] party, so I opened a newspaper." As reported by Elaine Sciolino, *Persian Mirrors: The Elusive Face of Iran* (New York: Basic Books, 2000), p. 257.

28. For a short history of *Salam* and its mission, see *Khamushi-ye darya* (The silence of the sea), assembled by Mehrdad Farid (Tehran: Ruznameh-ye Salam, 1999).

29. Of course, the idea of a government simultaneously banning the publication of a short public statement critiquing government actions in all newspapers and giving license to the publication of a whole alternative newspaper intent on critiquing government policies is just yet another example of how difficult it is to pigeonhole the Islamic Republic of Iran as one of the more familiar types of regimes usually discussed in the field of political science.

30. According to the statistics offered by the Ministry of Culture and Islamic Guidance, the amount of foreign currency received by *Salam* between 1991 and 1999 was $5,558,148. This is in comparison to over $105 million received by the *Keyhan* conglomerate (with nine publications), over $101 million received by *Ettela'at* (with eight publications), and over $11 million received by *Resalat*. Comparable figures can be found regarding the amount of paper supplied. *Keyhan* and *Ettela'at* received ten times as much as *Salam* while *Resalat* received twice as much. The comparison to *Resalat* is particularly important since that paper had a lower circulation (never above 30,000). These figures were reprinted in *Daricheh*.

31. The circulation of *Salam* never exceeded 50,000. Nevertheless *Salam* was able to create a stable pool of readership, especially among university students.

32. Farid, *Khamushi-ye darya*, p. 10.

33. For a more detailed discussion of this idea, see Farideh Farhi, "Political Islam in Iran," *Brown Journal of World Affairs* 6, no. 1 (winter/spring 1999), pp. 121–34.

34. *Salam*'s most important exposé came in its 1994 pursuit of the so-called missing 123–billion-tumans scandal at the Saderat Bank.

35. Other *Salam* journalists, such as Rajab'ali Mazru'i and Karim Arghandehpur, became founders of the Association of Iranian Journalists.

36. The use of opinion polls by people intent on making the claim that public opinion is on their side should not come as a surprise. In its later years, *Salam* began to rely for its opinion polls on the work of emerging nongovernmental research centers such as *Adineh*, interestingly run by many of the people associated with *Salam*. In more recent years, many of the polls conducted have been done by the National Research Institute for Public Opinion (Mo'aseseh-ye Melli-ye Pazhuhesh-e Afkar-e 'Omumi) affiliated with the Ministry of Culture and Islamic Guidance, a reformist stronghold. No matter the possibility of potential bias, the point is that poll taking and reportage have been made into common practice in the newspapers, now even put to use by the more conservative papers.

37. *Salam*'s facilities were put to use by *Bayan* once the former was shut down. With the closure of *Bayan*, the same printing facilities were put to use by *Aftab-e Yazd* after a short break. The same dynamics operated for *Sobh-e Emruz*'s printing facilities, which were used to print *Bahar* after the closure of the former. Government aid in terms of favorable foreign currency loans as a means to set up printing factories, according to some critics, has been so extensive that it has led to excess capacity. See interview with 'Ezatollah Sahabi in *Daricheh*.

38. In the editorial of its first issue on 29 November 1992, *Hamshahri* explains its mission, among others, as one of informing citizens of the rights they have and responsibilities they carry in their social life in large cities. Identifying itself as a "communication bridge," it offers itself as an arena in which citizens can express their views about "the problems of the environment," explain their views about "the implementation of programs and how they can be improved," and make possible "their multifaceted participation" in large cities such as Tehran.

39. The latest figures offered by the Ministry of Culture and Islamic Guidance put the circulation of *Hamshahri* at close to 300,000 while that of *Keyhan* has dropped to around 60,000. These figures are primarily for the period following the closure of many reformist papers in April 2000, although they hold for the preclosure period as well. During the preclosure period, however, some papers, such as *Jame'eh* (or one of its reincarnations: *Tus, Neshat*, and *'Asr-e Azadegan*) and *Sobh-e Emruz* did hit circulation numbers above 300,000 on some days. For instance, it is said that right after *'Asr-e Azadegan* was closed, along with other papers, the remaining two reformist papers still running hit very high numbers, with *Sobh-e Emruz* reaching a circulation of 700,000 before it was also closed. I have not been able to confirm these figures and this is important to do, given the fact that newspaper circulation has been used as a marker for claiming the popularity of the reform movement and as such the figure itself can be open to political manipulation. In his analysis of the reformist press in *Gunagun,* Jalaeipour men-

tions *Sobh-e Emruz, Jame'eh, Tus,* and *'Asr-Azadegan* as having a circulation of above 200,000 on a daily basis and *Khordad* and *Fath* as having a circulation of above 100,000.

40. A few words about Shamsolva'ezin's vision: I met Shamsolva'ezin and a few other well-known journalists at a conference in Cyprus in the summer after Khatami's election and several months before the launch of *Jame'eh*. He was well into planning the paper and asserted with his usual jubilant confidence that in a few short months after its publication *Jame'eh* would exceed all expectations in terms of circulation, with numbers well into the hundreds of thousands. Needless to say, while everyone there wished him luck, no one expected his predictions about public reception to come true so rapidly.

41. A perfect example of this dynamic can be seen in the numerous exchanges that occurred between reformist writers such as Akbar Ganji and 'Emadeddin Baqi, on the one hand, and Hoseyn Shari'atmadari, *Keyhan*'s editor, on the other. Trying to unravel the way of thinking that made the murder of intellectuals and political activists possible, both Ganji and Baqi pointed to the close relationship between those who ran the prisons for the Intelligence Ministry and sought confessions from political opponents, and those who were on the editorial team of *Keyhan*. Shari'atmadari and *Keyhan*'s editorial team, in general, responded by questioning the "suspicious" political activities and character of the reformist writers. These exchanges usually led to the participation of others—some of whom were members of the families of those murdered or had, themselves, been tortured in prison—in the conversation, leading to further revelations about the connection of *Keyhan*'s editorial team to the Intelligence Ministry. Some of these exchanges are reproduced in Akbar Ganji's *Tarik-khaneh-ye ashbah* (The ghosts' dark house) (Tehran: Tarh-e Naw, 1999); *'Alijenab-e Sorkhpush;* and 'Emadeddin Baqi's *Trazhedi-ye demokrasi dar Iran,* vols. 1 and 2.

42. By this I do not mean the state security secrets but rather news about the way the state and the personalities who are influential in it operate. For examples of this type of writing, see a regular column by Mohammad Quchani called "Faces of the Week," published in *Neshat,* and "Newsmakers" in *'Asr-e Azadegan,* both later reincarnations of *Jame'eh*. In his columns, Quchani not only discussed the political history of some of the main players on the Iranian political scene but also expanded on how they were positioned and were repositioning themselves vis-à-vis each other. Editors were well aware of the fact that these revelatory kinds of writing were attractive to readers. The following editorial in *Neshat* on 7 July 1998, a day after *Salam* had published a headlined article about the fact that the person arrested for the serial murder of intellectuals happened to be the same person who had conceived the bill that was being debated in the parliament about press limitation, clearly shows the point:

> Yesterday, from the point of view of many analysts, *Salam* came to a position for which perhaps the most apt name would be professional success. According to a well-known chief editor, "With yesterday's act, *Salam* took

a professional step ahead of other publications, in particular [those known as the] Dovvom-e Khordad publications." The expression "a professional step ahead" is generally used when several newspapers, in a parallel effort to pursue the news, are faced with the success of one [in breaking the news]. Perhaps it was this same realization that led *Salam*'s editors to increase the circulation of the paper in the newsstands in anticipation, and of course *Salam* subscribers (who had been choosing other papers for a while) once again, admitting that "*Salam* was still something else," went back to their old paper.

43. See note 34 above.

44. As quoted in Daniel Belgrad, *The Culture of Spontaneity: Improvisation and the Arts in Postwar America* (Chicago: University of Chicago Press, 1998), p. 2.

45. Morteza Mardiha, "Maslahat az haqiqat bartar ast," *'Asr-e Azadegan,* 3 February 2000.

46. This is something that even Mohammad Khatami seems to acknowledge. "Let me remind you that I did not come in the name of reform" were his words to reporters in New York. Quoted in Elaine Sciolino, "The Visiting Mullah," *New York Times,* 8 September 2000.

47. For a very interesting discussion of the history of elite conflict and factionalism during and since the constitutional revolution, see Sa'id Barzin's interview with Homa Katouzian in Sa'id Barzin, *Jenahbandi-ye siyasi dar Iran az daheh-ye 1360 ta dovvom-e Khordad 1376* (Political factionalism in Iran from the 1980s to 23 May 1997) (Tehran: Nashr-e Markaz, 1998).

48. Indeed, the players themselves openly complained about the absence of rules. According to 'Ali Nazari, managing editor of *Arzesh,* "Every time the press in Iran is warned by officials, we are told we have crossed a red line, although no one has bothered to tell us where that red line is." *RFE/RL Iran Report* 2, no. 15 (12 April 1999).

49. 'Emadeddin Baqi best puts the importance of risk-taking within the Islamic discourse. In response to the question of what drives writers to push the limits, he responds: "When you see your country unwell, it is your natural obligation to treat it. And when you enter the press, this is a case of life and death. Once you make that decision, you know no fear . . . We don't call it martyrdom, in which [case] you lose your life for God . . . we call it *isar,* which means you sacrifice your power, influence, title, and prosperity in a religious way." As quoted in the *Christian Science Monitor,* 9 November 1999.

50. Astutely aware of the pull-and-push dynamics that marked the print media/public relations, this is what 'Abbas 'Abdi, a member of *Salam*'s editorial board and a leading reformist journalist, has to say about the criticism made of the print media in general, and of Akbar Ganji in particular. Responding to allegations that the press was too radical, revealing too much information, and hence was at least partially responsible for the closures that befell it later, he writes:

> Politics, like other spheres, has a market. In this market people determine the price and people pay the necessary cost on the basis of what satisfies their needs. We cannot easily consider this as extremist. This argument does not suggest that one should follow the people or that people [necessarily] demand every extremist topic or product. In Iran today, there are many other people who speak even more strongly than Ganji and people like him, but are not as well received. Yet the circulation of only one of Ganji's books probably exceeds 150,000. Let us assume that what he has written is extremist; in this case what product can satisfy people's demand, which is [after all] generated from a need? The issue of the high circulation of Ganji's books is not something that can be easily overlooked. Under conditions in which people have economic problems, what could the sale of hundred million tumans of these kinds of books mean? Is this a false need?

'Abbas 'Abdi, introduction to a collection of essays by Akbar Ganji, *Eslahat-e Me'mar-garaneh* (translated by the publisher as Constructive Reformation) (Tehran: Tarh-e Naw, 1379).

51. Here I am not making a claim that this shift will be permanent. But I am arguing that for now, given the perceived irrationality of the structure of Iranian authority, there has been a shift of trust toward a more open public sphere, which is in turn conceived as an institutional mechanism for rationalizing political domination by rendering states accountable to their citizenry. Presumably once political domination becomes "rationalized," the possibility that critical scrutiny of the state will give way to public relations, mass-mediated staged displays, and the manufacture and manipulation of public opinion, as in the case of many long-standing democracies, will arise.

52. Interview with Hashemi Rafsanjani as reported in *Hamshahri* (22 December 1999).

53. Quoted from a political brochure distributed by the Servants of Construction Party titled *Amniyat, Refah, Azadi* (Security, welfare, and freedom).

54. Newspapers on 23 December 1999 were filled with reactions. See, for instance, *Azadi,* which ran an article "Saheb-nazaran vakoneshha-ye motefavet-i darbareh-ye mosahebeh-ye Hashemi Rafsanjani neshan midahand" (Experts show different reactions to Hashemi Rafsanjani's interview). "Saheb-nazaran" can be translated as experts but literally means someone who has an opinion about something.

55. For an in-depth and day-to-day reportage of how the debate on Hashemi Rafsaajani's candidacy progressed, see *Payam-e Emruz,* nos. 36 and 37. The monthly *Payam-e Emruz,* itself, should be considered an important contribution to an array of journalistic analyses available to Iranian readers until it was shut down in March 2001. Its lead articles were always devoted to events of the month, relayed in a language accessible to a body of readers who may not have had the time to keep up with all the news on a daily basis. It reported on politics and

presented a record of the public mood as revealed in the public media, using the straightforward and direct language of political reportage.

56. For an explicit comparison of prerevolutionary and postrevolutionary patriarchal ways as exemplified by the shah and Hashemi Rafsanjani, see 'Abbas 'Abdi, "Enqelab 'aleyh-e tahqir" (The revolution against humiliation), *'Asr-e 'Azadegan,* 2 February 2000.

57. See, for instance, Sadeq Zibakalam, "Hashemi Rafsanjani: eslahtalab ya mohafezehkar" (Hashemi Rafsanjani: Reformist or conservative), *'Asr-e 'Azadegan,* 26 January 2000.

58. Questions about the war shifted the conversation to another era during which Ayatollah Khomeini was alive. This shift was significant insofar as it created the potential for opening the way for a serious and highly volatile discussion of many issues on which all factions, otherwise competing, had a tentative agreement, including the brutal way the Islamic Republic dealt with its opposition before Ayatollah Khomeini died. The closure of many reformist newspapers and journals predictably ended the encroachment of this conversation, at least for the time being.

59. In "Sitasar va Gofr-o-gu" (Politics and dialogue), a very interesting article about the debate over Hashemi Rafsanjani, Bijan Hekmat argues that Ganji's stance as a "searcher for truth" made him behave more like a political party. *Goft-o-gu,* winter 2000. Hekmat's article is intended to be a critique of Ganji's position, as he distinguishes between the role of a public intellectual and that of a politician and posits the former as the "searcher for truth." Hekmat argues that by not making clear why Hashemi's candidacy increased the chances of authoritarian rule in Iran, Ganji actually closed down the space for debate and entered the dangerous arena of mass politics.

60. The notion that some of the people opposed to reform, particularly those in control of the judiciary, simply do not care about public opinion seems to be the conclusion reached by some reformers. This view was reflected in the headline of the reformist paper *Bahar,* which reported the acquittal of the main suspects in the police beatings of the students. On 12 July 2000, the paper carried the word "acquittal" in huge letters accompanied by the picture of the acquitted former head of the regional security forces, Farhad Nazari, wearing a mocking smile.

61. According to Guillermo O'Donnell and Philippe Schmitter, "Democracy is produced by stalemate and dissensus rather than prior unity and consensus." *Transitions from Authoritarian Rule: Tentative Conclusions about Uncertain Democracies* (Baltimore, Md.: John Hopkins University Press, 1986).

62. Adam Przeworski, "Democracy as a Contingent Outcome of Conflicts," in *Constitutionalism and Democracy,* Jon Elster and Rune Stagstad, eds. (Cambridge: Cambridge University Press, 1988); see also Adam Przeworski, *Democracy and the Market: Political and Economic Reforms in Eastern Europe and Latin America* (Cambridge: Cambridge University Press, 1991).

8

Sacral Defense of Secularism

Dissident Political Theology in Iran

Mahmoud Sadri

Continuity between Premodern and Modern Political Theologies of Iran

Although this essay is devoted to the political theology of twentieth-century Iran, I would like to begin by highlighting some of the continuities that this theology shares with traditional Iranian political thought. Iran, as I have argued elsewhere, may be dubbed the cradle of theocracy just as Greece is known as the cradle of democracy.[1] Three instances should suffice to illustrate the precedence in Iranian history for the idea of government by divine approval. First, there is the mythological notion of *farr-e izadi* (divine grace) germane to the sources that the tenth-century poet Ferdawsi used to compose his *Shahnameh* or Book of Kings. Second, the sixteenth-century juxtaposition of the Shi'i utopian belief in the charismatic government of the infallible Imams with the ideology of the righteous stewardship of the Safavid kings, dubbed *zilollah* (the shadow of God), can be considered another manifestation of the same idea.[2] Finally, the concept of clerical guardianship on behalf of the absent Imam as crystallized in the notion of *velayat-e 'ammeh* (general trusteeship) is another case in point. Thus, one could argue that Ayatollah Khomeini's thesis of *velayat-e motlaqeh-ye faqih* (the absolute mandate of the jurisconsult), while being a theological innovation, is not entirely alien to the Iranian political culture. However, the counterforce to this belief, as seen in the burgeoning antiauthoritarian political theology of the last two decades, also draws upon Iran's premodern political philosophy, in the form of the traditionally Shi'i pluralistic and historically rebellious tendencies.[3] With this as background, I will consider three distinct voices from among the innovative discourses of secularism in Iran's postrevolutionary political theology.[4]

ʿAbdolkarim Sorush: The Luther of Islam

ʿAbdolkarim Sorush was born in 1945 into a traditionally learned merchant family. Educated at ʿAlavi high school (which in hindsight has proved to be the intellectual incubator of most of the Islamic revolution's lay elite) and the pharmacology school of the University of Tehran, he emerged at the dawn of the Islamic revolution from his postgraduate studies in England, where he had integrated the theories of Willard Van Orman Quine, Pierre Duhem, Karl Popper, and others into the framework of his vast Islamic learning. Sorush soon came to be known as one of the most prolific and eloquent intellectuals of the nascent Islamic Republic and then as one of the most ebullient and learned critics of clerical rule in Iran.[5]

It is difficult to do justice to Sorush's multifarious project; he is the most significant, the best known, and the most prolific of the three theologians under discussion here.[6] In this essay I will outline his major contributions to three fields, namely sociology of knowledge; philosophical anthropology; and ethics and social criticism.

Sorush's magnum opus, *The Theoretical Contraction and Expansion of Shariʿa*, brings his almost encyclopedic knowledge of jurisprudence, history of ideas, hermeneutics, epistemology, philosophy of science, and sociology of knowledge to bear on such questions "as to what extent we ought to take the edicts deduced by Islamic jurisconsults as literal, and immediate divine commandments?" His argument is that religion, per se, should be separated from religious knowledge. Religion, that is, the essence of religion, is perceived as being beyond human reach, hence eternal and divine, whereas religious knowledge is, by contrast, a sincere and authentic but finite, limited, and fallible form of human knowledge. The clergy who have dealt with similar quandaries in their professional circles do not object to these discussions as such. They are, however, outraged by Sorush's recklessness for exposing the laity to such sensitive subjects. Sorush, in turn, criticizes the practice of protecting humanly formulated knowledge by censoring its wider circulation.[7]

Sorush's political theory starts with a philosophical anthropology concerning human nature. In his rather pessimistic view of human nature, Sorush appears to have been influenced by a modern tradition that starts with Thomas Hobbes and finds expression in the ideas of the framers of the American Constitution.[8] That is, human beings are weak and susceptible to temptation, even predation. As such, they need a vigilant and transparent form of government. However, Sorush softens the pessimistic edge of this view of human nature with verses from the Qur'an and the poems of Rumi and Hafez concerning the fragility of the human condition. Sorush believes that the assumption of the innate goodness of mankind, shared by anarchists, radical Marxists, and Islamic fundamentalists alike, underestimates the staying power of social evil, fosters the false hope that it can be extinguished, and discounts the necessity of a government of checks and balances to rein in the weaknesses of human nature.

Sorush's political philosophy remains close to the heart of the liberal tradition, ever championing the basic values of reason, liberty, freedom, and democracy. The main challenge is not to establish their value but to promote them as "primary values," as independent virtues, and not handmaidens of political maxims and religious dogma. In his essay "Reason and Freedom,"[9] Sorush is at pains to demonstrate that freedom and justice are values in their own right, regardless of their performance as instruments of attaining other ends.

Sorush is one of the boldest social critics of postrevolutionary Iran. As such, he has not minced his words about the questionable office of the clergy *(rawhaniyat)* within the Islamic tradition where they perform no sacraments and have no mediating position in the relationship between man and God. He has also criticized the hegemony of what could be called clerocracy and its encroachment on the autonomy of the academy in Iran. More specifically, he sees contemporary Iran as a society in the grip of massive disenchantment. His own political theology is an expression of this despair that has come about as a result of the official Islam advocated by the government.

In short, Sorush is the intellectual face of a new kind of philosophical revivalism in Iran. Its political face can be seen in the sweeping victory of President Mohammad Khatami in 1997 and 2001 and the election of the new liberal-minded Parliament (Majles) in 2000. But the significance of Sorush's work goes beyond the realpolitik of contemporary Iran. He belongs to a new and sophisticated brand of Islamic reformation that has its origins in the works of the late Mohammad Iqbal. Sorush's views, informed by the Western experiences of modernization and secularization and influenced by the revolutionary and reform movements in the Islamic world, are not only illustrative and instructive from an intellectual point of view, but they are also potentially capable of revolutionizing Muslim theology and mass religiosity.

Mohammad Mojtahed-Shabestari: Harbinger of the New *Kalam*

Born in Tabriz in 1936 into a clerical family, Mohammad Mojtahed-Shabestari[10] was educated as a seminarian in Qom. He stayed in the seminary for seventeen years, achieving the degrees of *ejtehad* and doctor of philosophy. He was invited by Mohammad Beheshti (who was to become one of the main architects of the Islamic revolution of Iran) to take his place as the director of the Islamic Center of Hamburg. Shabestari remained in that position from 1970 to 1979. While in Germany, he immersed himself in German philosophy and Catholic as well as Protestant theology.[11] After the revolution he was briefly elected to the First Consultative Assembly (Majles) following the establishment of the Islamic Republic, but thereafter he avoided politics and turned his attention, instead, to editing journals, teaching, and writing. At present, he holds a position as professor of theology at the University of Tehran.

Shabestari has made a modest contribution to the introduction and application of modern hermeneutics to traditional Shi'i theology and jurisprudence[12] and thus to the proposition of the variability of religious knowledge. However, his most significant contribution seems to be his authoritative commentary on the essentially limited nature of religious knowledge and rules and, therefore, the necessity of complementing it with extrareligious sources. He argues that distinguishing the eternal (values) from the changeable (instances and applications) in religion requires a kind of knowledge that is not itself contained in the rules of jurisprudential adjudication as developed in Islamic law *(feqh)*. He laments the lack of such a body of knowledge in Islamic society: "Today, we are deprived of a systematic legal philosophy, a comprehensive philosophy of ethics, a political philosophy, and a sound science of economics. Is it possible to talk about universal and eternal rules and values when we don't have any definitive or defensible views of such disciplines?"

In the same vein, Shabestari underscores the limited nature of religious knowledge in general, and religious jurisprudence in particular. He argues, "The role of the Qur'an, the tradition *(sonnat)*, and religious jurisprudence *(feqh)* in economic transactions and politics has been one of organizing and orienting, not one of establishing. . . . The science of jurisprudence emerged . . . [in order] to channel the flow of change . . . not to initiate it." He thus concludes, "We are permitted, nay obligated to cast a new glance at the current problems of life and to expose the Qur'an and the tradition to the questions of the modern man."[13]

In Shabestari's view, therefore, what is essential and eternal are the general values of Islam, not the particular forms in which they are realized at any given time (including the time of the Prophet).[14] He writes, "When we talk about *kamal-e din* (the perfection of religion), we do not mean that everything and anything has to be found in religion, and that if we don't find a specific item in religion, then we should call it 'imperfect.' The perfection of religion does not imply that it should be seen as a substitute for science, technology, and human deliberation."[15]

Shabestari goes a step further than any of his clerical colleagues by suggesting that there has been a divine decree for a separation of religious values and secular realities. "God has accepted the world for what it is (in the secular sense of the term). He has decreed that the world just be."[16]

Having established the foundation of his argument concerning the boundaries of religious knowledge, Shabestari then proceeds to explore the link between freedom, democracy, and Islam. Here, Shabestari makes an innovative leap:

> It is high time that we let the people know the extent to which they can rely on religion to solve their worldly problems and expect it to [help them] establish an advanced society.... The need for a democratic government cannot be derived from the meaning of faith or of the religious texts. However, since social realities demand such a form of government, people of faith must forge a relationship with this reality, reconcile themselves with its requirements, and follow a faithful life along its riverbed.[17]

In his latest book, *Naqdi bar qera'at-e rasmi az din* (A critique of the official reading of religion), Shabestari pursues his critique of religious absolutism as hermeneutically naïve and realistically unworkable. He also launches a major defense of the modern concept of human rights, although they have not been articulated in religious sources.[18]

Still, as he told me in an interview in January 2001,[19] his endeavor is one undertaken from within the Islamic tradition, not from without. He hopes to transform the nature of religiosity without destroying its essential contours. This reminds one of the profound and far-reaching accomplishments of the Christian theologians with whose works he is so intimately familiar. He has chosen the path of quiet, learned—and brave—persuasion and argumentation to achieve his goal.

The Political Theology of Mohsen Kadivar: The Two-Edged Sword

Mohsen Kadivar, born in Fasa in central Iran in 1959, left the University of Shiraz after a brief stint as a student of electrical engineering and moved to the holy city of Qom to pursue classical clerical learning.[20] He graduated at the top of his cohort and entered postgraduate studies *(dars-e kharej)* from which he emerged with a "license" to practice *ejtehad,* the highest level of Shi'i learning. His family was politically active; his grandfather was a dissident under Reza Shah, and his father, similarly, was considered a dissident under Mohammad Reza Shah.

Compared with Sorush and Shabestari, Kadivar's views are less well known in the West, but they are by no means less significant. There is a pronounced convergence and complementarity between his ideas and those of Sorush and Shabestari. What is distinct about Kadivar, however, is his sole reliance on Islamic sources of scholarship. Even his use of Farsi sources is minimal. This constitutes, at once, his weakness as well as his strength.[21]

Of the nine books that he has published, four are on political theology. Of these, one is a collection of essays, lectures, and articles, and the other three comprise a trilogy. The first volume of the trilogy, *Nazariyehha-ye dawlat dar feqh-e shi'eh* (The theories of state in Shi'i jurisprudence), encompasses a broad typology of religious opinions on the desired or permissible types of government in Shi'i theology. Every single instance in this typology is either proposed or endorsed by the highest authorities in Shi'i jurisprudence. Kadivar suggests two reasons for the underdevelopment of Shi'i political philosophy: the messianic hope for the imminent return of the Hidden Imam and the stipulation of infallibility for the charismatic leaders (the twelve Imams) in the traditional Shi'i casuistry. He discerns four periods in the history of Shi'i cogitation concerning political matters: (1) the era of the development of the private and individual aspects of *feqh* from the eleventh to the sixteenth centuries; (2) the era of the coexistence of the clerics and kings; (3) the era of the constitutional government along with clerical supervision in the early twentieth century; and (4) the era of the Islamic Republic of Iran, from 1963 to the present. The most important feature of the first volume of Kadivar's trilogy is a typology of the forms of government adumbrated in Shi'i jurisprudential sources. Given the significance of this typology, I will summarize it here.

Theories of state based on immediate divine legitimacy (four theocratic types, in chronological order)

1. Appointed mandate of the jurisconsult in religious matters (Shari'a), along with the monarchic mandate of Muslim potentates in secular matters *(saltanat-e mashru'eh)*

Proponents: Mohammad Baqer Majlesi, Mirza-ye Qomi, Seyyed Kashfi, Sheykh Fazlollah Nuri, Ayatollah 'Abdolkarim Ha'eri Yazdi

2. General appointed mandate of the jurisconsults *(velayat-e entesabi-ye 'ammeh)*

Proponents: Molla Ahmad Naraqi, Sheykh Mohammad Hasan Najafi (Saheb Javaher), Ayatollah Borujerdi, Ayatollah Mohammad Reza Golpayegani, Ayatollah Ruhollah Khomeini (before the revolution)

3. General appointed mandate of the Council of the "Sources of Imitation" *(Velayat-e entesabi-ye 'ammeh-ye shawra-ye marja'-e taqlid)*

Proponents: Ayatollah Javadi Amoli, Ayatollah Beheshti, Ayatollah Taheri-Khorramabadi

4. Absolute appointed mandate of the jurisconsults *(velayat-e entesabi-ye motlaqeh-ye faqihan)*

Proponent: Ayatollah Ruhollah Khomeini (after the revolution)

Theories of state based on divine-popular legitimacy (five democratic types, in chronological order)

1. Constitutional state (with the permission and supervision of jurisprudents) *(Dawlat-e masruteh)*

Proponents: Sheykh Esma'il Mahallati, Ayatollah 'Abdollah Mazandarani, Ayatollah Aqa Bozorg Tehrani, Ayatollah Ahmad Tabataba'i, Ayatollah Kazem Khorasani, Ayatollah Hoseyn Na'ini

2. Popular stewardship along with clerical supervision *(Khelafat-e mardom ba nezarat-e marja'iyat)*

Proponent: Ayatollah Mohammad Baqer Sadr

3. Elective limited mandate of jurisprudents *(Velayat-e entekhabi-ye moqayyadeh-ye faqih)*

Proponents: Ayatollah Motahhari, Ayatollah Hoseyn'ali Montazeri

4. Islamic elective state *(Dawlat-e entekhabi-ye eslami)*

Proponents: Ayatollah Mohammad Baqer Sadr, Ayatollah Mohammad Javad Moghniyeh, Ayatollah Mohammad Mehdi Shams al-Din

5. Collective government by proxy *(Vekalat-e malekan-e shakhsi-ye moshaʿ*
Proponent: Ayatollah Mehdi Ha'eri Yazdi

This typology does not include completely the apolitical views of the grand ayatollahs such as Sheykh Morteza Ansari, Seyyed Jaʿfar Kashef al-Gheta', and Abolqasem Kho'i, who opposed any legitimate or clerically legitimized form of government in the absence of the infallible Imams or on the basis of clerical mandate over mature and sane individuals. Through their negative political theology, they lend support to the purely democratic and objectively secular form of government (the last form enumerated in the above typology) as proposed by Ayatollah Mehdi Ha'eri Yazdi.[22]

The significance of this typology in the context of the contemporary Iranian political discourse cannot be overestimated. The corpus of Shiʿi political theology, which the ruling clerics present as a monolith, an obelisk on which the hieroglyph of the absolute mandate of the jurisconsult, *"velayat-e motlaqeh-ye faqih,"* is etched, turns into a fascinating prism in Kadivar's adroit hands, reflecting no less than nine distinct possible forms of government, all proposed and supported by the most revered religious scholars and texts. Having revealed a menu of authoritative options for Islamic society, Kadivar launches his criticism of the most absolutist thesis.

The second volume of the trilogy is *Hokumat-e velaʾi* (Government by mandate). This 432–page opus, which Kadivar considers the heart of his trilogy and the most scholarly book he has written,[23] comprises a frontal and unabashed attack on the thesis of the *velayat-e motlaqeh-ye faqih* introduced by Ayatollah Khomeini and enshrined in the Constitution of the Islamic Republic of Iran. The work unfolds in two stages. The first lays bare the presuppositions of the concept of *velayat,* which concerns the etymology of the term and its interpretation in mysticism *(erfan),* philosophy *(kalam),* jurisprudence *(feqh),* the Qur'an, and tradition *(sonnat).* In every instance, Kadivar discounts political implications of the term. He traces the first indication of his thesis to the writings of a number of eighteenth- and nineteenth-century jurists, namely Mohaqqeq Karaki, Shahid Thani, and Ahmad Naraqi. Kadivar thus determines the age of the concept as less than two centuries, a mere blinking of an eye compared with the age of Shiʿi jurisprudence.[24] But he reserves his most devastating attacks for the second part of the book, which is devoted to the critical analysis of the proofs and confirmations of the principle of government by divine mandate. Here, Kadivar proceeds in four sections. Tracing the sources of adjudication in Shi'i theology, he sets up and knocks down the arguments for the *velayat-e faqih* adduced from the Qur'an, tradition *(sonnat)*, consensus of the 'ulama *(ijma'a)*, and reason *('aql)*. He then concludes:

> The principle of *velayat-e faqih* is neither intuitively obvious nor rationally necessary. It is neither a requirement of religion *(din)* nor a necessity for denomination *(mazhab)*. It is neither a part of the Shi'i general principles *(osul)* nor a component of the detailed observances *(foru')*. It is, by near consensus of Shi'i 'ulama, nothing more than a jurisprudential minor hypothesis, and its proof is contingent upon reasons adduced from the four categories of the Qur'an, tradition, consensus, and reason.[25]

The third volume of Kadivar's trilogy, *Hokumat-e entesabi* (Government by appointment), deals with the practical consequences, disappointments, and disenchantment brought about by the government based on a divine mandate.

In Kadivar's career, we witness not only the voice of a gifted and brave clergyman but also a tradition of pluralism and debate in Shi'i theology that allows such utterances. Having achieved the status of *ejtehad*, one is allowed, indeed expected, to contest the opinions of colleagues and the received wisdom of one's predecessors. Indeed, as radical as Kadivar's political theology is, due to his status as a *mojtahed* with the right to issue verdicts and edicts, he has not been molested for these crucial writings that constitute the most specific and explicit refutation of the cornerstone of the theocratic element in Iran's Constitution and form of government. Instead, he was arrested, tried, and sentenced to eighteen months' imprisonment because of a sermon in which he railed against the so-called serial murders of Iranian intellectuals and an interview in which he implied that the Islamic Republic could be said to have partially reproduced the absolutist authority relations reminiscent of the monarchic rule.[26] He was thus charged with having implicitly implicated the clerical leadership of Iran in authorizing the murders, and his comparison of the Islamic Republic to the imperial regime of Iran had, it was charged, verged on sedition. Yet in spite of such accusations, Kadivar continued to cite his authority as a *mojtahed* to adjudicate and to inform. He argued, "As a student of religion, who according to the explicit statement of my professors has achieved the right to express jurisprudential opinion, I have announced that terrorism is religiously prohibited."[27]

Even though this essay is limited to a comparison of Sorush, Shabestari,

Table 8.1. Comparative philosophies of three prominent theologians

Theologian	Primary discipline	Dialogue of influences	Primary contribution
Sorush	Philosophy	Islam—critical rationalism (British)	Variable nature of religious knowledge
Shabestari	Theology	Islam—hermeneutics (German)	Limited nature of religious knowledge
Kadivar	Jurisprudence	Islam—casuistry of application	Plural nature of religious knowledge

and Kadivar, I would be remiss if I failed to mention an intriguing related line of reasoning in Iran's postrevolutionary political theology. That is the sophisticated and, one might argue, almost sophistic position of Sa'id Hajjarian and 'Abdollah Nuri, who endorse the letter of the principle of *velayat-e motlaqeh-ye faqih* but argue that "logically" it cannot be an autocratic institution, for in that case it would be indistinguishable from tyranny. They suggest that the principle be upheld in literal terms but given a thoroughly democratic interpretation. Table 8.1 provides a brief comparative outline of the above-mentioned theologies.

Conclusion

The complementarity and convergence of the three political theologies discussed in this chapter are evident in the above table. Whereas Sorush emphasizes the variable nature of religious knowledge and Shabestari underlines its limited nature, Kadivar substantiates the multiple nature of religious theses. Each theologian questions the absolutist and totalitarian theology of the ruling clerical elite in the Islamic Republic, and each utilizes the indigenous sources of scholarship and erudition to oppose the hegemony of "clerocracy" in Iran. Sorush and Shabestari represent the maturing of the dialogue of Iranian-Islamic thought with Western social and political philosophy and theology, while Kadivar represents the coming of age of indigenous Islamic political theology, reclaiming and reinterpreting its pluralistic and democratic elements and relying on the contested nature of the knowledge it produces.

As I pointed out earlier, people like Shabestari and Sorush are the intellectual faces of the massive disenchantment of Iranians with the promises of theocracy, while President Khatami and the new reformist Majles represent its political face. As we enter a new millennium, the intransigence of the clerical establishment against the decisive electoral will of the people, as expressed in the election of Khatami and the reformist Majles, its crackdown against reform-minded newspapers, its jailing of journalists and intellectuals, and its increasingly belligerent and bellicose tone against democracy and reform is radicalizing the reform movement and its theological and political rhetoric. It may have been a portent of the darkening horizons of peaceful political reform when Kadivar in an interview remarked that the attempt by Khatami to compromise with and to rehabilitate the regime of the *velayat-e faqih* might have reached an impasse.[28]

Notes

A version of this essay has appeared in *International Journal of Politics, Culture and Society* 15, no. 2 (winter 2001).

1. At least, this is the way Greek philosophers understood the contrast between the two cultures. See Mahmoud Sadri, "Tahlil-e jameʻeh-shenakhti-ye mafhum-e 'farr-e izadi' dar Shahnameh-ye Ferdawsi" (The sociological implications of the notion of 'farr-e izadi' in Ferdawsi's *Shahnameh*), *Kiyan* 5, no. 22 (fall 1996), pp. 54–9.

2. Said Amir Arjomand, *The Shadow of God and the Hidden Imam* (Chicago: University of Chicago Press, 1984).

3. Hamid Algar, *Religion and State in Iran: 1785–1906: The Role of the ʻUlama in the Qajar Period* (Berkeley: University of California Press, 1969).

4. By secularism I mean the so-called objective secularism of Daniel Bell, Robert Bellah, and Peter Berger, in the sense of the modern differentiation of institutions, not the subjective secularism in the sense of cultural and psychological decimation of religion. I define the term political theology, following Leo Strauss's notion of political philosophy, as a form of theology that concerns religious legitimacy or admissibility of government. Coining this term for the case of Iran, and maybe for other Oriental cultures as well, is useful in view of the fact that secular philosophical thought in the form of political philosophy is not indigenous to most non-Western societies and thus political mediation has befallen theologians and religious thinkers.

5. The American journalist Robin Wright and many others after her have referred to Sorush as the "Luther of Islam," a designation that indicates, above all, the level of attention that Sorush's thought has deservedly found in the West.

6. *Reason, Freedom, and Democracy in Islam: The Essential Writings of ʻAbdolkarim Sorush*, trans. and ed. Mahmoud Sadri and Ahmad Sadri (Oxford and New York: Oxford University Press, 2000). This book includes eleven of his essays, as well as an introduction and interview concerning his intellectual biography.

7. See Sorush's essay, "What the University Expects from the Hawzeh," in Sadri and Sadri, *Reason, Freedom, and Democracy in Islam*, pp. 171–83.

8. Thomas Hobbes, *Leviathan* (New York: Penguin, 1985), part 1; Alexander Hamilton and John Jay, *Federalist Papers,* no. 10 (New York: Modern Library, 1888), p. 51.

9. "Reason and Freedom," in *Reason, Freedom, and Democracy in Islam,* pp. 88–104.

10. Mojtahed-Shabestari identifies himself as a "motekallem," that is, a practitioner of *kalam,* a discipline shared by Judaism, Christianity, and Islam that seeks to determine the "relationship between the consciousness of divine revelation and the consciousness of human philosophy." Shabestari calls for a renewal of *kalam (kalam-e jadid).* Such a discipline would undertake a new assessment of the relationship between the divine and the human. *Iman va azadi* (Faith and freedom) (Tehran: Tarh-e Naw, 1998), p. 64.

11. There is ample evidence in his works that he not only has come into contact with the works of such contemporary Protestant theologians as Paul Tillich and Karl Barth, as well as Catholic thinkers like Tyrell, but that he has also engaged in comparing their contributions and opinions with such Islamic thinkers as Ibn 'Arabi. See, for example, Mojtahed-Shabestari, *Hermenutik, ketab va sonnat: farayand-e tafsir va vahy* (Hermeneutics, the Book, and the Tradition: The process of exegesis and revelation) (Tehran: Tarh-e Naw, 1999), p. 132. He has also published an essay, "Christian Theology," which has been reprinted in *Iman va azadi,* pp. 157–62.

12. For example, he unabashedly posits two of the most revered components of Shi'i theology, that is, *ejtehad* (religious adjudication) and *tafsir* (exegesis), as instances of the discipline of hermeneutics and urges the Islamic seminaries to "welcome hermeneutics with all their power and with utmost enthusiasm." True to this hermeneutic stance, he argues, "It is a delusion to believe that one can empty the mind of all assumptions and suppositions and to access the Qur'an and tradition directly. Nobody can show an example of the success of such an endeavor . . . all commentators have reached conclusions based on their necessary mental limitations." *Iman va azadi,* pp. 8, 31, 135.

13. *Hermenutik, ketab va sonnat,* pp. 47, 49, 56, 54, 62.

14. He writes, for example, "The Qur'an and the tradition (of the Prophet and the Imams) are to inspire us, as [they provide] the eternal source of values; they are not to instruct us as to the specific forms and manners of life." *Hermenutik, ketab va sonnat,* p. 90. It is in this context that Shabestari argues that such issues as *qesas,* that is, the laws pertaining to revenge and restitution, were not legislated by the Qur'an but simply regulated, modified, and rationalized.

15. Ibid., p. 234. It is here that he comes closest to the theology of Harvey Cox, Reinhold Niebuhr, Tillich, and Barth.

16. *Iman va azadi,* p. 67.

17. Ibid., pp. 134, 192.

18. Mojtahed-Shabestari, *Naqdi bar qera'at-e rasmi az din* (A critique of the official reading of religion) (Tehran: Tarh-e Naw, 2000), pp. 18, 22–9, 199–312.

19. Unpublished interview, Tehran, 3 January 2001.

20. In the text of his defense in the Special Court of the Clergy, Kadivar made a statement that symbolizes both the source of his authority and the potential danger that he poses to the theocratic rule in Iran: "To attribute to the *mojtahed* who rejects the veracity of the principle of the trusteeship of the jurist *(velayat-e faqih)*, a basic lack of jurisprudential knack is wielding a two-edged sword, for the accused *mojtahed* has the power to pay back in kind." *Baha-ye azadi: defa'iyat-e Mohsen Kadivar* (The price of freedom: The text of Mohsen Kadivar's defense in the Special Court of the Clergy) (Tehran: Nashr-e Ney, 1999).

21. His most pivotal book, *Hokumat-e vela'i* (Government by mandate), has eleven pages of Arabic references and only three pages of Farsi references. Infrequent references to Western sources (as in, for example, his book *Nazariyehha-ye hokumat dar feqh-e shi'eh* [Theories of government in the Shi'i jurisprudence]) tend to be to translations. Kadivar's lack of contact with the West may explain why he is more conservative than Sorush and Shabestari with regard to social issues, even though he is in complete agreement with them on political matters.

22. Kadivar elaborates on this view in the second book in his trilogy, under the rubric of "the principle of no mandate" *(asl-e 'adam-e velayat)*. See *Hokumat-e vela'i* (Government by mandate) (Tehran: Nashr-e Ney, 1999), chaps. 7 and 8.

23. *Baha-ye azadi*, p. 97.

24. Those in favor of this concept include Seyyed Mohammad Hasan Najafi, Seyyed Mohammad Hoseyn Borujerdi, Mohammad Reza Golpayegani, and Ayatollah Ruhollah Khomeini. The opposing camp is equally replete with religious authorities, such as the following grand ayatollahs: Sheykh Morteza Ansari, the author of one of the most revered advanced texts of Shi'i jurisprudence, Akhund Molla Mohammad Kazem Khorasani, Seyyed Mohsen Hakim, Seyyed Ahmad Khonsari, and Seyyed Abolqasem Kho'i.

25. *Hokumat-e vela'i*, p. 237. Kadivar reiterates the same statement in a variety of other arguments in this book (see, for example, pp. 81, 98, 107, 232, 334). From among those who recognized any kind of trusteeship for jurists, the verdict of the obvious majority of the experts limited such a mandate only to the cases of death *(vali-ye dam, vali-ye ers)* or when a client is a minor or an imebecile *(vali-ye seghar, vali-ye majnun)* (p. 74).

26. The sermon, "The Religious Prohibition of Terrorism," was delivered in the Hoseynabad Mosque of Esfahan in December 1998, and the interview was granted to the reformist newspaper *Khordad* in January 1999. The charges against Kadivar as specified in the court verdict against him included propagandizing against the Islamic Republic of Iran and spreading falsehoods and disturbing the public opinion. See *Baha-ye azadi*, p. 121.

27. Ibid., p. 129.

28. Interview with Christiane Hoffman, *Frankfurter Allgemeine* (2 August 2000).

9

Women's Rights and Clerical Discourses

The Legacy of 'Allameh Tabataba'i

Ziba Mir-Hosseini

The debate over women's rights has been one of the most contentious in twentieth-century Iran, its roots entangled with anticolonial and nationalist discourses. At the start of the century, positions and dividing lines were more or less clear-cut. Those who raised the issue were identified with secular discourses and modernism, and those who avoided it adhered to religious discourses and traditionalism. The 1978–79 revolution, which led to the convergence of political and religious power, also changed the context and dynamics of the debate.[1] Once in power, the clerical establishment could no longer evade the issue of gender inequalities as it had done before. The establishment now had to deal with on-the-ground realities, including women's presence in virtually every field of activity in society and their increasing demand for equal rights. By the late 1980s, prominent ayatollahs in the Qom seminaries—the bastion of traditionalism—were already addressing these issues in their scholarship. In March 1992, the Propagation Office of the Qom Seminaries (Daftar-e tablighat-e hawzeh-ye 'elmiyyeh-ye Qom) launched a women's journal, *Payam-e Zan* (Women's message). Run by young male clerics, it contains the latest clerical thinking on the notion of equal rights for women.[2]

In this chapter, I examine the ways in which the notion of equal rights for women has been conceptualized and debated in *Payam-e Zan*, by discussing and contextualizing an article titled "Women in *al-Mizan*," featured in the magazine in November 1995 (issue 44). The article, commemorating the fourteenth anniversary of 'Allameh Tabataba'i's death, discusses his views on women and their rights in Islam. The author, Ahmad Heydari, is a young cleric who contributes to *Payam-e Zan* on themes of sacred history and religious legends.

This article is important for two reasons. First, 'Allameh Tabataba'i was the first and the most prominent twentieth-century cleric in Iran to address women's rights from the perspective of Islamic philosophy. His views on the "naturalness" of Shari'a laws and their compatibility with human nature shaped the prerevolutionary religious discourse on gender rights and provided a new philosophical justification for the unequal construction of gender rights in Islamic law. After the revolution, Tabataba'i's views came to form the core logic of the Islamic Republic's early discourse on women, reproduced in myriad oral and written texts. His views continue to be invoked by all who attempt to defend, justify, or explain away the gender biases of Shari'a laws. Second, an examination of "Women in al-Mizan" not only reveals how 'Allameh's views on women's rights in Islam are represented and reconstructed in mid-1990s Iran but also betrays a hidden disagreement among the clerics contributing to the journal. It was published immediately after three extended debates I conducted with the editors of the journal between 7 September and 16 November 1995, on the subject of the construction of gender rights in Islamic law. During these sessions, edited transcripts of which were to be published in the journal in the first half of 1996, the question of the "naturalness" of Islamic laws was a major topic of contention between us. The timing of the publication of an article on 'Allameh's views, I believe, was not unconnected to the issues raised in these sessions. In order to get a sense of the background, some preliminary notes on 'Allameh Tabataba'i's original text on gender rights, and on *Payam-e Zan*'s own gender discourse and place within the Qom seminaries, may be useful.

'Allameh Tabataba'i and Equal Rights for Women

'Allameh Seyyed Mohammad Hoseyn Tabataba'i, who died in November 1981 at the age of 78, was the most renowned Shi'i philosopher of the twentieth century. Despite his command of *feqh* (Islamic jurisprudence), which could have earned him great prestige and authority in the seminaries, he chose not to pursue it but to devote his scholarship instead to philosophy and exegesis, in which he excelled, and became 'Allameh, the highest title reserved for nonjurist scholars.[3] He was a great teacher and mentor, recognized not only in both Shi'i and Sunni religious circles but also among academics both inside and outside Iran. In the late 1950s he began a lifelong dialogue with Henri Corbin, the French Orientalist; and in 1963 he was asked to write the volume on Shi'ism for a series intended to present Oriental religions through their authentic representatives.[4]

Tabataba'i's views on gender are to be found in his monumental, twenty-volume Qur'anic commentary, *al-Mizan fi tafsir al-Qur'an* (The balance in the exegesis of the Qur'an). His guiding principle was that "certain parts of the Qur'an are defined by certain other parts"; that is, he used the Qur'an as a balance (*mizan,* literally meaning scales) to unravel its inner meaning and the relation between various verses.[5] Known commonly as *al-Mizan,* some regard it as "the greatest achievement in the history of Koranic commentaries."[6] He wrote the work in Arabic between 1954 and 1972; it was later translated into Persian and English. A small book, *Polygamy and the Position of Women,* published during his lifetime, contains the gist of Tabataba'i's philosophical argument on gender rights in Islam.

Throughout his life, Tabataba'i kept away from politics, both in the seminaries and outside; in the massive opus he left behind he is concerned solely with intellectual and philosophical issues and questions. Yet he came to contribute to the founding political and gender discourses of the Islamic Republic. This was managed by his students, who developed and spelled out the ideological dimension of his writing.[7] Some of his students assumed high office when the Islamic Republic was established; most distinguished of them was Morteza Motahhari, a close ally of Ayatollah Khomeini. During Khomeini's exile in Najaf (1964–78), Motahhari became his sole representative in Iran, and after the victory of the revolution in February 1979, he became a member of the Revolutionary Council, though his role in shaping the future of the Islamic Republic was abruptly terminated by his assassination in May that year.

Motahhari used and elaborated Tabataba'i's philosophical arguments when debating gender rights with secular proponents of women's rights. His celebrated text, *Nezam-e hoquq-e zan dar Eslam* (The rights of women in Islam),[8] has its origin in thirty-three articles published in 1966 in *Zan-e Ruz* (Today's woman), the popular women's magazine of the Pahlavi era. The magazine was then supporting a campaign that eventually led to the enactment of the Family Protection Law in 1967, giving women and men more or less equal access in matters of divorce and child custody. Motahhari's articles were a response to those written by Ebrahim Mahdavi-Zanjani, a secular judge who argued for women's equal rights in law and sought radical reform of the Civil Code, which reflected dominant opinions within Shi'i *feqh* on marriage and divorce. Mahdavi's sudden fatal heart attack ended the debate after six weeks, but Motahhari's articles, which had found an eager audience, continued, and in 1974, they were published as a book.[9]

Payam-e Zan and Its Gender Discourse

Motahhari dismissed gender equality as a Western concept with no place in Islam; instead, he put forward the notion of complementarity in gender rights and duties, both in marriage and in society. This was the notion that Seyyed Zia Mortazavi, the young cleric who had been editor of *Payam-e Zan* since its launch in 1992, supported and aimed to promote. A student of Ayatollah Yusef Sane'i, a senior cleric well known for his progressive views on women, Mortazavi had to tread a sensitive path, avoiding offense to prevailing sensibilities in the Qom seminaries, where, until the revolution, discussion of women's rights was frowned upon. For example, in 1970 Motahhari was reprimanded by his seminary colleagues for publishing his first book, *Mas'aleh-ye hejab* (The question of hejab), which indirectly raised the issue of women's presence in society. An eminent cleric wrote his objections on the margins of his own copy and returned it to Motahhari, who wrote a long response. The objections and Motahhari's response, published as a book after the revolution, make fascinating reading—and indicate the distance that seminary debates on women's rights have covered since then.[10]

Today, young clerics like Mortazavi are keen to understand the logic of feminist critiques of Islamic law, though they do not accept their legitimacy and deal with them as *shobheh-shenasi* (doubt-ology).[11] It was in this spirit that, in September 1995, the editorial board of *Payam-e Zan* welcomed a debate on women's rights in Islam. It soon became evident that their gender perspective was a modified version of Motahhari's reworking of 'Allameh Tabataba'i's theory of the "naturalness" *(fetri budan)* of Shari'a laws. I centered my critique on the contradictions in and the anachronism of "nature theory," contending that what 'Allameh Tabataba'i and Motahhari took as a "law of nature" was in fact cultural. I said that their arguments were formulated as a response to the previous regime's secularization of family laws and policies, when the Shari'a was under threat. Didn't the editorial board think that, seventeen years after the establishment of the Islamic Republic, with the Shari'a in force, one could approach these arguments critically? If not, how could the Shari'a, with its patriarchal legal logic, improve the lot of women?

This first discussion turned into a debate, which the editor suggested we should continue on the basis of greater preparation. I was asked to provide them with my questions in advance of the next meeting, which I did, but I also posed new questions as our debate progressed. Issue 44 of *Payam-e Zan*, which appeared in early November 1995, before our final session, carried an editorial titled "Women's Issues, Seen from Our Angle," which was described by the editor as the first of a series in which he intended to clarify the magazine's position. The same issue also published the first of the two installments of the article "Women in *al-Mizan*," covering the philosophical basis and rationale of the gender discourse that the editor of *Payam-e Zan* was now trying to modify. The article is prefaced by an editorial introductory note informing the reader that 'Allameh's views are to be discussed in three parts, with the headings (1) Women in Human and Spiritual Dimensions, (2) Social Laws and Rights, and (3) Familial Laws and Rights; and that the last and most extended part would appear in the subsequent one or two issues.

In what follows, I will translate—and contextualize with my own commentary—the first installment of "Women in *al-Mizan*," which deals with women's spirituality and social rights. It is written in a style, common in *Hawzeh* scholarship, known as *hashiyeh-nevisi* (lit. marginal commentary), when a writer airs his own views in the process of introducing the text of an established authority. He might support and elaborate the arguments of the text, or he might challenge or refute them. Ahmad Heydari, author of "Women in *al-Mizan*," does the former. In translating his article, I try not only to retain his style but also to separate his text from that of 'Allameh. I keep his convention of presenting 'Allameh's text in quotation marks.

Reading and Reconstructing "Women in *al-Mizan*"

In his own introduction, Heydari declares his objectives in publishing 'Allameh's views on women. His motive, he tells us, is politico-religious: he writes to defend Islam and its laws on women and to offset the unfair attacks and "poisonous propaganda" that Islam faces because of these very laws. He explains:

> At the present time, especially after the collapse of the Eastern Bloc and the obstreperous school of communism, one can witness a revival of and return to religion. Disillusioned by kaleidoscopic human schools, many people are finding religion to be the only stable foundation, and once again religious inclinations have gained momentum. Among these, Islam has had a faster rhythm to the extent that the currents of Islamism have been causing tension in Christian America and Europe, and these colonialist regimes have become alarmed and forced to find a solution to combat [Islam]. The

"headscarf war" in France is an example of this hostile struggle. The revival of the fortunes of Islam in Europe and America in the past decade is due to the Islamic revolution.

After the revolution, many turned their attention to Iran and wanted to find out about this religion that, contrary to world propaganda, which defines "religion as the opiate of the masses," has become the source of such a revolution. Realizing that Islam is the source of the revolution and a bulwark against their domination, the enemies of the revolution started their propaganda against Islam. But with God's will their propaganda has produced the opposite effect, as it motivated many to learn more about Islam and its ideas, which they found to echo the voice of their conscience.

Interestingly, in their propaganda, from the very beginning, the enemies of Islam and the revolution put their finger on discrimination between men and women in Islam. They brought up some of the [Islamic] rules on women, such as the ban on becoming a judge or a ruler, and their inheriting half [the share of men], and declared them unjust and discriminatory. But in spite of all this negative propaganda, in Europe and America women were more attracted to Islam than men. This, on its own, is strong evidence of the infallibility and naturalness of these laws, and proof of the claim that Islam is a natural religion. (p. 29)

It is here that 'Allameh Tabataba'i's Qur'anic commentary serves its purpose: that is, "the naturalness of Islam" and "the compatibility of its rules *(ahkam)* with human nature," as developed in *al-Mizan*, provide clerics like Heydari with their prime and most potent argument in defense of the gender inequality in Shari'a laws. To add an element of political correctness to 'Allameh and his Qur'anic commentary, Heydari quotes Motahhari, praising 'Allameh and referring to his work as "one of the best commentaries that have been written in both Shi'i and Sunni worlds since the advent of Islam."

In order to guide the reader through 'Allameh's text, Heydari then outlines its primary propositions:

1. The rules of Islam *(ahkam-e Eslam)* are enacted on the basis of nature and the laws of creation, and ultimate benefits are inherent in all its rules. Each rule corresponds to the exact need, capacity, aptitude, and condition of its subject; and this is a solid, serene, and indestructible foundation. This noble principle has been taken into account in all issues that relate to women, and those rules are legis-

lated according to this solid foundation.

2. The criteria for evaluating and judging rules are sound reason, together with pure and uncorrupted nature, not hollow emotions stemming from one's surroundings, social customs, time, and space. If a group, a people, people of a certain time and place, under the influence of their hollow emotions and social customs and practices, do not favor a certain rule, and see it as unjust, this cannot be taken as proof that the rule itself is unjust or condemned. A rule is unjust and condemned when it is rejected by sound reason and pure nature.

3. Islam is not the same as the practice and action of Muslims. Unfortunately, from the very beginning, the management of the Islamic community came into the hands of those who were unworthy and incapable and could not educate Muslims according to Islamic rules or fully enforce the implementation of Islamic rules, and thus pre-Islamic thought and conduct persisted among Muslims. Therefore one cannot attribute the incorrectness that exists in Muslim societies to Islam. (p. 30)

These three propositions not only provide a philosophical rationale for gender inequality but, further, silence and eliminate any objection, in the name of "sound reason" and "pure and uncorrupted nature." Heydari dismisses social practice and custom as irrelevant, and his failure to praise the achievements of the Islamic Republic in the area of women's rights is an implicit rejection of postrevolutionary developments.

In these three propositions, Heydari grafts his own argument onto those of 'Allameh. He proceeds to divide women's rights into three distinct realms: the spiritual, the social, and the familial—as alluded to in *Payam-e Zan*'s introductory note to the article. Definitions and constructions of equality and women's rights differ in each of these realms. In the first realm, equality is defined as the supreme Islamic principle; men and women are treated in the same way according to the laws of nature and creation. In the other two realms, equality becomes a "corrupted and Western" concept and anti-Islamic; it is thus rejected at the behest of the Qur'an. Such a contradictory position is sustained and argued on Islamic grounds, through an interplay of narrative and rhetorical devices that both Heydari and 'Allameh employ.

Part 1, "Women in Human and Spiritual Dimensions," is divided into four sections, each advocating absolute equality between the sexes. The first section, under the heading "Women and Men Are of the Same Rank and Kind," begins with an account of the status of women in the pre-

Islamic era. Here Heydari argues that, in the majority of pre-Islamic societies, both primitive and civilized, women were not considered to be human beings, but animals, created for men's pleasure and benefit. He chooses three short passages from volumes 2 and 4 of *al-Mizan,* juxtaposed and linked by three short sentences to show how badly women were treated and how much Islam improved their lot. He thus writes:

> For a better appreciation of women's status in Islam, at the outset *al-Mizan* gives accounts of women's status among various peoples.
>
> "Among peoples and primitive tribes such as those inhabiting Africa, Australia, the Pacific Islands and [pre-Columbus] America, and others, women's life in relation to that of men was like the life of domestic animals. Men viewed women as they viewed their own domestic animals.... They [men] would say that the survival, existence, and life of women depended on that of men, and that just like animals, women had no independence and no rights in life; an unmarried woman was under the authority and control of her father, and after marriage she was under the authority of her husband—the authority, in each case, being unconditional and unfettered.... In India, it was believed that a woman followed her husband and was like a part of his body. Due to such a belief, after her husband's death a woman was burned as part of his body, and if she was not, she suffered utmost humiliation and indignity.[12]
>
> "Among nations such as India and China, women were neither human nor animal, but midway between the two. Chaldeans and Assyrians also considered a woman to be dependent on her husband and bereft of independence. According to the laws of Hammurabi, women had freedom neither of will nor of action.
>
> "In ancient Rome, all members of the household had to worship its head and guardian, and women were not considered part of society, thus their complaints were not heard and their transactions were not valid.[13]
>
> "In ancient Greece, women were considered to be unclean and raised by the devil. The Romans and some Greeks believed that women did not have a human soul whereas men did. Even in the year 586 in the Christian calendar, in France a congress was held to discuss whether women were human or not, and after long discussions the conclusion was reached that, yes, women were also human, although not independent like men but human with the purpose of serving men. In England, too, up until a hundred years ago, women

were not considered part of the social organization. Arab treatment of women was a mixture of the above."[14] (pp. 30–1)

The picture painted here is horrendous, unjust, inhuman, exaggerated, and selective. It is a rhetorical style, which works well in oral argument, and is employed by all clerics in their sermons on women's rights. Likewise, every Shari'a-based text that argues for inequality begins with a similar account. Why? Clearly, to divert attention from the actual situation, to persuade the reader or listener, if she is a woman, to appreciate what she has, reminding her how bad things once were; thus implying that instead of complaining, she should be grateful for what Islam has done for her. If the reader or listener is a man, it gives him a sense of power and control, as well as generosity and pride that, as a Muslim, he does treat women as human beings.

To complete the desired effect and reinforce the message, Heydari makes four observations, taken from another passage from *al-Mizan* and prefaced by his own linking sentence:

As for the beliefs and practices of these societies in relation to women, a few points should be added:

1. Before Islam, humans had two kinds of views on women: one considered women to be at the level of dumb animals, and the second considered them to be human but with a weak and inferior humanity; humans whose freedom would endanger men, [regarded as] the perfect humans. For this reason, women needed to remain under the domination and control of men.

2. With regard to women's social condition, there also existed two perspectives. Some considered women not to be a part of human society but to be necessary for men's comfort, like the shelter that every man needs and cannot do without. Others considered women as slaves who had to follow the society that enslaved them, required their labor, and at the same time protected them from being hurt and harmed.

3. Women's deprivation in these societies was multifaceted; women were denied all the rights that they could have had, apart from those that were in the interest of men, who saw themselves as their guardians and keepers.

4. Men's treatment of women was based on the domination of the weak by the powerful, that is, men used women for their own purposes and exploited them to the full. This was the practice of uncivi-

lized peoples, but civilized peoples also believed women to be defective humans who were incapable of running their own affairs independently and dangerous beings who were a threat to humanity.[15] (p. 31)

These four observations—presented in 'Allameh's words—are speculations and gross distortions and have been invalidated and dealt with in early feminist literature. Heydari unintentionally admits that women's low status and predicament have an ideological and material basis. Sometimes women were dehumanized and denied a soul, sometimes they were considered dangerous, or weak and incapable of running their own affairs. However, he tells us, the end result was the same: they needed to be controlled and dominated by men. What made this domination possible was women's physical weakness and its exploitation by men and society, which needed women's productive and reproductive faculties. What changed the situation was Islam. He writes:

> It was at such a time that the Qur'an showed women to be of the same kind and on a par with men. In proving women's humanity and their equality with men in the human dimension, *al-Mizan* argues as follows: "Observation and experience have shown that men and women are different individuals of the same kind and of the same essence, called humanity, since all human attributes found in the class of men are also found in the class of women, without any difference. Surely the manifestation of [human] attributes in one kind is the proof of fulfillment of that kind. Therefore, the class of women is also human. Yes! These two classes differ in the degree and extent of their possession of some of these common attributes—not specific ones, such as pregnancy, etc.—but the mere difference of degree in some human attributes does not justify saying that the inferior class [women] is no longer human."[16] (p. 31)

This passage ends the first section of this part of the article. In the remaining sections, Heydari relies more on 'Allameh's actual Qur'anic commentary than on his own assertions, and he organizes the material into three topics: "The Creation of Woman," "Was Eve the Means for Adam's Deception?" and "Equal to Men in Spiritual Dimensions." The subtext of Heydari's discussion of the first two is a theological refutation of the Old Testament account of creation, which according to him is the root of the worldview underlying women's protest against religion in the West. That is, women in the West have a reason to protest, since they are not treated as equal in their account of creation, whereas women in Islam are treated as equals in creation.

> The creation of women is one of those issues that have been brought up from ancient times. According to the Old Testament, God separated one of Adam's ribs and created Eve, the first woman, thus the existence of woman [from the very beginning] was as an extra and a dependent. With regard to the opening verse of the Qur'anic chapter on women (Surah Nisa'), "Oh people! Be careful of (your duty to) your Lord, Who created you from a single being and created its mate of the same (kind)," *al-Mizan* says:
>
> "The manifest meaning of the verse is that Adam's mate was of his kind and was human like him. Thus when some commentaries suggest that Adam's mate was made out of his body, it is incorrect, even though there are some hadiths in which it is said that Eve was made of Adam's rib. But the verse itself is not referred to and there is nothing in it to support [those hadiths]."[17] (pp. 31–2)

Heydari cites another passage from *al-Mizan* in which 'Allameh refutes all the hadiths that state that Eve was created of Adam's rib, as a variation of the Old Testament version. In his refutation, 'Allameh invokes a hadith by Imam Baqer (fifth Shi'i Imam) in which the Imam denies that Eve was created from Adam's rib, instead citing the Prophet, who said that Eve was made of the remainder of the clay out of which Adam was made. 'Allameh also refutes the Old Testament account of the expulsion of Adam and Eve from Paradise, in which the bulk of the blame is put on Eve. Citing a hadith from Imam Reza, 'Allameh holds them equally responsible in committing the Original Sin.

This ends Heydari's discussion of the second topic, and he turns his attention to the section in *al-Mizan* that argues that men and women are equal in the spiritual realm and that differences between them are confined to earthly ones. He starts with 'Allameh's commentary on verse 34 of the Surah Nisa', which 'Allameh interprets with the aid of another. This much-debated verse is commonly understood and frequently invoked as a clear support for men's control over women in Islam. Heydari quotes the following passage from *al-Mizan*:

> "From the concluding part of verse 13 of the Qur'anic chapter 'Hujurat,' 'The most honored of you in the sight of God is (he who is) the most righteous of you,' it is evident that the verse 'Men are the maintainers of women because God has made some excel others'

refers to ways in which worldly matters, that is, earning a livelihood, are best accomplished and managed. It does not signify the real virtue and superiority, which come from closeness to God, because in the eyes of Islam physical and material privileges have use only in material life; they are of no consequence unless they become a means for attaining a place in the other world. The criterion for real superiority is piety (*taqva*); if it is in men, [then] men are superior, and if it is in women, [then] women are superior."[18] (p. 33)

As further evidence, Heydari refers to 'Allameh's commentary on verse 124 of Surah Nisa': "And whoever does good deeds whether male or female and has faith—they shall enter Heaven, and not the least injustice will be done to them." Here 'Allameh states that, unlike in the past and in other religions, in Islam there is no difference between men and women, they are equal in the eyes of God and subject to the same rewards and punishments in the other world.

Heydari concludes part 1 of his article by drawing the reader's attention to 'Allameh's observation that in four Qur'anic verses the term "man" (*rajul*) is used in a gender-free sense, referring to a pious and wise person, be it man or woman, who has attained human perfection.[19] Likewise, in two other verses, *rajul* denotes a person who has taken on an evil dimension, regardless of being male or female.[20]

Unlike part 1, which focuses on parity and the spiritual and eternal worlds, part 2, on the theme of social rights and rules, deals with differences and the ephemeral world. Earlier, Heydari invoked Qur'anic verses together with 'Allameh's commentary on them to argue that, despite their natural and physical differences, men and women are created from the same substance, share the same humanity, are held equal in the eyes of God, and are subject to the same spiritual rules in this and the next world. Here, however, he invokes the same authorities to argue the opposite. He does this by shifting the paradigm and changing definitions and concepts, which enables him to bypass—and in a way to negate—what was argued for and established on a Qur'anic basis. The paradigm shift occurs abruptly and is achieved with a single linking sentence, a long one without much punctuation. In this sentence Heydari first restates the equality principle, then qualifies it with the phrase "and yet." He writes:

> Given what was said in the previous part, it became evident that women, from the perspective of *al-Mizan*, are human beings who can attain all the stages of perfection on the same footing as men. In

the human and spiritual dimensions, there is no difference between men and women, and as to rewards and punishments, they are subject to the same system, *and yet* men and women each have specific rights and duties in accordance with their nature and their special conditions. (p. 33, emphasis and punctuation added)

There then follow three sections in which Heydari adjusts the definitions so far used. All three are short assertions and contain no reasoning. The first section is titled "The Difference between *Haqq* (Right) and *Hokm* (Rule)."[21]

A distinction has been made between *haqq* and *hokm*; *haqq* has been defined as a kind of dominion over persons or things, which entails certain effects and obligations. For example, the right of God over the universe, whose effects are the obligation of gratitude and worship; and the right of humans over each other, such as the right of authority of the Imam or father over a person, or the right of ownership over one's possessions which enables one to sell or transfer them.

Some rights, such as guardianship or marital rights, are not transferable, whereas others, such as ownership rights, are.

In contrast to rights, there are rules, [these being] injunctions that entail advisability, incumbency, and choice. For example, a command is an injunction that entails obligation and a prohibition is its opposite.

Some also define rights as what can be attained, and rules as duties and obligations. (pp. 33–4)

The second section, "The Source of Rights and Rules," is even shorter. Here, Heydari writes:

As stated in the introduction to this discussion, the source of rights and duties in Islam is natural and intrinsic needs. In accordance with men and women's physical and psychological conditions, God has instituted duties for each according to their natural and intrinsic needs. Therefore, since men and women differ in their nature and constitution, their rights and duties must also differ.

The third section, "Men's Intrinsic Privileges," is longer and contains the core of Heydari's argument, based on his reading of *al-Mizan*. Building on the premises of the two previous sections, this core argument consists of three elements. The first, stating that men are superior to women, derives legitimacy from the two Qur'anic verses that form the main evidence for those who argue that the Qur'an privileges, in clear terms, men over women. Like others, Heydari neither quotes these verses in their entirety nor mentions the context in which they were revealed. The second element holds that men and women are created to fulfill certain preordained natural and social tasks and that social life is possible and sustainable only by adhering to the divine and natural division of labor. The third element once again invokes the two Qur'anic verses to close the door on any change in gender roles in this world and to argue that what matters is the next world. He writes:

> The Qur'an refers to man's physical superiority and his dominion over woman, when it says:
>
> 'And they [women] have rights similar to those against them [men] according to what is equitable; but men have a degree (of advantage) over them' (Surah Baqara, v. 228).
>
> 'Men are maintainers of women because God has made some of them excel others' (Surah Nisa', v. 34).
>
> As is [well known], men's superiority is due to the fact that they have more reason. In addition, men enjoy greater power, stamina, strength, and aggression to run society and conduct war and difficult tasks.
>
> Of course, whereas men have a greater spirit of reason, power and strength for defense, war, protecting property and tolerance of life's hardships, without which social life could not exist, and women by nature cannot manifest these characteristics, women have other qualities that society also needs. For instance, women are superior to men in delicate feelings and tender emotions, and society does not take hold without these, because those important matters relating to fondness, love, peace of heart, pregnancy, caring and rearing of children, and so on are to do with emotions and feelings. Given the aggression and toughness of men, without women's delicacy and softness human life could not continue, and, in sum, the fact that men are equipped with the power of reason and defense and women are equipped with emotions and feeling is what balances the scales of life in society.
>
> On the basis of the above, it is clear that men's privilege in some faculties over women, and vice versa, is not a spiritual privilege to be desired. The imperative of nature is that, in order to assume different tasks, the faculties and abilities are divided differently and God has

created each class to carry out certain duties. What is real privilege, and worth desiring, is what brings closeness to God, and that is possible only by correct conduct of the assigned duties, and for this reason the Qur'an has forbidden [us] to desire these physical and unreal privileges:

'And do not covet that by which God has made some of you excel others' (Surah Nisa', v. 32).

"From the appearance of the verse it is understood that it wants to forbid certain desires, that is, the desire for privilege that is fixed among people. These privileges arise from the difference between classes of people. Some are of the class of men and for this reason they have certain privileges, and some are of the class of women and they have other privileges, due to the criterion of womanhood."[22]

Heydari then adds in his words, "Each man or woman who employs his/her faculties and capacities better, and carries out his/her specific duty, is closer to God's throne, [thus] what is worth desiring is that one fulfills one's duty well and does not wish to be in the place of others" (pp. 34–35).

Having in this section presented the framework underlying *al-Mizan*'s arguments on gender, in the remainder of part 2 Heydari offers a defense of Shari'a laws. He does this in four sections, whose headings and contents reflect postrevolutionary debates and divisions among the clerics over women's participation in society.[23] Unlike the earlier sections, Heydari here reproduces long extracts from *al-Mizan,* linking them with brief sentences of his own. His concern is to present a case for "difference." He argues how and why "difference in rights and duties" is not in contradiction with divine justice but is in fact a manifestation of it; in short, difference does not negate equality but creates it. The arguments are repetitive, at times flawed, frequently qualified, and difficult to sustain if one accepts Heydari's—or 'Allameh's—own premises and does not take issue with their primary assertions: that men are superior to women; that gender roles must be fixed, otherwise, social order collapses; and that desire for change is forbidden.

The first section is titled "Specific Rules and Their Bases," a euphemism for the gender biases in Shari'a laws. It consists of two long quotations from *al-Mizan,* introduced by two sentences from Heydari, who interestingly refers to differences in rights only in passing and ignores current debates about them. He writes:

The general principle is that men and women share all ritual rules (*ahkam-e 'ebadi*) and social rights, except in instances where the natures of men and woman demand a difference. Islam's view is not that rights and duties are equal in all respects, but that rights and duties are proportionate to nature, capabilities, and merits. *Al-Mizan* defines the basis of specific rules as follows:

"The basis on which Islam has legislated the named laws (banning women from the judiciary, government, jihad, and so on) is nature and creation. What nature demands is that rights and duties, namely, that which is earned and that which is granted among human beings, must be equal; but this equality in rights does not entail that all social positions in society belong to all its members; for instance, how is it possible for a child or a madman to undertake affairs that demand strong and wise men? Therefore, what social justice demands, and what demonstrates the meaning of equality, is that each person in society obtains the rights he or she deserves, and each person progresses according to his or her capacity, and this is the meaning of the verse, 'And they [women] have rights similar to those against them [men] according to what is equitable; but the men have a degree (of advantage) over them' (Surah Baqara, v. 228), because this verse, while admitting equality in rights between men and women, accepts men's intrinsic difference with and superiority over women. According to the evidence of the science of physiology, average women—with exceptions—are different from average men in terms of brain, heart, arteries, nerves, body muscles, and weight; that is, they are weaker, and it is this that makes women's bodies more delicate and tender and men's rougher and stronger; and delicate feelings, such as friendship, kindheartedness, and a disposition to beauty and luxury, are more prominent in women than men, while the power of thinking and rationalization are more prominent in men. Therefore women's lives are emotional lives just as men's lives are rational. Because of this natural difference, Islam has made a general distinction among men and women and their social duties and obligations. Whatever has more to do with reason than emotion is allocated to men, such as government and the judiciary, and whatever duties have more to do with emotions than reason are allocated to women, such as child rearing, housekeeping, and so on; then [Islam] has compensated for men's greater burden of having more duty by doubling their share of inheritance. Of course here, although men's share is two-thirds of this world's wealth, women are the owner of one-third, as well as the beneficiary of the other two-thirds, as they have the right of maintenance.²⁴ Therefore, the management of wealth is more in the hands of men, but its use is more the concern of women; on the basis of what is said, it is clear that the majority of men are stronger in management and therefore most of the worldly management, or, in other words, production—the circulation of wealth—is in the hands of men, and most of the consumption of the products and profits is by women, because women's emotions dominate their reason."²⁵

Heydari adds, "The desired [form of] equality, in Islam's view, is that whoever has a duty should also have alongside it a right. It should not be that all rights go to one [party] and all duties to another." He quotes *al-Mizan*:

"In Islam women share with men all ritual rules and social rights. Like men, women can be independent and they are no different from men except in instances where difference is demanded by women's nature. The main exceptions concern the issues of taking responsibility in matters of government, the judiciary, jihad, and attack on enemies, and also inheritance. Another one is *hejab* and covering the attractive parts of the body, and another is obedience to the husband in matters of sexual and marital pleasures.

"Against these deprivations and duties, women have been given certain compensations:

1. Maintenance is imposed on the husband and the husband is made to do his best to protect his wife.
2. The right of child care and education *(hezanat)* is given to women.²⁶
3. During the period of menses and bleeding due to childbirth, she is exempt from ritual prayer, and in all conditions she is given consideration."²⁷ (pp. 34–5)

What is curious in this section is not so much the flaw in the assumptions on which Heydari builds his defense (based on *al-Mizan*) of Shari'a gender biases, so much as the flaw in its internal logic. On the one hand, in line with *al-Mizan*, Heydari argues that men and women are equal in both ritual rules and social rights and that differences between men and women, whether natural or social, do not put one above the other; on the other hand, when it comes to the social realm, he conceptualizes and talks of these differences in terms of superiority and inferiority. What happened to the principle of equality? If these differences are irrelevant in the eyes of God and in the next world, then why are they transformed into discrimination in the social realm? Is this not to do with the rules of society, which are not eternal and are subject to change? If these rules are eternal and based on "nature," then can we really talk of equality, and if we do, how can we reconcile it with difference?

The three concluding sections suggest that Heydari was aware of these questions, but instead of addressing them, he puts his intellectual energy into avoiding them—he clearly classes them as doubts *(shobheh)*. Not surprisingly, the next passage is titled "The Error of the West in the Meaning of Equality."

> It became evident that from the standpoint of *al-Mizan*, the correct meaning of equality is that in society, every holder of a right achieves his or her right and every person progresses according to his or her capacity. It is not that one has the opportunity to progress and the other is barred from it; but the West has not founded its laws on this sound and solid basis:
>
> "Westerners have based their method on equality between men and women in all aspects of rights, and their general consensus is that a woman's backwardness in learning and accomplishments is not due to her nature but to centuries of incorrect socialization and the artificial deprivation in which she has lived since the beginning of creation of the world. The reality in the West contradicts this claim. Although they have tried for many years and have done their utmost to free woman from backwardness and to facilitate the elements of her advance, so far they have not succeeded in establishing equality between men and women, and world statistics confirm that in those occupations from which women are excluded in Islam, that is, in the judiciary, government, and war, the majority [of posts] are held by men, and always [only] a small number of women occupy them."[28]
>
> Therefore, apart from the above specific rules, in others, women are like men, and no man, be he father, husband, or other, has the right to forbid women to do a thing that is not contrary to the Shari'a, and a woman, like a man, can make independent decisions and conduct her own affairs. Freedom in choice of spouse, employment, and place of residence and so on, as guaranteed for men, is also guaranteed for women.

In the next section, "Men's Guardianship," Heydari immediately qualifies the women's sphere of freedom and choice and makes them subordinate to men, not only in family matters but also in all others. After a linking sentence, he invokes a long passage from *al-Mizan,* which has little punctuation but is crystal clear in meaning.

> "From the universality of the cause (that is the cause *['ellat]* for men's guardianship is their privilege and superiority, which is a general privilege and exists in men as a class), is derived the rule *(hokm)* that men's guardianship over women is also universal, and men not only have guardianship over their wives but it is a rule that is made for mankind in relation to womankind; of course, in general matters that relate to the two classes, such as leadership and judgment, on which society's life depends and these two responsibilities are based on the power of thinking, which is naturally stronger in men, and also the armed defense of the country requires both bodily and mental force, which is stronger among men than women, and one of the subsidiaries of guardianship is women's obedience to men in the house and in all affairs related to marriage. Therefore, just as men's guardianship over women in society does not harm women's independence and their personal choice and individual action, men have no right to say, 'Why do you like this, or why do you do that?' unless [a woman's] action is ugly and forbidden, because it is said, 'You are not to be blamed for what women do in their personal affairs, if their actions are not wrong.' Also, a man's guardianship of his wife does not mean that he deprives her of choice and of control of her wealth. A woman also has her own freedom and independence and can preserve her individual and social rights and defend them and take the preliminary steps to reach her objective.
>
> "Therefore the meaning of men's guardianship over women in the house is that, because [he] pays for the expenses, therefore his wife, in what relates to enjoyment and intercourse, must obey her husband and in his absence preserve his honor *(namus)* and not let a strange man into his bed and not allow strangers to take pleasure in the beauties of her body, which is her husband's."[29] (p. 36)

It is intriguing that a philosopher of the caliber of 'Allameh does not ask how a woman can keep her independence and free choice when she has to obey her husband in all respects. 'Allameh's notion that women's freedom and free choice can exist within men's rule contradicts his own assertion that women, both as individuals and as a class, come under the guardianship of men, not only at home but in society. The contradiction becomes clearer in the final section, "A woman's jihad is to be a good wife." Heydari prefaces the subject matter in the following way:

> As we have seen, jihad is obligatory only for men, and women are free from this duty. Now we must see how Islam has compensated for this command. The section in *al-Mizan* in which the hadiths are examined mentions the following:
>
> "Isma', the daughter of Yazid Ansari, approached God's Prophet when he was sitting amongst his Companions, and asked:
>
> 'May my father and mother be sacrificed for you, I have come to you on behalf of women. Prophet of God, know that every woman from the East or the West of this world that is aware that I am coming to you shares my opinion. God Almighty has justly sent you as a Prophet for men and women and we have believed in you and the God who has sent you [that is, we have converted to Islam]. We womenfolk are confined to the four walls of the house under the domination of men, yet at the same time we are the foundation and basis of life for you men. It is we who satisfy your lust and carry your children. But you men in the religion of Islam have gained certain privileges over us. You attend Friday and collective prayers, visit the sick and attend funerals. Each successive year you can go on pilgrimage (Hajj to Mecca), and more importantly, you men can do jihad for God's sake, and when you go on pilgrimage or jihad, we look after your property, weave cloth, make your clothes, look after your children, and educate them; are we not then entitled to the same share of rewards and punishments as you?'
>
> "The Prophet, hearing these interesting words, turned his face to his Companions and said: 'Have you ever heard any women utter a better word on the commands of her religion?'
>
> "The Companions said, 'O Prophet of God, we never expected a woman to understand such matters.'
>
> "Then God's Prophet turned to the woman and said, 'Woman, go back and tell all women who ask this question, "if you care for your husband, satisfy him, agree with him, the reward for all this equals men's reward for all that you listed for them."'
>
> "The woman went back, weeping for joy, and constantly praising God for His Unity and Greatness."[30]

In line with 'Allameh Tabataba'i, Heydari is either unaware, or chooses to ignore, that there is another way to read this hadith: as a protest by women. Isma' does not talk for herself but for the class of women. The Prophet accepts her logic and her objections and tells her that not much can be done about the practice, but that in the next world God will not discriminate against women as society does in this world. Heydari, however, quotes *al-Mizan* in reference to this hadith:

"If one examines this hadith and its like, it is clear that, although women are veiled, and their duty is to engage in affairs inside the home, they are not forbidden to go out to see the Islamic ruler and to try to solve the problems they might encounter. From the abovementioned hadith and its like, three points are derived:

"1. The praiseworthy way for women in Islam is to engage in housekeeping and child rearing. While this meritorious tradition is nonobligatory, it has been so much praised and recommended that it has been preserved—because Muslims were in the state of fear of God and preferred reward in the other world to this world—women's engagement in the household and their effort to keep their pure feeling untarnished, by raising children with reserve, modesty, love, and affection, did not give [women] time to enter men's society and to mix with them even at the level endorsed by God, until the lawlessness of the West in the name of [modern] civilization penetrated among [women] and so on.

"2. Without any doubt, banning women from taking part in jihad, the judiciary, and government was an obligatory tradition and remains so.

"3. [God] has not neglected the banning of women from taking part in jihad and . . . has compensated for it. For instance, if women are deprived of the privilege of jihad in the way of God, God Almighty compensated them with an equal privilege that is a true honor; Islam has designated being a good wife as women's jihad, and perhaps this matter is such that its true value is not manifest among us, but in the cup of life in which Islam flows, no [occupation] is superior to another. In plain words, in such a cup the privilege of a man, who goes to the battlefield and sacrifices his blood with generosity, is not more than that of a woman who is a good wife; and likewise a man who is a ruler and holds the reins of society and the affairs of life has no distinction above that woman; and a man who is sitting in the seat of judgment is not superior to a woman who looks after her child; serving in government or as a judge brings nothing but heartache and hardship for a person who acts according to justice; because in the cup of Islam to accept such responsibilities is to expose oneself to danger and annihilation, it is possible to be the cause of injustice to a poor human being who has no protector other than God, and God is in search of oppressors.

"Therefore it is no honor for men to be given these responsibilities over women; it is because God of the two worlds has not requested them to do so and has designed another line for [women to follow]. . . . In an Islamic society, if a man is told, 'You must go to the front or manage the country,' he accepts the burden for the sake of God, and if a woman is told, 'You must stay at home and educate the [next] generation,' she also accepts it for God's will, and it is an honor for both and neither is privileged over the other."[31]

The passage also clearly shows Tabataba'i's detachment, his disdain for the affairs of the world, and his idealistic notion of Islam. With this section, the first installment of the article on *al-Mizan* comes to an end. The second installment of the article appeared in the next issue of *Payam-e Zan* (no. 45, Azar 1374/December 1995). Here, the exposition of 'Allameh's views is terminated abruptly; the discussion of women's rights in the family domain, which the editor had earlier adumbrated (in his introductory note to issue 44) as the most important and extended part of the article, is not brought to an end in any conclusive way—the article does not even have a concluding paragraph. Issue 46 (Dey 1374/January 1996) featured the first installment of the transcript of my debate with the magazine, starting with the second session, in which I—unwittingly—challenged and refuted the kind of arguments and logic underlying the "Women in *al-Mizan*" articles. Were they trying to get me to articulate a critique that they felt necessary to air but which, as clerics, they could not articulate themselves? Perhaps, after the debates, the editor felt that a detailed analysis of 'Allameh's views was no longer needed? Perhaps he used our debate as a reply? The views and arguments contained in the second installment of Heydari's article are precisely those that I was arguing against in my debate with the journal.[32]

Conclusion

The Shari'a rules defended by 'Allameh Tabataba'i in *al-Mizan* as eternal and in line with human nature have faced many challenges in the Islamic Republic, which eventually has had to allow many of them to be circumvented. During the eight years of war with Iraq, women took part in jihad;

afterward, they continued to hold posts in government, and the ban on women acting as judges has been gradually relaxed. Since 1992, women have served as advisory judges, and some prominent jurists have issued decrees that Islam does not bar women from being judges. Ayatollahs Yusef Sane'i and Musavi Bojnurdi have declared that they see no reason for a woman not to occupy the supreme office of *vali-ye faqih* if she has the right qualifications.

But those expressing such views in Qom in the mid-1990s were in a minority. The majority shared the conception of women's rights as argued by 'Allameh Tabataba'i in his Qur'anic commentary and reproduced by Heydari in his article, "Women in *al-Mizan.*" *Payam-e Zan*'s editorial introductory note to this article tells us something of the dilemmas of the journal and the clerics who work there, of the dead weight of established scholarship, and of their attempt to find a space to maneuver within it. These young clerics have to bow to the rules of seminary scholarship, but they have set themselves the task of defending women's rights and feel an acute need for debate. The editorial, as a result, is full of double meaning and double thinking.

The editor makes a hesitant attempt to dissociate himself and the journal from some of the views expressed in the article, yet he neither questions the very premises on which these views are constructed nor challenges their authority and legitimacy. He draws the readers' attention to 'Allameh's high position and achievements as thinker, philosopher, mentor, and scholar and to the hidden levels of meaning in the work he left behind. He says, "Although today one might not be in total agreement with 'Allameh's views and perspectives on women, one can neither dismiss nor bypass them." He goes on to qualify them and makes a number of points. First, 'Allameh's views on women must be placed in the context of prerevolutionary Iran: Today they might seem outdated and outmoded, but in their own time they were daring and pioneering, paving the way for the reform and correction of popular and negative beliefs about women. Secondly, *Payam-e Zan* sees its "first mission" to be to introduce and present "in a scientific [that is, objective] way the various perspectives, analyses, and studies on women"; critical appraisal of them is of secondary importance. That is, the journal does not necessarily agree with the views expressed in its articles, or at least sees them as open to question; as, for example, with 'Allameh's view that women are banned from positions as judges and leaders and from taking part in jihad. Third, 'Allameh Tabataba'i's actual practices in his personal life and in relation to his wife are the best examples of the ways in which one can honor women and respect their humanity. The last point is interesting as it implies that even 'Allameh himself did not practice what he preached in the sphere of family law; that is, he did not do what he considered to be allowed according to Shari'a law.

So the debate over women's rights continues. But as the twentieth century drew to a close, the concept of gender equality remained as contentious and as underdeveloped in intellectual discourses in Iran as when the century opened, though the battle lines shifted. With the convergence of religious and political authority under the Islamic Republic, the ball fell squarely into the seminary court, which is the very raison d'être for the appearance of a women's journal run by clerics. *Payam-e Zan* has a formidable task ahead of it in the twenty-first century.

Notes

1. There is an extensive literature on the debate; for instance, see H. Hoodfar, *The Women's Movement in Iran: Women at the Crossroads of Secularization and Islamization*, (Grabels, France: Women Living under Muslim Laws, 1999); Z. Mir-Hosseini, "Emerging Feminist Voices," in *Women's Rights: A Global View*, ed. L. Walter (Westport, Conn.: Greenwood Press, 2000); A. Najamabadi, "Hazards of Modernity and Morality: Women, State, and Ideology in Contemporary Iran," in *Women, Islam, and the State*, ed. D. Kandiyoti (London: Macmillan, 1991); P. Paidar, *Women and the Political Process in Twentieth Century Iran* (Cambridge: Cambridge University Press, 1995); E. Sanasarian, *The Women's Rights Movement in Iran* (New York: Praeger, 1982).

2. See Z. Mir-Hosseini, *Islam and Gender: The Religious Debate in Contemporary Iran* (Princeton, N.J.: Princeton University Press, 1999), part 2, passim.

3. For a biography, see Seyyed Hossein Nasr's preface to his English translation of Tabataba'i's *Shi'ite Islam* (Albany: State University of New York Press, 1975), pp. 22–5.

4. A meeting with the editor, Professor Kenneth Morgan of Colgate University, was arranged by Seyyed Hossein Nasr, one of Tabataba'i's students, who undertook the task of translating 'Allameh's text. See *Shi'ite Islam*, p. 18.

5. Hamid Dabashi, *The Theology of Discontent: The Ideological Foundation of the Islamic Revolution in Iran* (New York: New York University Press, 1993), p. 308.

6. Ibid., p. 309.

7. Ibid., pp. 273–323.

8. The book was translated into English under the title *The Rights of Women in Islam* (Tehran: World Organization for Islamic Services, 4th ed., 1991).

9. See preface to the English translation, pp. xxxvii–xl.

10. *Pasokhha-ye ostad beh naqdha-i bar ketab-e Mas'aleh-ye Hejab* (The master's response to critiques of the book *The Question of Hejab)*, 5th ed. (Qom: Entesharat-e Sadra, 1994).

11. In seminary terminology, *shobheh,* which can be translated as "doubt," is a question that comes into the mind of a believer and goes beyond the accepted body of religious knowledge. Once a question is termed a *shobheh,* it must be suppressed and intellectual energy has to be directed at what caused it. See Mir-Hosseini, *Islam and Gender,* p. 146.

12. The translations from *al-Mizan* that occur in Heydari's article are my own; they appear in Persian in the article.

13. *Al-Mizan,* Persian translation, vol. 2, pp. 394–6. Here, and hereafter, I reproduce Heydari's footnoted references.

14. Ibid., 4:140.

15. Ibid., 2:404.

16. Ibid., 4:140.

17. Ibid., 4:215.

18. Ibid., 4:344.

19. These verses as cited in Heydari's footnotes are as follows: Surah A'raf, v. 46; Nur, v. 37; Tawba, v. 108; Ahzab, v. 23.

20. Jinn, v. 6; Sadd, v. 62.

21. Both these terms are technical, complex, and difficult to translate; see my *Islam and Gender,* pp. xxiii–xxiv.

22. *Al-Mizan,* 4:532.

23. See Mir-Hosseini, *Islam and Gender,* pp. 45–7, 65–9, 155–8.

24. For another version of the argument, see *Islam and Gender,* pp. 150–1.

25. *Al-Mizan,* 2:412–4.

26. This is true as long as the marriage is extant, otherwise, Shi'i *feqh* limits a woman's right to custody to sons up to the age of two, and seven for daughters.

27. *Al-Mizan,* 2:410–1.

28. Ibid., 2:417.

29. Ibid., 4:543–4.

30. Ibid., 4:554. The hadith saying that a woman's jihad is to be a good wife is from Musa b. Ja'far, the seventh Imam.

31. *Al-Mizan,* 4:555–7.

32. For this debate, see *Islam and Gender,* chapter 4.

Select Bibliography

Works in Persian

Ahmadi, Hamid, ed. *Khaterat-e Bozorg 'Alavi* (The memoirs of Bozorg 'Alavi). Spanga, Sweden: Nashr-e Baran, 1997.

'Alavi, Bozorg. *Panjah va seh nafar* (The fifty-three). Tehran: Amir Kabir, 1978.

Al-e Ahmad, Jalal. *Dar khedmat va khiyanat-e rawshanfekran* (On the service and betrayal of intellectuals). Tehran: Ravaq, 1978.

——. *Gharbzadegi*. Tehran: Ravaq, 1978.

Amir Khosravi, Babak. *Nazar az darun beh naqsh-e hezb-e Tudeh-ye Iran* (An inside look at the role of the Tudeh Party of Iran). Tehran: Entesharat-e Ettela'at, 1996.

Baqi, 'Emadeddin. *Trazhedi-ye demokrasi dar Iran* (The tragedy of democracy in Iran). Tehran: Nashr-e Ney, 1999.

Ganji, Akbar. *'Alijenab-e sorkhpush va 'alijenaban-e khakestari* (The red eminence and the gray eminences). Tehran: Tarh-e Naw, 1999.

Hedayat, Mehdi Qoli (Mokhber al-Saltaneh). *Tohfeh-e mokhberi ya kar-e bikari* (The gift of reporting or a leisurely profession). Tehran: Chapkhaneh-e Majles, 1954.

Kadivar, Mohsen. *Hokumat-e vela'i* (Government by mandate). Tehran: Nashr-e Ney, 1999.

——. *Baha-ye azadi: defa'iyat-e Mohsen Kadivar* (The price of freedom: The text of Mohsen Kadivar's defense in the Special Court of the Clergy). Tehran: Nashr-e Ney, 1999.

Katouzian, Homa, ed. *Khaterat-e siyasi-ye Khalil Maleki* (The political memoirs of Khalil Maleki). Tehran: Sherkat-e sahami-ye Enteshar, 1989.

Katouzian, Homa, and Amir Pichdad, eds. *Yadnameh-ye Khalil Maleki* (Essays in memory of Khalil Maleki). Tehran: Sherkat-e sahami-ye Enteshar, 1991.

——. *Khalil Maleki: barkhord-e 'aqayed va ara* (Khalil Maleki: The conflict of ideas and opinions). 2d ed. Tehran: Nashr-e Markaz, 1997.

Khameh'i, Anvar. *Panjah nafar va seh nafar* (The fifty and three). Tehran: Entesharat-e Hafteh, 1982.

——. *Forsat-e bozorg-e az dast rafteh* (The big opportunity that was lost). Tehran: Entesharat-e Hafteh, 1983.

———. *Az Enshe'ab ta kudeta* (From the secession to the coup d'état). Tehran: Entesharat-e Hafteh, 1984.

Mojtahed-Shabestari, Mohammad. *Iman va azadi* (Faith and freedom). Tehran: Tarh-e Naw, 1998.

———. *Hermenutik, ketab va sonnat: farayand-e tafsir va vahy* (Hermeneutics, the Book and the Tradition: The process of exegesis). Tehran: Tarh-e Naw, 1999.

———. *Naqdi bar qera'at-e rasmi az din* (A critique of the official reading of religion). Tehran: Tarh-e Naw, 2000.

Saghafi, Morad. "Bab-e Goftogu," *Goft-o-gu: rawshanfekri dar Iran* (Goft-o-gu: Special issue on intellectualism in Iran). Winter 2001.

Sorush, 'Abdolkarim. "Qabz va bast-e te'orik-e Shari'at" (The theoretical contraction and expansion of the Shari'a). *Keyhan-e Farhangi* 7, no. 73 (1990), pp. 12–9.

Taqizadeh, Seyyed Hasan. *Khatabeh-ye Aqa-ye Seyyed Hasan Taqizadeh dar akhz-e tamaddon-e khareji* (Seyyed Hasan Taqizadeh's address on the adoption of Western civilization). Tehran: Entesharat-e Bashgah-e Mehregan, 1960–61.

Works in English and French

Abrahamian, Ervand. *Iran between Two Revolutions*. Princeton, N.J.: Princeton University Press, 1982.

Alam, Asadollah. *The Shah and I: The Confidential Diary of Iran's Royal Court, 1967–1977*. Edited by Alinaghi Alikhani. London and New York: I. B. Tauris, 1991.

Amir Arjomand, Said. *The Shadow of God and the Hidden Imam*. Chicago: University of Chicago Press, 1984.

Ashraf, Ahmad, and Ali Banuazizi. "Iran's Tortuous Path toward 'Islamic Liberalization.'" *International Journal of Politics, Culture and Society* 15, no. 2 (winter 2001), pp. 237–56.

Atabaki, Turaj. *Azerbaijan, Ethnicity and the Struggle for Power in Iran*. London and New York: I. B. Tauris, 2000.

al-Azmeh, Aziz. *Islams and Modernities*. London: Verso, 1993.

Bayat, Mangol. *Mysticism and Dissent: Socioreligious Thought in Qajar Iran*. Syracuse, N.Y.: Syracuse University Press, 1982.

Behrooz, Maziar. *Rebels with a Cause: The Failure of the Left in Iran*. London and New York: I. B. Tauris, 1999.

Benda, Julien. *La trahison des clercs*. 5th ed. Paris: Grasset, 1975.

Berlin, Isaiah. "The Birth of the Russian Intelligentsia." In *Russian Thinkers*, edited by Henry Hardy and Aileen Kelly. London: Hogarth Press, 1978.

Boroujerdi, Mehrzad. *Iranian Intellectuals and the West: The Tormented Triumph of Nativism*. Syracuse, N.Y.: Syracuse University Press, 1996.

Dabashi, Hamid. *The Theology of Discontent: The Ideological Foundation of the Islamic Revolution in Iran.* New York: New York University Press, 1993.

Davison, Roderic H. "Westernized Education in Ottoman Turkey." *Middle East Journal,* vol. 15 (summer 1961).

Debray, Régis. *Le scribe.* Paris: Éditions Grasset et Fasquelle, 1980.

Gheissari, Ali. *Iranian Intellectuals in the Twentieth Century.* Austin: University of Texas Press, 1998.

Giddens, Anthony. *The Consequences of Modernity.* Stanford, Calif.: Stanford University Press, 1990.

Haas, William S. *Iran.* New York: AMS Press, 1966.

Intellectual Change and the New Generation of Iranian Intellectuals. Washington, D.C.: Woodrow Wilson International Center for Scholars, October 2000.

Jacoby, Russell. *The Last Intellectuals: American Culture in the Age of Academe.* New York: Basic Books, 1987.

———. *The End of Utopia: Politics and Culture in an Age of Apathy.* New York: Basic Books, 1999.

Jennings, Jeremy. "Mandarins and Samurais: The Intellectual in Modern France." In *Intellectuals in Twentieth Century France,* edited by J. Jennings. New York: St. Martin's Press, 1993.

Katouzian, Homa. *The Political Economy of Modern Iran: Despotism and Pseudo-Modernism, 1926–1979.* London and New York: Macmillan and New York University Press, 1981.

———. *Sadeq Hedayat: The Life and Legend of an Iranian Writer.* London and New York: I. B. Tauris, 1991.

———. "Problems of Democracy and the Public Sphere in Modern Iran." *Comparative Studies of South Asia, Africa and the Middle East* 18, no. 2 (1998).

———. *Musaddiq and the Struggle for Power in Iran.* 2d ed. London and New York: I. B. Tauris, 1999.

———. "European Liberalisms and Modern Concepts of Liberty in Iran." *Journal of Iranian Research and Analysis* 16, no. 2 (November 2000).

———. *State and Society in Iran: The Eclipse of the Qajars and the Emergence of the Pahlavis.* London and New York: I. B. Tauris, 2000.

Laroui, Abdallah. *The Crisis of the Arab Intellectual: Traditionalism or Historicism?* Berkeley: University of California Press, 1976.

Lévy, Bernard-Henri. *Éloge des intellectuels.* Paris: Bernard Grasset, 1987.

Lipset, Seymour M. *Political Man: The Social Bases of Politics.* New York: Doubleday, 1960.

Milani, Abbas. *Tales of Two Cities: A Persian Memoir.* Washington, D.C.: Mage, 1996.

———. *The Persian Sphinx: Amir Abbas Hoveyda and the Riddle of the Iranian Revolution.* Washington, D.C.: Mage, 2000.

Mir-Hosseini, Ziba. *Islam and Gender: The Religious Debate in Contemporary Iran.* Princeton, N.J.: Princeton University Press, 1999.

Nabavi, Negin. "The Changing Concept of the 'Intellectual' in Iran of the 1960s." *Iranian Studies* 32, no. 3 (summer 1999), pp. 333–50.

Sadri, Mahmoud, and Ahmad Sadri, eds. *Reason, Freedom, and Democracy in Islam: The Essential Writings of 'Abdolkarim Sorush*. Oxford and New York: Oxford University Press, 2000.

Said, Edward. *Representations of the Intellectual: The 1993 Reith Lectures*. London: Vintage, 1994.

Schalk, David. "Are Intellectuals a Dying Species? War and Ivory Tower in the Post-Modern Age." In *Intellectuals in Politics: From the Dreyfus Affair to Salman Rushdie,* edited by J. Jennings and A. Kemp-Welch. New York: Routledge, 1997.

Sharabi, Hisham. "Modernity and Islamic Revival: The Critical Task of Arab Intellectuals." *Contention: Debates in Society, Culture, and Science* 2, no. 1 (fall 1992).

Shils, Edward. "The Intellectuals and the Powers: Some Perspectives for Comparative Analysis." *Comparative Studies in Society and History,* vol. 1 (1958–59), pp. 5–22.

———. "The Intellectuals in the Political Development of the New States." In *Political Change in Underdeveloped Countries: Nationalism and Communism,* edited by John H. Kautsky. New York: John Wiley and Sons, 1963.

Tavakoli-Targhi, Mohammad. "Refashioning Iran: Language and Culture during the Constitutional Revolution." *Iranian Studies* 23, nos. 1–4 (1990), pp. 77–101.

Vahdat, Farzin. "Return to Which Self? Al-e Ahmad and the Discourse of Modernity." *Journal of Iranian Research and Analysis* 16, no. 2 (November 1999), pp. 55–71.

Vakili, Valla. *Debating Religion and Politics in Iran: The Political Thought of Abdolkarim Sorush*. New York: Council on Foreign Relations, 1996.

Young, T. Cuyler, Jr. "The Social Support of Current Iranian Policy." *Middle East Journal* 6, no. 2 (spring 1952).

Contributors

Mehrzad Boroujerdi is associate professor of political science at the Maxwell School of Citizenship and Public Affairs, Syracuse University.

Hamid Dabashi is associate professor of Iranian studies and a member of the executive committee of the Center for Comparative Literature and Society at Columbia University.

Golriz Dahdel is managing editor of the *Columbia Review*, Columbia University's oldest literary journal, and is pursuing a degree in comparative literature at Columbia University.

Farideh Farhi is adjunct scholar at the Middle East Institute, Washington, D.C., and is researching the changing political landscape of Iran for a project funded by the United States Institute of Peace.

Hamidreza Jalaeipour is a journalist and publisher of a number of reformist newspapers including *Jame'eh, Tus, Neshat,* and *'Asr-e Azadegan,* all of which were closed down in summer 2000.

Homa Katouzian is a member of the faculty of Oriental studies at the University of Oxford and an honorary fellow of the Department of Politics at the University of Exeter, England.

Ziba Mir-Hosseini, a freelance anthropologist, is a research associate at the Center for Near and Middle Eastern Studies, School of Oriental and African Studies, University of London.

Negin Nabavi is assistant professor of Near Eastern studies, Princeton University.

Mahmoud Sadri is associate professor of sociology at Texas Women's University and the Federation of North Texas Area University.

Morad Saghafi is founder and editor of *Goft-o-gu* (Dialogue), a quarterly journal on culture and society, published in Tehran.

Index

'Abdi, 'Abbas, 142, 145n.3, 156, 177n.50
Adorno, Theodor, 16
Akhavan-e Sales, Mehdi, 53
Akhundzadeh, Mirza Fath 'Ali, 2, 13
'Alam, Asadollah, 42
'Alavi, Bozorg, 30
Al-e Ahmad, Jalal, 25, 31; and *gharbzadegi* (Westoxication), 107, 113–18, 132n.4
Amini, 'Ali, 43–44, 52n.44
Amir Kabir, Mirza Taqi Khan, 13
Anglophobia, 13, 36
Anjoman-e Senfi-ye Ruznamehnegaran-e Iran (Association of Iranian Journalists), 154
Ansari, Sheykh Morteza, 187
Anti-imperialism, 35, 115
Arani, Taqi, 30, 75
Aron, Raymond, 25
Arya (newspaper), 148
Ashuri, Daryush, 99–101, 107n.27, 145n.2
'Asr-e Azadegan (newspaper), 138, 142, 148
'Asr-e Ma (newspaper), 142
Association of Combatant Clerics. *See* Majma'-e Rawhaniyun-e Mobarez
Association of Iranian Journalists. *See* Anjoman-e Senfi-ye Ruznamehnegaran-e Iran
Authenticity, notion of, 92, 94, 95, 97–98
Ayandegan (newspaper), 115
Azerbaijan, 31; secession crisis of 1946, 26, 29
Al-Azmeh, Aziz, 19

Bahar (newspaper), 138, 142
Bamdad, A. *See* Shamlu, Ahmad
Baqa'i, Mozaffar, 32

Baqi, 'Emadeddin, 142, 148, 177n.49
Bashiriyyeh, Hoseyn, 145n.2
Bayat, Mangol, 13
Bazargan, Mehdi, 33, 137
Beheshti, Mohammad, 183
Behnud, Mas'ud, 152
Benda, Julien, 25, 123, 125
Berlin, Isaiah, 3
Berman, Marshall, 19n.3
Boroujerdi, Mehrzad, 4

Césaire, Aimé, 93
Cherikha-ye Fedayi-ye Khalagh Aksariyat, 120
Cheshmandaz (intellectual journal), 134n.44
China, 18, 163; position of women in, 200
Christianity, 18, 103–4
Clemenceau, Georges, 24
Communism, 26, 107n.27, 108n.43, 127–28
Communist Party, 26, 113; French, 104
Corbin, Henry, 21n.16, and dialogue with 'Allameh Tabatab'i, 194
Counterculture, 104
Coup of August 1953, 15, 33
Crisis of the Arab Intellectual (Laroui), 15
Cultural Revolution, 112
Culture, definitions of, 91–98

Dabashi, Hamid, 5
Dahdel, Golriz, 5
Darwin, Charles, 27
Dawlatabadi, Mahmud, 118
Debray, Régis, 1, 123
Dehkoda, 'Ali Akbar, 3
Democracy, 114, 126, 168

Dialectic of Enlightenment (Adorno and Horkheimer), 16, 22n.23
Dovvom-e Khordad movement, 136–38, 141, 142
Dreyfus affair, 1–2, 24
Duhem, Pierre, 181

Eastern bloc, 26, 197
Eastoxication, 100
Einstein, Albert, 27
'Elm va zendegi (Science and life) (journal), 28, 39
Éloge des intellectuels (Lévy), 1
Enayat, Mahmud, 106n.26
Encyclopedists, the, 24
Enlightenment, 2, 55
Entekhab (newspaper), 138, 143
Eshag, Eprime, 31
Ettela'at (newspaper), 118, 153–56

Fanon, Frantz, 21n.16, 93
Farber, Ann, 159
Fardid, Ahmad, 113
Farhi, Farideh, 6
Fathers and Sons (Turgenev), 11
Ferdawsi (periodical), 94
Ferdawsi, Abol-Qasem, 90n.32, 180
Festivals, 95–96
Fifteenth Majlis, 31
Fifth development plan, 97
Foruhar, Daryush, 33
France, Anatole, 24
Freedom Movement, 33
Freemasonry, 37–38
Fromm, Erich, 21n.16
Fuladvand, 'Ezzatollah, 145n.2

Galileo, 27
Ganji, Akbar, 142, 145n.3, 147–48, 150, 160, 167
Garaudy, Roger, 103, 108n.43
Gharbzadegi (Westoxication), 100, 107n.35, 113
Gol Aqa, 158
Golesorkhi, Khosraw, 58, 91, 105n.1, n.5
Gramsci, Antonio, 123
Great Britain, 35, 37

Group of Fifty-three, 30
Guénon, Réné, 21n.16
Guevara, Che, 21n.16

Hafez, 88n.3
Hajjarian, Sa'id, 140, 142, 189
Hamidi, Mehdi, 61, 90n.90
Hamshahri (newspaper), 148, 154
Hedayat, Mehdi Qoli (Mokhber al-Saltaneh), 16–17, 22n.22, n.24
Heidegger, Martin, 21n.16, 113
Heydari, Ahmad, 193–205
Hezarkhani, Manuchehr, 93
Hezb-e zahmatkeshan-e mellat-e Iran (Toilers Party of the People of Iran), 32, 41
High Council of Culture and Art, 95, 125
Hobsbawm, Eric, 14
Horkheimer, Max, 16
Human rights, concept of, 184
Hus, Jan, 27
Hussein, Saddam, 119

Imperialism, British, 35–37
India, 18, 36, 200
Intellectuals, 3, 15–16, 25–27, 114–15, 123, 136–44; and arts, 28; definition of, 1, 2, 4–7, 24–25, 144n.1; and Islamic Republic, 111–31; and Islamic Revolution, 4, 7, 126; in politics, 128–29, 136–41; religious, 136–44
Iqbal, 182
Iran-e Farda (journal), 137–38
Iran-Iraq War, 111, 118–20, 141, 153, 167
Iran Liberation Movement, 119
Islam, 3, 14, 18, 91, 107n.43, 113, 182, 189; and laws on women, 197–98
Islamic Center of Hamburg, 183
Islamic Republic, 111, 118–21, 141, 154, 185, 195; and advent of public intellectuals, 131; Constitution of, 187–88; Leftist movements in, 128–29

Jacoby, Russell, 1, 131
Ja'far Khan az farang amadeh (Ja'far Khan is back from Europe) (Moqaddam), 11
Jahanbeglu, Ramin, 145n.2

Jahan-vatani (universalism), 102
Jalaeipour, Hamidreza, 6, 145n.3, 151
Jame'eh (newspaper), 138, 148, 150, 158
Jennings, Jeremy, 4

Kadivar, Mohsen, 143, 145n.3, 185–90
Kanun-e nevisandegan-e Iran (Writers' Association of Iran), 116–17, 122, 125, 129
Karbaschi, Gholamhoseyn, 157
Kashani, Ayatollah Seyyed Abolqasem, 32, 41
Kashef al-Gheta', Seyyed Ja'far, 187
Kasravi Ahmad, 26
Katouzian, Homa(yun), 5, 145n.2
Kermani, Mirza Aqa Khan, 2, 58
Keyhan (newspaper), 45, 124, 150, 153, 155–57
Khatami, President Mohammad, 112, 118, 126, 130, 138, 140, 189–90; election of, 154, 165, 182; as political face of theocracy, 189–90
Kho'i, Esma'il, 117
Khomeini, Ayatollah Ruhollah, 58, 121, 164–65, 195; and thesis of *velayat-e motlaqeh-ye faqih* (the absolute mandate of the jurisconsult), 180, 187, 189–90
Khordad (newspaper), 138, 159
Khorramabad, 33
Kiyan (journal), 137
Komeleh, 119
Kuhn, Thomas, 27
Kurdistan, Democratic Party of, 119

Land reform, 39, 119
Laroui, Abdallah, 15–16
Lenin, Vladimir, 21n.16
Lévy, Bernard-Henri, 1
Luther, Martin, 27

Mahdavi-Zanjani, Ebrahim, 195
Majma'-e Rawhaniyun-e Mobarez (Association of Combatant Clerics), 154–55
Maleki, Khalil, 5, 26–52, 107n.27
Marcuse, Herbert, 21n.16
Mardiha, Morteza, 160

Marx, Karl, 19
Marxism, 4, 25, 38; "Islamic," 91–92
Mende, Tibor, 22n.18
Meskub, Shahrokh, 115
Ministry of Culture and Islamic Guidance, 125
Mir-Hosseini, Ziba, 6
Mirza Malkam Khan, 13
Mo'ayyeri, Rahi, 88n.3
Modernity, definition of, 12–13, 19n.2
Mojahedin-e Khalq, 119
Mojtahed-Shabestari, Mohammad, 183, 189
Mokhtari, Mohammad, 129–30
Monavvar al-fekr, 2–3, 24–25
Moqaddam, Hasan, 11
Mosaddeq, Mohammad, 29, 31–32, 40, 42–43
Mosharekat (newspaper), 138
Motahhari, Ayatollah Morteza, 65, 137, 195
Mysticism, 102, 104, 187

Nabavi, Ebrahim, 158
Naqd va Nazar (monthly journal), 137
National Front Coalition, 39, 119
Nehzat-e Melli (Popular Movement), 29, 31–32, 35, 44
Neshat (newspaper), 138, 142, 148
Nezami Aruzi, 66
Nietzsche, Friedrich, 123
Niru-ye sevvom (newspaper), 37, 50
Nuri, 'Abdollah, 143, 145n.3, 189

Oil, 101–2; Anglo-Iranian Oil Company, 34, 40; nationalization of, 38; Supplemental Agreement, 31

Pahlavan, Changiz, 115
Pahlavi, Mohammad Reza Shah, 3, 106n.13, 112–13, 185
Pahlavi, Reza Shah, 15–16, 58
Parham, Baqer, 130, 145n.2
Parham, Mehdi, 99, 101–3, 107n.28
Payam-e Hajar (newspaper), 150
Payam-e Zan (woman's journal), 6, 196–97, 199, 214–16

People of Iran Party, 33
Perfect Man, notion of, 13
Pirniya, Hasan, 3
Poetry, 38; of Shamlu, 54–90
Popper, Karl, 27, 181
Popular Movement. *See* Nehzat-e Melli
Przeworski, Adam, 169
Purdavud, Ebrahim, 3

Qavam, Ahmad, 31–32
Qazvini, Mohammad, 65
Qom, 138, 183; seminaries, 193
Qorrat al-ʿAyn, Tahereh, 58
Quine, Willard Van Orman, 181
Qurʾan, 182–83, 187–88, 199; references to women, 203, 206–7

Rafsanjani, ʿAli Akbar Hashemi, 150, 163–67
Rawshanfekr (intellectuals), 2–4, 24–25; *rawshanfekr-e dini* (religious intellectuals), 4, 144–45n.1. *See also* Intellectuals
Razi, Shams al-Din Muhammad ibn Qays, 66
Religion, 103–4
Resalat (newspaper), 150, 155
Revolution: Algerian, 93; Cuban, 93; English, 28; French, 28; Islamic (1978–79), 35, 38, 54, 111, 115, 128, 152, 181, 183
Revolutionary Guards, 119, 125
Ricoeur, Paul, 131
Russell, Bertrand, 22n.18
Russophobia, 13

Saberi, Kiyumars, 158
Sadiqi, Gholam Hoseyn, 42–43
Sadri, Mahmoud, 6
Saghafi, Morad, 5–6, 145n.2
Said, Edward, 1
Salam (newspaper), 138, 142, 148, 154–58, 163, 175n.34–n.36
Sanjabi, Karim, 33, 43
Sartre, Jean-Paul, 5, 22n.18, 25
SAVAK (secret police), 37, 43

Second National Front, 29, 33, 41–42, 44
Sepahsalar, Mirza Hoseyn Khan, 13
Servants of Construction Party, 166
Seventeenth Majlis, 32
Shahed (weekly newspaper), 32
Shalamcheh (newspaper), 156
Shamlu, Ahmad, 5, 53–90
Shamsolvaʿezin, Mashallah, 145n.3, 159
Sharabi, Hisham, 18
Shariʿati, ʿAli, 137
Sharqzadegi (Eastoxication), 100
Shayegan, Daryush, 145n.2
Shils, Edward, 14
Shiraz, 116; University of, 185
Siahkal, 94
Siéyès, Abbé, 28
Sixth Parliament, 138, 166
Sobh (newspaper), 156, 159
Sobh-e Emruz (newspaper), 138, 142
Socialist League of the Popular Movement of Iran, 33, 39–40
Soleyman Mirza, 30
Soltanpur, Saʿid, 58
Sorush, Abdolkarim, 124, 127, 133n.31, 134n.39, 181–82, 189
Soviet Union, 15, 26, 31, 35, 127–28, 169
Special Court for the Press, 126
Spengler, Oswald, 22n.18

Tabatabaʾi, Allameh Seyyed Mohammad Hoseyn, 193–216
Tabatabaʾi, Javad, 145n.2
Tabriz, 30, 116
Talebof, Mirza ʿAbd al-Rahim, 2, 13
Taleqani, Ayatollah Mahmud, 137
Taqizadeh, Seyyed Hasan, 38
Tavalloli, Fereydun, 90n.26
Technocracy, 114
Tehran, 30–32, 37–38, 53, 56, 157–58
Tehran University, 33, 82, 116, 181, 183
Third Force Party, 32, 40–41
Third National Front, 29, 33
Third-worldism, 100
Toilers Party of the People of Iran. *See* Hezb-e zahmatkeshan-e mellat-e Iran

Tudeh Party, 2–3, 15, 26, 28–29, 35, 40, 42; and freedom of speech, 122; and Iran-Iraq war, 119–20
Turgenev, Ivan, 11
Tus (newspaper), 138, 142, 148

United States, 35, 104; constitution, 182; embassy, 115

Vietnam war, 104

West, 3–5, 11–13, 14–18, 94, 96, 101, 104; technology of, 11–12, 18
Western imperialism, 18, 36, 93
Westoxication. *See Gharbzadegi*

White Revolution, 46
Williams, Raymond, 92
Women: suffrage of, 41; notion of equal rights of, 193–217
Writers' Association of Iran. *See* Kanun-e nevisandegan-e Iran

Yalfani, Moshen, 117, 128
Yazdi, Ayatollah Mehdi Ha'eri Yazdi, 187
Yazdi, Farrokhi, 58
Yousefi Eshkevari, Hasan, 145n.3
Yushij, Nima, 53, 55

Zola, Émile, 24
Zoroastrianism, 3